THE IDEA OF JUSTICE
AND THE PROBLEM OF ARGUMENT

International Library of
Philosophy and
Scientific Method

EDITOR: A. J. AYER
ASSISTANT EDITOR: BERNARD WILLIAMS

INDUCTIVE PROBABILITY by John Patrick Day.

SENSATION AND PERCEPTION: A History of the Philosophy of Perception by D. W. Hamlyn.

TRACTATUS LOGICO-PHILOSOPHICUS: Ludwig Wittgenstein's *Logisch-philosophische Abhandlung* with a new Translation by D. F. Pears & B. F. McGuinness and with the Introduction by Bertrand Russell.

PERCEPTION AND THE PHYSICAL WORLD by D. M. Armstrong.

HUME'S PHILOSOPHY OF BELIEF: A Study of His First *Inquiry* by Antony Flew.

KANT'S THEORY OF KNOWLEDGE: An Outline of One Central Argument in the *Critique of Pure Reason* by Graham Bird.

CONDITIONS FOR DESCRIPTION by Peter Zinkernagel, translated from the Danish by Olaf Lindum.

AN EXAMINATION OF PLATO'S DOCTRINES by I. M. Crombie. I: Plato on Man and Society, II: Plato on Knowledge and Reality.

PHENOMENOLOGY OF PERCEPTION by M. Merleau-Ponty, translated from the French by Colin Smith.

THE IDEA OF JUSTICE AND THE PROBLEM OF ARGUMENT by Ch. Perelman, translated from the French by John Petrie.

LECTURES ON PSYCHICAL RESEARCH by C. D. Broad. Incorporating the Perrott Lectures given in Cambridge University in 1959 and 1960.

THE VARIETIES OF GOODNESS by Georg Henrik von Wright.

METHOD IN THE PHYSICAL SCIENCES by G. Schlesinger.

SCIENCE, PERCEPTION AND REALITY by Wilfrid Sellars.

THE IDEA OF JUSTICE
AND THE
PROBLEM OF ARGUMENT

by
Ch. Perelman
Professor of Logic and Ethics, University of Brussels

With an Introduction by
H. L. A. Hart
Professor of Jurisprudence, University of Oxford

Translated from the French by
John Petrie

LONDON
ROUTLEDGE & KEGAN PAUL
NEW YORK: THE HUMANITIES PRESS

Published 1963
by Routledge & Kegan Paul Limited
Broadway House, 68–74 Carter Lane
London, E.C.4

Printed in Great Britain
by Richard Clay & Company Ltd
Bungay, Suffolk

CONTENTS

ACKNOWLEDGEMENTS for permission to publish papers appearing in this volume, some in translation and some in their original English, are gratefully made to the following publishers and journals: Presses Universitaires de France. Les Editions du Griffon, Neuchatel. *Dialectica*, Neuchatel. *Revue Internationale de Philosophie*, Brussels. *Etudes Philosophiques*, Paris. *Cahiers Internationaux de Sociologie*, Paris. *Philosophy*, London. *Ethics*, Chicago. *Proceedings of the Thirtieth Indian Philosophical Congress, 1955*, Nagpur. *Philosophy Today*, Carthagena. *Journal des Tribunaux*, Brussels. Sansoni, Florence.

INTRODUCTION

M. CH. PERELMAN, some of whose important work is now
made accessible to English readers in this volume, is a master of
two disciplines: philosophy and law. It is therefore altogether
natural that many of his writings should be concerned with the
concept of justice and with forms of discursive argument other
than deductive reasoning. For both these are subjects of philosophical inquiry which have an intimate connection with law.
Not only do we talk of justice according to law and of the justice
or injustice of laws; but even when we make use of these terms,
as distinct from other moral epithets, in the criticism of conduct
or arrangements which have nothing to do with the law we do so
usually when we are concerned with the way in which competing
claims of different persons have been or should be met, and questions arise very like those which the lawyer is accustomed to
answer. The connection between law and the study of argument—
rhetoric in the old non-pejorative sense of that word—is no less
clear. Legal reasoning characteristically depends on precedent and
analogy, and makes an appeal less to universal logical principles
than to certain basic assumptions peculiar to the lawyer; it therefore offers the clearest and perhaps most instructive example of
modes of persuasion which are rational and yet not in the logical
sense conclusive. The reader should, however, be warned that
though he will find in this volume all M. Perelman's most important writings on justice, he must turn for the full statement of
his theory of argument to the two-volume *Traité de l'Argumentation*, which he published jointly with Mme L. Olbrechts-Tyteca
in 1958. That work has for its sub-title 'La nouvelle rhétorique',
and the author's principal concern was to redirect philosophical
attention to the problems investigated in antiquity under the title
of rhetoric. This was not a study of matters of mere style or
literary form, but of the varied techniques of argument which
made appeal to those 'proofs' which Aristotle characterised as
dialectical in contrast to the analytic proofs of formal logic.

INTRODUCTION

There is a special reason why M. Perelman's study of justice should interest English readers, legal and philosophical. For neither English jurisprudence nor English philosophy have contributed very much to the elucidation of the specific idea of justice. Many legal theorists write as if 'just law' and 'good law' were interchangeable expressions, and have ignored the distinct form of criticism usually intended when 'just' and 'unjust' are used in the criticism of law. Hume's chapter 'On Justice and Injustice' in the Treatise is rightly famous among philosophers. Yet little of it is specifically concerned with justice. In it there are truths of great importance about the institution of property, but we could not learn from it what it is for one system of property to be just and another to be unjust. Bentham was too preoccupied with the wish to exhibit justice as a subordinate aspect of utility to appreciate its special characteristics, and perhaps Sidgwick, in his Method of Ethics, was the first to pay due attention to them. It may be that the need for a searching analysis of justice was not felt because in England philosophers have always been ready to turn back to Aristotle's discussion of it in Book V of the Nicomachean Ethics. Here certainly much light is thrown in spite of the difficult apparatus of mathematical ratios used in the exposition. Aristotle rightly discriminates particular justice (ἡ ἐν μέρει δικαιοσύνη) as a special concept to be distinguished from morality in general (ἡ ὅλη δικαιοσύνη) thus making clear something which Plato had obscured or ignored. He also shews himself well aware of the fact that though justice has several diverse forms or types of application, a common element runs through these. This he characterises as a proper proportion (ἀναλογία) or relationship between individuals: and it is something to be maintained or, if disturbed, restored in three cardinal transactions of social life: distribution, compensation and exchange.

M. Perelman in his first and longest essay on justice makes a clarifying fresh start. For him, as for Aristotle, justice is a concept of complex structure within which we should distinguish a constant formal element and a varying material element. This distinction might be presented in terms used in recent English moral philosophy as one between the constant *definition* of justice and the varying *criteria* for its application in different situations or to different subject matters. The constant formal or defining element is the principle that 'like persons be treated alike'. This by itself

viii

cannot be used to characterise any arrangements just or unjust, since all human beings are alike in some respects and different in others. It must therefore be supplemented by a variable material criterion determining what resemblances or differences between human beings are to be regarded as relevant. So the slogans 'To each according to his need', 'To each according to his deserts', 'To each according to his legal rights' are for M. Perelman formulae of concrete justice. They are different specifications of the formal principle of justice that like persons be treated alike. The latter is made specific by reference to some characteristic (need, merit, etc.) selected as relevant for determining 'likeness'. Such a characteristic M. Perelman refers to as an *essential* characteristic and the classification of human beings made by reference to it as essential categories.

It is obvious that disagreement may arise concerning the characteristics to be taken as essential in the application of formal justice. Such disagreements will necessarily result in different concrete formulae of justice like the slogans quoted above. In this first essay M. Perelman took the view that such disagreements could not be resolved by anything deserving the name of reasoning. For the choice of an essential characteristic used in classifying men as alike is a value judgment and as such 'utterly arbitrary'. 'Any value may serve as a foundation for a system of justice.' Of course an initial disagreement may prove to be rationally resoluble. For one disputant may be able to show that wider moral principles which both disputants share logically require the use of his formula of concrete justice rather than his opponent's. But if the dispute cannot be so resolved it cannot be rationally resolved at all. 'We can only note the disagreement.' Indeed, in this essay M. Perelman goes far towards a position not unlike Hobbes'. He allows that both particular actions and rules of concrete justice may be rationally criticised in terms of justice; the former will be just where they conform to the rules and the latter will be just when they accord with what in the last resort are arbitrarily chosen values. But in this essay M. Perelman expresses the view that an attempt to judge law in the name of justice 'is possible only by means of a confusion'.

In his later work, as the reader will find, M. Perelman modifies these views and especially the doctrine that judgments of value rest on arbitrary choices. It is possible to identify a number of different influences which lead him to qualify the rigorous doctrine that reason has no longer a part to play where there is disagreement over the values which in the last resort determine what characteristics are taken as essential in the formulae of concrete justice. It is apparent from his essay on *Three Aspects of Justice* that historical study of what the author there terms 'the well tried formulae of the Roman jurists, the rational systems of Greek philosophers and the impassioned invocations of the Jewish prophets' may well have led him to reconsider what it is for rules of conduct to 'be justifiable by reason'. But the major influence leading him to the view that there may be 'reasoning about values' was the revision and expansion of the concept of reasoning produced by his study of the varied techniques of actual argument. For once we command a clear and detailed view of the way in which in living discourse conclusions are supported by arguments and arguments are evaluated as 'strong' or 'weak', or as having or lacking 'force' or 'weight', it seems dogmatic to confine the term reasoning to logical demonstration or inductive generalisation or the apprehension of self-evident truths.

The foregoing is perhaps enough to show the general connection between M. Perelman's two chosen subjects: the study of justice and the theory of argument. But there is a more specific connection to be noticed. In his essay on *The Rule of Justice* M. Perelman draws an instructive parallel between the principle of formal justice and the principle which in his view underlies the use of inductive procedures even in the sciences. The latter like the former consist in treating like cases alike; for it regards each phenomenon as 'a manifestation of an implicit rule according to which essentially similar phenomena manifest the same properties'. In the interplay between observation and theory by which science advances a shifting classification of phenomena may play a part analogous to that of the varying characteristics taken to be relevant in different specifications of the formal principle of justice. Moreover, in his essay on *The Social Contexts of Argumentation* M. Perelman exhibits a connection between justice and one of the most salient features of argument in every field: namely, the primary role played by precedent. No argument, least of all moral argument, takes place in a void; when the disputants approach each other they already owe allegiance to certain common principles of both thought and conduct and are eager to classify the instant case under familiar traditional general rubrics and then to treat it as other cases so classified in the past have been treated. Argument most often proceeds by linking a disputed thesis to precedents already acknowledged, and their use in this way is another application of the formal principle that like cases be treated alike.

Many other important themes run through M. Perelman's work besides the two which I have discussed. He has illuminating criticisms to make both of the Cartesian theory of knowledge resting on the criterion of self-evidence and of empiricist theories which conceive knowledge as a structure at the base of which is an indubitable experience of sense-given data. Both of these, in M. Perelman's view, share a common error, and have generated misconceptions of the rôle of language and the methodology of the sciences, and a misleading contrast between knowledge and opinion. In this part of his work M. Perelman has reached, by an independent route, conclusions similar to those of contemporary English philosophers who have also been critical of both the rationalism and the empiricism of the past. Many English readers therefore will certainly be now disposed to agree with M. Perelman's dictum that 'reasoning is infinitely more varied than anything to be found in the manual of logic or scientific methodology', but they cannot fail to be instructed by the range of novel and important considerations which M. Perelman urges in its support.

H. L. A. HART

I

CONCERNING JUSTICE[1]

(i) SETTING OF THE PROBLEM

THIS study has for its object the analysis of the idea of justice. There is no intention whatever of appealing to the reader's innate generosity, to the goodness of his heart or to the noble part of his soul with a view to drawing him on directly or indirectly to the conception of one ideal of justice to be revered above all others.

There is no desire whatever to convince him that such a conception of justice is the only good one, the only one answering to that ideal of justice of which mankind is emotionally in search, whereas all the others are mere cheats, imperfect pictures which give a false image of justice, a simulacrum which misuses the word 'justice' in order to win assent to conceptions which are really and profoundly unjust. No, this study makes no claim to appeal to the good feelings of the public. It aims neither at uplift, nor at moralising, nor yet at pointing out to the reader those values that confer on life all that makes it precious.

The warning contained in this preface may not seem strictly necessary: it is, however, extremely useful. In effect, every time we meet a word with emotive overtones—one of those words written with a capital letter in order to show how much respect is paid to it—whether it be Justice, Virtue, Liberty, Duty, the Good, the Beautiful or what have you, then we must be on our guard. Only too often our interlocutor, knowing how much store we set by the values these words connote, will try to make us accept the definition of them he offers us as the only true, only adequate, only admissible definition of the idea under discussion. Sometimes he

[1] Originally appeared as *De La Justice*, Office de Publicité, Brussels, 1945.

I

will do his best to lead us directly into acquiescing in his reasoning. More often he will go a long way round in order to conduct us to the end he proposes to attain.

The fact is that, unless forewarned, the mind does not attach the importance it should to the choice of a definition. Thinking that it has merely yielded over the meaning of a word, it throws away all that is at stake in the debate. And this mishap will occur the more readily if the mind in question is imbued with the spirit of geometry, habituated by training to rigorous deductions based on arbitrary definitions.

It is a grave mistake to think that all definitions are entirely arbitrary. If logicians grant the arbitrary character of definitions it is because these constitute for them no more than an operation which makes it possible to replace a group of known symbols by a new symbol which is shorter and more manageable than the group of signs which it defines. The sole meaning of this new symbol, in itself completely arbitrary, is that of the collection of signs which serves as its definition. It has no other meaning, and to allow it another meaning is to commit the error known in classical logic as double definition. We are, in fact, landed in the worst of sophistries if we employ an idea in two different senses, without proving that they coincide. Now the result is normally a sophistry every time a definition is offered of a 'capital letter idea'. The logical error thus committed is imperceptible to all those who confine themselves to purely geometrical forms of reasoning. In fact, this error does not consist in a double definition which is explicit and readily detectable, but in coupling with the proposed definition of a prestige-ridden term (Justice, Liberty, the Good, Virtue, Reality) the *emotive sense* of the term in question, with the result that one accords a *value* to that which is defined as being justice, liberty, the good, etc.[1]

Every time the question arises of defining an idea which does not constitute a new sign, but which already exists in the language, with all its emotive meaning and all the glamour attaching to it, one is not performing an arbitrary and logically indifferent act. It is by no means indifferent that justice, the good, virtue, reality should be defined in one way or in another. For we thereby settle the meaning which is accorded to recognised and accepted values,

[1] Cf. C. PERELMAN, 'Une Conception de la Philosophie', *Revue de l'Institut de Sociologie*, 20th year, Vol. XXVI, No. 1, Brussels, 1940.

to instruments that are extremely useful in action and constitute real social forces.[1] In granting a definition of an idea of this kind, so far from performing an indifferent act, we are saying what we esteem and what we despise. We are determining the direction of our action, attaching ourselves to a scale of values that will enable us to steer our course in life.

Every definition of an idea which is strongly coloured from the affective point of view transfers that affective colouring to the conceptual meaning we decide to attribute to it. In so far as we consider any definition as the affirmation of an analytic judgment which can be arbitrarily made, we overlook this transfer of emotive content from the term defined to the conceptual meaning which serves it as a definition. Every time such a transfer takes effect, the definition is neither analytic nor arbitrary, for, by means of it, we affirm a synthetic judgment, the existence of a link joining a concept to an emotion.

It follows that a definition is analytic, and therefore arbitrary, only in so far as no emotive meaning is attached to the term defined.

The essential distinction between the disciplines of philosophy and the disciplines of science lies in the degree of emotivity attached to their basic ideas. The sciences have detached themselves from philosophy to the extent that, by using exact methods, experimental or analytic, they have succeeded in laying stress, and securing agreement, less on the emotive meaning of words than on their conceptual meaning. The more the conceptual meaning of words acquires substance in the generality of minds, the less discussion there is of the meaning of those words, the more their emotive colouring fades.[2] When it is more worth while to reach agreement on the conceptual meaning of a term than to take sides for differing definitions the emotive meaning of the term fades into the background. This is what has happened in the case of the basic ideas of the experimental and mathematical sciences.

The difficulty in establishing themselves which has been experienced by the so-called social sciences—what the Germans call *Geisteswissenschaften*, or sciences of the spirit—is above all due to

[1] E. DUPRÉEL, *La pensée confuse*. Extract from *Annales des Hautes Etudes de Gand*, Ghent 1939, Vol. III, pp. 17–27.
[2] Cf. C. L. STEVENSON, 'Persuasive Definition', *Mind*, July 1938.

the fact that the affective colouring of their basic ideas is so strong as to render very slight the chances of agreement on their conceptual meaning.

A fortiori these same considerations apply to philosophy. In effect, the proper object of philosophy is the study of those value-laden ideas which are so strongly coloured from the emotive point of view that agreement on their conceptual meaning is almost unattainable. For these ideas, by reason of their well-marked emotive meaning, constitute the battlefield of our spiritual world. It is about them, about the conceptual meaning which is to be accorded to them, that philosophical disputes have constantly arisen.

It is when it comes to defining these terms which are charged with emotive meaning that argument arises over the true sense of words. Now arguments of this kind would be absurd if every definition were arbitrary. If, however, there is agreement in granting them a certain significance, it is because their conclusion establishes an agreement on values. It is in trying to secure acceptance of one's own definition of these prestige-ridden ideas that one seeks to impose one's own conception of the world, one's own decision on what has value and what has not. Each man will therefore define these ideas in his own way, and this will lead to irremediable confusion about them.

From this one might draw the conclusion—disrespectful though it may appear—that the proper object of philosophy is the systematic study of confused ideas. In effect, the more an idea symbolises a value, the more numerous are the conceptual meanings that seek to define it, and the more confused it appears. So much so indeed that one sometimes wonders, and not without reason, whether it is not the emotive meaning alone that defines these eulogistic ideas, and whether one ought not once and for all to resign oneself to the fact that their conceptual meaning is confused.

In seeking to secure agreement on the conceptual meaning of an idea of this kind, one will inevitably be led to play down its affective role: only so will one succeed, if ever, in solving the problem. By the same token, the idea will cease to be philosophical and will admit of a scientific analysis which is devoid of passion but yields more satisfaction to the logician. By this very fact, the field of science will be enlarged, without, however, that of philosophy being diminished. As will be seen from the example

4

of this study, the emotive colouring which is dissociated from an idea that has become more scientific will attach itself to some other idea which will enrich the field of philosophic controversies. As an idea is cleared of all emotive colouring, the emotivity is reflected back on to another idea which is complementary to the first. Thus it is that the efforts of philosophic thought, which opens to science a new domain of knowledge, recall those of the Dutch engineers, who, in order to hand over to the ploughman a pocket hand-kerchief of dry land, drive back the waters of the sea without causing them to disappear.

A logical analysis of the idea of justice would seem to be a very hazardous business. Indeed, among all the evocative ideas, that of justice appears to be one of the most eminent and the most hope-lessly confused.

Justice is considered by many people as the principal virtue, the source of all the others.

'Thought and terminology,' says Professor Dupréel,[1] 'have al-ways incited men to confuse with the value of justice that of morality as a whole. Ethical and religious literature recognise in the just man the man who is utterly and entirely honourable and given to well-doing. Justice is the common name of all forms of merit, and the classics might be said to express their fundamental idea in saying that moral science has no other object than to teach that which it is just to do and that which it is just to forbear. Moral science might also be said to assert that reason ought to teach us the distinction between the just and the unjust, a distinc-tion in which the whole science of good and evil consists. Thus justice, which on the one hand is one virtue among the others, on the other embraces the whole of morality.'

It is when taken in this latter sense that justice outweighs all other values. *Pereat mundus, fiat justitia.*

For Proudhon 'justice, under various names, governs the world —nature and humanity, science and conscience, logic and morals, political economy, politics, history, literature and art. Justice is that which is most primitive in the human soul, most fundamental in society, most sacred among ideas, and what the masses demand today with most ardour. It is the essence of religions and at the same time the form of reason, the secret object of faith, and the

---

[1] E. DUPRÉEL, *Traité de Morale*, Brussels, 1932, Vol. II, p. 483.

beginning, middle and end of knowledge. What can be imagined more universal, more strong, more complete than Justice?'[1]

It is always useful and important to be able to qualify as just the social conceptions which one advocates. Every revolution, every war, every overthrow has always been effected in the name of Justice. And the extraordinary thing is that it should be just as much the partisans of a new order as the defenders of the old who invoke with their prayers the reign of Justice. And when a neutral voice proclaims the necessity of a just peace, all the belligerents agree, and affirm that this just peace will come about only when the enemy has been annihilated.

Let us note that there need be no bad faith in these contradictory affirmations. Each of the antagonists can be sincere and believe that his cause alone is just. And no one is wrong, for each is speaking of a different justice.

'An ethical idea,' writes Professor Dupréel,[2] 'corresponds neither to a thing which has only to be seen in order for one's assertion to be verified, nor to a demonstration to which one cannot but yield, but rather to a *convention* which is designed to define the idea in a certain manner. Accordingly, when an opponent has taken the offensive and, in doing so, has ranged the appearance of Justice on his side, then the other party will tend to give such a definition of justice as is admittedly agreeable to his cause.'

Each will defend a conception of justice that puts him in the right and his opponent in the wrong.

One has only to remind oneself that for thousands of years every antagonist, in public and private conflicts, in wars, in revolutions, in lawsuits, in clashes of interest, has always declared, and has done his best to prove, that justice is on his side; that justice is invoked every time recourse is had to an arbiter—and at once one realises the unbelievable multiplicity of meanings attached to the idea, and the extraordinary confusion provoked by its use.

It is vain to try to enumerate all the possible meanings of the idea of justice. Let us, however, give a few examples which constitute the most current conceptions of justice, and whose irreconcilable character is at once obvious:

[1] PROUDHON, *De la Justice dans la Révolution et dans l'Eglise*, new edition, Brussels, 1868, p. 44.

[2] *Traité de Morale*, Vol. II, p. 484.

1. To each the same thing.
2. To each according to his merits.
3. To each according to his works.
4. To each according to his needs.
5. To each according to his rank.
6. To each according to his legal entitlement.

Let us take a closer and more precise look at each of these conceptions.

1. *To each the same thing*

According to this conception, all the people taken into account must be treated in the same way, without regard to any of their distinguishing particularities. Young or old, well or sick, rich or poor, virtuous or criminal, aristocrat or boor, white or black, guilty or innocent—it is just that all should be treated in the same way, without any discrimination or differentiation. In popular imagery the perfectly just being is death, which touches every man on the shoulder regardless of any of his privileges.

2. *To each according to his merits*

Here we have a conception of justice that no longer demands universal equality, but treatment proportional to an intrinsic quality —the merit of the human person. How are we to define this merit? What common measure are we to find between the merits or demerits of different beings? Is there, generally speaking, such a common measure? What are the criteria we must have regard to in establishing this merit? Should we have regard to the result of the action, to the intention behind it, to the sacrifice made, and, if so, how far? Ordinarily we do not answer all these questions: indeed, we do not even put them to ourselves. If we are driven into a corner we tell ourselves that it is after death that all beings will be treated in accordance with their merits; that their 'weight' of merit and demerit will be established by means of a balance; and that the result of this 'weighing' will indicate automatically, so to speak, the fate in store for them. Life beyond the grave, heaven and hell, constitute the just recompense or the just punishment for life on earth. The intrinsic moral worth of the individual will be the sole criterion of the judge, who will be blind to all other considerations.

7

3. *To each according to his works*

This conception of justice also does not call for equal treatment, but for proportional treatment. Only the criterion is no longer ethical, for regard is no longer had either to intention or to sacrifices made, but solely to the result of action.

This criterion, in that it ceases to make demands relative to the agent, we find less satisfying from the ethical point of view. But it becomes infinitely easier to apply in practice, and, instead of constituting an ideal practically impossible of realisation, this formula of justice makes it possible to take account, for the most part, only of elements which can be reckoned up, weighed and measured. It is this conception—of which incidentally several variants are possible—that underlies the payment of workers' wages, whether at time-rates or at piece-rates, and which also underlies examinations and competitions in which, regardless of the effort exerted, account is taken only of the result—the candidate's answers and the work he has shown up.

4. *To each according to his needs*

This formula of justice, instead of having regard to the merits of the man or of his output, seeks above all to lessen the sufferings which result from the impossibility in which he finds himself of satisfying his essential needs. It is in that respect that this formula of justice comes nearest to our conception of charity.

It goes without saying that this formula, if it is to be socially applicable, must be based on formal criteria of the needs of each person, the divergence between these criteria giving rise to the differing variants of the formula. Thus regard will be had to a basic minimum of which each man must be assured, to his family responsibilities, to the more or less precarious state of his health, to the care and attention required in his youth or his old age, etc., etc. It is this formula of justice which, making itself felt more and more in contemporary social legislation, has reversed the liberal economy in which labour, treated as though it were an article of sale, was subject to the fluctuations resulting from the law of supply and demand. Protection of labour and the worker, all the laws on the minimum wage, the limitation of hours of work, insurance against unemployment, sickness and old age, family allowances and so on—all these spring from the desire to assure to each human being the satisfaction of his most essential needs.

5. *To each according to his rank*

Here we have an aristocratic formula of justice. It consists in treating human beings, not in accordance with criteria intrinsic to the individual, but according as they belong to such or such a determined category of beings. *Quod licet Jovi non licet bovi*, says an old Latin saw. The same rules of justice do not apply to beings springing from categories which are too widely separated. Thus it is that the formula 'to each according to his rank' differs from the other formulas in that, instead of being universalist, it divides men into various categories which will be treated differently.

In antiquity different treatment was reserved for the native and the foreigner, for the free man and the slave. At the beginning of the Middle Ages the Frankish masters were treated differently from the native Gallo-Romans. Later, distinction was made between the nobles, the bourgeoisie, the clergy and the serfs bound to the soil.

At the present day white and black are treated differently in the colonies. In the army there are different rules for officers, non-commissioned officers and private soldiers. There are well-known distinctions based on criteria of race, religion, wealth, etc., etc. The characteristic which acts as a criterion is of a social nature and, for the most part, hereditary, and so independent of the will of the individual.

If we regard this formula of justice as aristocratic it is because it is always maintained and bitterly defended by its beneficiaries, who demand or enforce favourable treatment for the categories of beings whom they put forward as being superior. And this claim is normally sustained by force, whether by force of arms, or by the fact of being a majority as against a defenceless minority.

6. *To each according to his legal entitlement*

This formula is the paraphrase of the celebrated *cuique suum* of the Romans. If to be just means to attribute to each what is his own, then, if a vicious circle is to be avoided, it is necessary to be able to determine what each man's own is. If we allow a juridical meaning to the phrase 'that which is each man's own' we arrive at the conclusion that to be just means to accord to each person what the law entitles him to.

This conception enables us to say that a judge is just, that is, impartial and uncorrupt, when he applies the same laws to the same situations (*in paribus causis paria jura*). To be just is to apply the laws of the country. This conception of justice, unlike all the previous ones, does not set itself up as a judge of positive law, but limits itself to applying it.

This formula in practice naturally admits of as many variants as there are different codes of law. Each system of law assumes a justice relative to that law. What may be just under one code may not be so under another. In effect, to be just is to apply the rules of a given juridical system, and to be unjust is to misapply them.

Professor Dupréel contrasts this conception with all the others.[1] He characterises it as 'static justice', because it is based on the maintenance of the established order; and he contrasts with it all the others which are considered as forms of 'dynamic justice' because they are capable of modifying that order and the rules which define it. 'Dynamic justice is a factor of change, and appears as an instrument of the reforming or, to take its self-given name, the *progressivist* spirit. Static justice, essentially conservative, is a factor of rigidity.'[2]

This summary analysis of the most prevalent conceptions of the idea of justice has demonstrated to us the existence of at least six formulas of justice, most of them admitting numerous variants, and all of them normally irreconcilable. True, by recourse to more or less forced interpretations and to more or less arbitrary assertions one can attempt to bring one of these different formulas into line with another. Nevertheless, they present aspects of justice which are quite distinct and are for the most part mutually opposed.

Given this state of affairs, there are three possible standpoints.

The first would consist in declaring that these differing conceptions of justice have absolutely nothing in common; that characterising them in one and the same manner is improper and creates hopeless confusion; and that the only possible analysis would consist in distinguishing the different meanings, it being accepted that these meanings are not united by any conceptual link.

[1] *Traité de Morale*, Vol. II, pp. 485–496.   [2] *Ibid.*, Vol. II, p. 489.

If this is the case we shall, if all misunderstanding is to be avoided, be driven to characterise in different fashion each one of these six conceptions. Either we shall deny the name of justice to any of them or we shall regard one of them as alone capable of being characterised as just.

This latter mode of action would lead indirectly to the second standpoint. This consists in choosing from among the various formulas of justice only one, and in trying to convince us that that is the only admissible, the only true, the only really and thoroughly just formula.

Now it is precisely this way of reasoning that we would wish to avoid at any cost; it is the one against which we have warned the reader. Whatever our reasons for choosing one formula, antagonists would advance equally valid reasons for choosing another. The debate, far from bringing about agreement, would serve only to provoke a conflict, which would be the more violent in so far as each party was more bitter in defence of his own conception. And anyway the analysis of the idea of justice would be little forwarded thereby.

That is why we give our preference to the third standpoint. This would shoulder the extremely delicate task of seeking out what there is in common between the various conceptions of justice that could be formulated. Or at least—to avoid the impossible requirement of seeking out the element which is common to an indefinite multitude of different conceptions—there would be an attempt to find what there is in common between the conceptions of justice most currently accepted, those, namely, that we have distinguished in the preceding pages.

(ii) FORMAL JUSTICE

For a logical analysis of the idea of justice to constitute an irrefutable step forward in the clarification of this confused notion, that analysis must succeed in giving a precise description of what there is in common between the various formulas of justice and in showing the points in which they differ. This preliminary discrimination will enable us to consider it a formula of justice on which unanimous agreement will be possible—a formula which will retain all that there is in common between the contrasting conceptions of justice.

This does not mean in the least that the disagreement prevailing between the champions of the various conceptions of justice will be reduced to nothing. The logician is not a conjurer, and it is not his job to spirit away that which exists. On the contrary, it is his duty to fix the point at which disagreement arises, bring it out into the light of day and demonstrate the reasons why, setting out from a certain common idea of justice, men nevertheless arrive at formulas that are not merely different but in fact irreconcilable.

To everyone the idea of justice inevitably suggests the notion of a certain equality. From Plato and Aristotle, through St. Thomas Aquinas, down to the jurists, moralists and philosophers of our own day runs a thread of universal agreement on this point. The notion of justice consists in a certain application of the notion of equality. The whole problem is to define this application in such fashion that, while constituting the element common to the various conceptions of justice, it leaves scope for their divergencies. This is possible only if the definition of the idea of justice contains an indeterminate element, a variable, whose various specific applications will produce the most contrasting formulas of justice.

In his treatise on 'The Three Kinds of Justice' [1] de Tourtoulon endeavours to establish a link between the differing conceptions of justice by having recourse to the notion of limit.

For him, perfect justice would consist in the complete equality of all mankind. The ideal of justice would correspond to the first of our six formulas. But this perfect equality, as everyone at once realises, cannot be achieved in practice. It can, therefore, only constitute an ideal towards which we may strive, a mathematical limit which we can seek to approach only within the bounds of the possible. On this theory, all other conceptions of justice are no more than imperfect attempts to bring about this equality. Men try at least to bring about a partial equality, which is the easier to attain as it is further removed from the stated ideal of complete equality.

'Logically,' says de Tourtoulon,[2] 'the various conceptions of justice equality, far from being contradictory, are essentially the

---

[1] P. DE TOURTOULON, Les Trois Justices, Paris, 1932.
[2] Ibid., p. 47.

same. They differ only in their potentialities. Perfect equality being a limit-idea, its potentiality for being realised in practice is nil. The potentialities increase in proportion as the other egalitarian conceptions depart from this point which is set at infinity.'

'One might,' he says,[1] 'call justice charity, or equality charity, when it tries to come to the help of those who are naturally unfortunate and to secure for them the largest possible share of the satisfactions others can enjoy.

'Distributive justice has for object another kind of equality which takes account of individual capacities and efforts in conferring benefits. Its motto is—to each according to his merits. Removed as it is from equality as a mathematical limit, it comes nearer to being something that could be realised in practice.

'Commutative justice, however, is not concerned with individual life taken as a whole. It seeks to establish equality in each and every juridical act, with a view to ensuring that a contract shall not ruin one party while enriching the other. With it we may associate compensatory justice, by means of which an equality prejudiced by the fault of others is redressed . . .

'The fact that the equality contained in the idea of justice appears under so many and so different guises is often employed as a weapon in order to reject all these conceptions *en bloc* as having no logical validity. But this is far too superficial an argument. Between these differing notions of equality there is no contradiction whatever. On the contrary, they are so many points that, taken on an abscissa whose limit is "perfect equality", come nearer and nearer to the ordinate constituted by the "potentiality of being realised".'

This conception undeniably represents a worthy attempt at the understanding of the idea of justice. Two objections may be advanced against it.

The first objection is this. The conception, faced with the various formulas of justice, makes the arbitrary choice of a single one; and this seems, with good reason, quite unacceptable to very many, if not most, consciences. Are all men to be treated in the same fashion without regard to their merits, their deeds, their origin, their needs, their talents or their vices? A great many moralists would be entitled to rise up against this pseudo-justice,

---

[1] P. DE TOURTOULON, *Les Trois Justices*, pp. 48–49.

of which the most that could be said is that from no point of view does it make itself felt as necessary.

The second objection is decisive from the point of view of logic. It is that the link which de Tourtoulon would like to establish between the different conceptions of justice is quite illusory. In effect, if it were the function of the different formulas of justice to promote partial equalities, then either they ought to have flowed one from another by syllogism, like a part contained in the whole; or else they should have been capable of complementing one another, like two different parts of one and the same whole. Now, whatever de Tourtoulon may say, the different formulas of justice frequently contradict one another. It is usually impossible to reconcile the formulas 'to each according to his merits' and 'to each according to his needs', not to mention the other formulas which ought, taken as a whole, to form a coherent system. In any case, the best proof of the impossibility of resuming all the formulas of justice in the one which advocates the perfect equality of all mankind is this: the champions of the other conceptions of justice rebel against it, regarding it not only as arbitrary but also as utterly opposed to our innate sense of justice.

In contrast to de Tourtoulon's idea (which regards the differing conceptions of justice as resulting from a different interpretation of the expression 'the same thing' in the formula 'to each the same thing') one might try to reduce the divergencies to a differing interpretation of the notion of 'each' in the same formula.

Aristotle observed long since that it was necessary that there should exist a certain likeness between the beings to whom justice is administered. Historically, indeed, it can be stated plausibly enough that justice began by being administered to the members of one and the same family, to be extended later to the members of the tribe, the inhabitants of the city, then of a territory, with, as the final outcome, the notion of a justice for all mankind.

In an interesting article [1] Tisset says, 'There must exist between individuals something in common whereby a partial identity may be established, if there is to be any attempt to realise justice as between them. Where there is no common measure, and therefore no identity, the question of realising justice does not

---

[1] TISSET, 'Les Notions de Droit et de Justice', *Revue de Métaphysique et de Morale*, 1930, p. 66.

even arise. And it may be noted that to this day the principle, in the human intellect, remains unchanged. There can, for instance, be no question of justice in the relations between men and plants. If today the idea of justice has been more widely extended and applies to all mankind, the reason is that man has come to recognise all his fellows as his fellows: the idea of humanity has little by little emerged . . .'

A priori, the field in which justice can and should be applied is not laid down. It is therefore susceptible of variation. Every time we speak of 'each' in a formula of justice we may be thinking of a different group of beings. This variation in the field of application of the idea of 'each' to variable groups will produce variants not only of the formula 'to each the same thing' but also of all the other formulas. But this is not the way in which it will be possible to solve the problem we have set ourselves. Indeed, far from demonstrating the existence of an element common to the different formulas of justice, the foregoing reflections prove, on the contrary, that each one of the formulas can in turn be interpreted in different ways and give rise to a very large number of variants.

Let us, then, after these unfruitful attempts, take up our problem again from the very beginning. The question is to find a formula of justice which is common to the different conceptions we have analysed. This formula must contain an indeterminate element—what in mathematics is called a variable—the determination of which will give now one, now another, conception of justice. The common idea will constitute a definition of *formal* or *abstract* justice. Each particular or *concrete* formula of justice will constitute one of the innumerable values of formal justice.

Is it possible to define formal justice? Is there a conceptual element common to all the formulas of justice? Apparently, yes. In effect, we all agree on the fact that to be just is to treat in equal fashion. Unfortunately, difficulties and controversies arise as soon as precision is called for. Must everyone be treated in the same way, or must we draw distinctions? And if distinctions must be drawn, which ones must we take into account in administering justice? Each man puts forward a different answer to these questions. Each man advocates a different system. No system is capable of securing the adherence of all. Some say that regard must be had to the individual's merits. Others that the individual's needs must be taken into consideration. Yet others say it is impossible to disregard origin, rank, etc.

But despite all their differences, they all have something in common in their attitude. He who requires merit to be taken into account wants the same treatment for persons having equal merits. A second wants equal treatment to be provided for persons having the same needs. A third will demand just, that is, equal, treatment for persons of the same social rank and so on. Whatever, then, their disagreement on other points, they are all agreed that to be just is to give the same treatment to those who are equal from some particular point of view, who possess one characteristic, the same, *and the only one to which regard must be had in the administration of justice.* Let us qualify this characteristic as *essential.* If the possession of any characteristic whatever always makes it possible to group people in a class or category defined by the fact that its members possess the characteristic in question, people having an essential characteristic in common will form part of one and the same category, the same essential category.

We can, then, define formal or abstract justice as *a principle of action in accordance with which beings of one and the same essential category must be treated in the same way.*

Be it noted at once that the definition we have just offered is of a purely formal idea, leaving untouched and entire all the differences that arise in respect of concrete justice. Our definition tells us neither when two beings participate in an essential category nor how they ought to be treated. We know that beings must be treated not in such or such a manner, but equally, so that it is impossible to say that one has been placed at a disadvantage by reference to another. We know, too, that equal treatment must be provided only for beings forming part of the same essential category.

The six formulas of concrete justice, among which we have been seeking as it were a common denominator, differ in as much as each one of them regards a different characteristic as the only one to be taken account of in administering justice. In other words, they determine membership of the same essential category in different ways. Equally, however, they indicate, with more or less precision, how the members of the same essential category ought to be treated.

Our definition of justice is formal for the reason that it does not lay down the categories that are essential for the administration of justice. It makes it possible for the differences to come into play at the point of transition from a common formula of formal justice to differing formulas of concrete justice. Disagreement arises as soon as it comes to settling the criteria essential for the administration of justice.

Let us take up again one by one our different formulas of concrete justice and show how they are all differing resolutions of the same conception of formal justice.

1. *To each the same thing*

The conception of justice advanced by this formula is the only purely egalitarian one, in contrast to all the others, which call for a certain degree of proportionality. In effect, all the beings to whom it is desired to administer justice form part of one single and unique essential category. Whether we are concerned with all mankind or merely with a few kinsmen taking part in the sharing of an inheritance, all those brought into consideration when we speak of 'each' have no other distinguishing characteristic. The view is taken that no characteristics other than those that have served to determine the totality of persons to whom the formula 'to each the same thing' must be applied can be taken into account; that the differences between these persons are not, from this point of view, essential.

This leads us, in considering the qualities that differentiate one person from another, to distinguish those qualities that are essential from the secondary qualities which are irrelevant for the administration of justice. Admittedly, the debate on distinguishing essential from secondary qualities could not be settled to everyone's satisfaction. Its solution would bring with it the solution of all other problems concerning values.

The formula 'to each the same thing' may establish an egalitarian conception of justice. It does not necessarily coincide with an egalitarian humanitarianism. Indeed, to make that true, it would be necessary that the class of beings to whom it was desired to apply the formula should consist of all mankind. It is, however, possible for this application to be limited to a much smaller category. Sparta applied this egalitarian formula to none but the 'homoioi', the aristocrats, the superior class of the population. It would never have occurred to the 'homoioi' of Sparta to try to apply this conception of justice to the other strata of the population, with which they felt they had nothing in common.

The same phenomenon is to be found in an analogous institution, notwithstanding that it arose in quite different circumstances of time and space—that of the peers of France and of England. The uppermost stratum of the aristocracy, recognising nothing higher than itself, expects the same treatment for all its members, as being equal one with another and superior to everyone else.

We see, then, that the egalitarian formula of justice, so far from manifesting an attachment to a humanitarian ideal, may constitute nothing better than a means of strengthening the links of solidarity within a class regarding itself as incomparably superior to the other inhabitants of the country.

In so far as we can arbitrarily determine the category of beings to whom egalitarian justice is applicable, we are enabled to show the points in which this formula, rather than the others, appears to give real effect to the ideal of perfect justice.

Indeed, on the basis of the formula we can succeed in framing a second definition of formal justice. All that is necessary is to specify that by 'each one' is meant the members of the same essential category. Thus we get the formula 'to each member of the same essential category, the same thing', which is equivalent in every point to the definition of formal justice we offered earlier. It was, perhaps, this possibility that was unconsciously glimpsed by de Tourtoulon when he thought to make of the egalitarian formula the unattainable ideal of perfect justice.

2. *To each according to his merits*

This formula of justice requires beings to be treated in proportion with their merits. That is, beings forming part of the same category so far as concerns their merit—and the degrees of merit will serve as criteria for settling the essential categories—are to be treated in the same way.

Let us observe that the application of justice in proportion with the degree of intensity of a quality susceptible of variation, such as merit, raises problems of logic which are elucidated in a striking work by Messrs. Hempel and Oppenheim.[1]

To form part of the same essential category is not merely a

[1] C. HEMPEL and P. OPPENHEIM, *Der Typusbegriff im Lichte der Neuen Logik*, The Hague, 1937.

matter of possessing one identical given characteristic. It must be possessed in the same *degree*. If two people are to be treated in the same way it is not enough that each should have merit. They must further have that merit to the same degree.

We must, then, have available for the application of this formula a criterion which will enable us either to measure the degree of merit—if we wish the rewards to be numerically comparable—or else to range beings according to the size of their merit, if we want higher merit to receive a higher reward. Naturally, the reward must be capable of varying to the same extent as the merit, if, that is, strict proportionality is desired.

If, in the administration of justice, we are not content with giving rewards but also wish to be able to punish, the idea of merit must be widened so as to take in demerit also.

In order that two people should have the same conception of concrete justice, it is not enough that they should both wish to apply the formula 'to each according to his merits'. They must also accord the same degree of merit to the same acts, and their system of rewards or penalties must be equivalent.

For two people to judge in the same way when applying the formula 'to each according to his merits', they must not only have the desire to apply the same formula of concrete justice. They must further have the same statement of the facts submitted to their consideration.

A judgment could be characterised as unjust—

1. Because it applied a formula of concrete justice which is not accepted.
2. Because its conception of the same formula of justice was a different one.
3. Because it was founded on an inadequate statement of the facts.
4. Because it infringed the specifications of formal justice requiring the same treatment for beings forming part of one and the same essential category.

Let us at once observe that the two first reasons are very often based on an equivocation. In effect, they are valid only in so far as the judge is bound to observe certain rules of justice, which is what happens in law, but never in ethics. In principle, a person cannot be considered unjust simply because he applies a different formula of concrete justice. For example, a man cannot be required to make an equal distribution when, according to him, the distribution ought to be made in proportion with the needs of each of the beneficiaries. Since injustice consists in violating the rules of concrete justice in accordance with which one is supposed to be judging, an act cannot be regarded as unjust if the formula of justice employed to criticise the judgment is not that of the judge.

If the judge violates the rules of concrete justice he has himself accepted, then he is unjust. He is so involuntarily if his judgment proceeds from an inadequate presentation of the facts. He is so voluntarily only when he infringes the specifications of formal justice.

3. *To each according to his works*

The formula of concrete justice 'to each according to his works' is arrived at by considering as forming part of the same essential category those whose production or knowledge have equal value in the eyes of the judge. If, from a certain standpoint, certain works or certain pieces of knowledge are regarded as equivalent, the same treatment must be accorded to those who have performed the work or whose knowledge is under examination.

This formula of justice is usually employed when it comes to remunerating workmen or marking candidates in an examination or competition.

Society has invented a tool for the common measure of labour and its products—namely, money. The ideas of 'just wage' and 'just price' are merely applications of the formula 'to each according to his works'. But it is very difficult to determine the just wage and the just price, seeing how disturbing are the effects of the law of supply and demand.

If it is desired to fix wages proportionally to the work carried out, account can be taken of the duration of the work, its output and its quality, this last usually varying with the length of the period of apprenticeship. But acceptable results can be obtained by proceeding in this way only so long as the work in question is such that its performance does not call for special capacity. For, as soon as there is need for a certain degree of talent, not to mention genius, to bring a task to completion, the common measure breaks down. That is why in such a case we usually prefer to judge the task on its own merits, with the help of its intrinsic qualities— to take stock of the result of the work rather than use as a basis the time necessary to carry out the task in question. The same applies to examinations and to competitions, where, instead of trying to measure the industry of the candidate, one is content to test his knowledge in the light of his answers or the work which he submits.

In all such cases we give up the attempt to establish a common measure for all tasks and remain content with comparing those for which a like criterion is accepted—tasks of the same kind. We will not attempt to compare pictures with works of literature, or symphonies with works of architecture. It may be true that at first sight the price of these works may seem to offer such a common measure, but that can be the case only when we are assured that this price is the just price, that is to say that it corresponds to their value. Now, if the price constitutes the sole element of comparison between works it is impossible to see how to determine their value in order to be able to know whether the price is just or not.

On the other hand, when it comes to comparing not works but knowledge, as in the case of an examination, recourse to money as a standard of measurement is not merely insufficient but quite impossible. The examiner can then judge the candidates only by reference to a purely internal criterion, the requirements which he himself formulates in the matter. The examination will make it possible to establish a relation between these requirements and the candidate's answers.

The examination postulates a kind of convention between the parties. In order to be able to submit to it, the candidate must be in a position to know the requirements of the judge. That is why the judge is accused of injustice every time he fails to observe the rules of the convention and sets a question 'which is not in the syllabus'.

In order to be able to compare candidates judged by different examiners on the basis of different syllabuses, we must be able to establish a relation between those syllabuses and also to assume that the judges evaluate the candidates' failings in the same way. As these comparisons are normally made only on practical and purely formal grounds—equivalence of diplomas, for example— the rival syllabuses ordinarily have reference to knowledge of the same kind, while, in the absence of special reasons, the differences between the examiners are disregarded.

Whereas the formula 'to each according to his merits' has its claims to universality in that it asserts its ability to constitute a common measure applicable to all men, the application of the formula 'to each according to his works' usually makes claims that are more modest and more immediately useful. When it comes to comparing work or knowledge, this latter formula of justice, which is one of the most common in social life, is limited, in the absence of a universal criterion and for purely practical reasons, to the comparison of work and of knowledge of the same kind.

4. *To each according to his needs*

The application of this formula calls for like treatment of those who form part of the same essential category from the point of view of their needs.

In social life it is only quite exceptionally that the application of this formula will be preceded by a psychological study of the needs of the men under consideration. In effect, we do not wish to take account of the individual's every whim, but only of his most essential needs, those alone that are to be retained in putting the formula into practical effect. The formula ought rather to be enunciated as 'to each according to his essential needs'. This limitation will at once give rise to argument about what is to be understood by 'essential needs', the differing conceptions producing variants of this formula of justice.

Often enough indeed, for the sake of facilitating the application of this formula, there will be a tendency to disregard needs that are considered important but whose existence is difficult either to discover or to check. Usually the attempt will be to determine these needs with the help of purely formal criteria, taking as a basis the requirements of the human organism in general. Only in so far as the application of this formula is restricted to a limited number of persons can the particular needs of each one be brought progressively into account. One of the most delicate problems of statistics in social affairs is to settle the details the inquiry is to concern itself with, given the number of persons to whom it extends. In its application to large numbers, such an inquiry will for preference take account only of numerically measurable elements, such as, for example, the number and ages of the persons in a family, the amount of money available to them, the number of calories in their diet, the cubic footage of air in their dwelling, the number of hours allotted to work, rest, leisure, etc.

Only rarely do we try to apply the formula 'to each according to his needs' to more refined and more individual needs. Indeed—and this is the difference between charity and this formula of justice which comes closest to charity—justice can be applied only to beings considered as elements of a whole, of the essential category. Whereas charity has regard to beings as individuals and takes account of the characteristics proper to them, justice, on the other hand, tends to discount the elements that are not common to a number of beings—their individual peculiarities, in fact. He who seeks out of charity to satisfy the desire of his neighbour will go to more trouble to take into account the individual and psychological factor than will the man moved by his conception of justice.

The man who desires to apply the formula 'to each according to his needs' will have not only to establish a distinction between essential needs and other needs but also to range the essential needs in an order of importance. Thus it will be known which needs call for priority in satisfaction, and the price of that satisfaction will be determined. This operation will lead on to the definition of the idea of the basic minimum.

Everyone knows what bitter controversies have been roused by this notion and all the ideas associated with it. Almost all the differences arising in this connection result from a different conception of the essential needs of man, that is to say, of the needs that ought to be taken into account by a social justice based on the principle 'to each according to his needs'—a justice that works towards settling the obligations of society towards each of its members.

5. To each according to his rank

The application of this formula assumes that the beings in respect of whom one would wish to be just are divided into classes, usually, though not necessarily, ranged in a hierarchical order. This formula regards it as just to adopt a different attitude towards the members of the various classes, provided that the same treatment is given to those who form part of the same class, that is to say, of the same essential category.

This division into classes, in the broad sense, can be effected in various ways. It can be based on the colour of the skin, on language, on religion or on the fact of belonging to a social class, to a caste or to an ethnic group. The subdivision of human beings can also be effected in accordance with their functions, their responsibilities and so on.

It is possible for the classes so distinguished not to be ranged in order. To treat the members of one class in a different way from those of another might not be favourable in all respects to a given category. Most often, however, the various classes are ranged in order. The upper classes, the privileged classes, enjoy more rights than the others. But ordered societies, according as they are in full flower or decadent, will impose greater burdens of duty on their élites or else will establish no correspondence between the rights accorded and the duties or responsibilities. The saying *noblesse oblige* is the expression of an aristocracy conscious of its specific duties and realising that it is only by paying that price that it will succeed in justifying its privileged situation.

Generally speaking, a régime is workable only if each member of its upper class is made to face his responsibilities, and if the rights accorded to him flow from the burdens laid on him. Where specific rights do not coincide with special responsibilities, the régime, thanks to the generalising of the factor of the arbitrary, will soon degenerate into a system of calculated favouritism—an 'old boy network'.

These reflections are applicable not only to régimes in which superior status goes by birth but also to quite different régimes, such as the democratic. In effect, in every régime there exists a superior class, the class which has at its disposal power and force in the state. A régime will be workable in the long run only if the demands laid on this class are quite specific and if the severity exercised in calling each individual's management to account is proportional to the responsibilities he has undertaken.

6. *To each according to his legal entitlement*

This formula of justice is to be distinguished from all the others in that the judge, the person made responsible for applying it, is not now free to choose the conception of justice he prefers: he is bound to observe the established rules. Classification, division into essential categories—these are laid down for him, and he must, as a matter of obligation, take account of them. Here we have the fundamental distinction between the ethical and the juridical conceptions of justice.

In ethics, there is freedom to choose the formula of justice that one intends to apply and the interpretation that one desires to give it. In law, the formula of justice is laid down, and its interpretation is made subject to the control of the highest court of the state. In ethics, the rule adopted is the result of the free adherence of the conscience. In law, it is necessary to consult the established order. In ethics, he who judges has first to settle the categories in accordance with which he will judge, then to see which are the categories applicable to the facts. In law, the sole problem to be entertained is that of knowing how the facts under consideration fit into the established juridical system, and how they are to be characterised. In modern law the two authorities—the one which settles the categories and the one which applies them—are rigorously kept apart. In ethics, they are united in the same conscience.

In law, how far has the judge, in the exercise of his functions, the means of bringing to bear his own particular conception of justice? How far is the law influenced by ethical conceptions?

The answer to the first question will be different according as by judge is meant any individual official whatever having the responsibility of administering justice, or jurisprudence as a whole. Even in the case of a judge who rests content with following the beaten tracks of jurisprudence and has no desire for innovation, his role is not entirely passive. Indeed, since every vision of reality is to some extent subjective—the more so in that it is a question of a reconstruction rather than of a direct vision—the upright judge will, even involuntarily, be led, in his evaluation of the facts, to make the law and his own inner feeling for justice coincide. By taking his stand on certain evidence or by denying its importance, by having regard to certain facts or by so interpreting them as to deprive them of all meaning, the judge is able to produce a different picture of reality and to deduce from it a different application of the rules of justice.

As for jurisprudence, in so far as it interprets the laws, it can even go farther. On it depends the definition of all the confused ideas, all the equivocal expressions, of the law. It will be for it an easy matter to define those ideas and to interpret those expressions in such fashion that the judge's feeling of justice and the exigencies of the law shall not clash too violently. In some cases, when laws were in question whose meaning was difficult to distort, jurisprudence has even been content quite simply to forget their existence, and by dint of not administering them has caused them to fall into desuetude. In Roman law the *praetor* could allow himself to take advantage of fictions so as to modify the application of the categories established by the law, whereas now the determination of those categories is the work of the legislator. He will make it his business to give legal force to the conception of justice of those who hold power in the state.

A priori, nothing can be said of the ethical character of the law, of the way in which the categories established by the legislator coincide with those of the mass of the population. Everything depends on the relation between that mass and those who hold power. According as these latter are or are not the true reflection of the majority of the nation, the juridical categories laid down will coincide more or less with popular feeling. In any democratic régime the law, albeit with some delay, follows the evolution undergone by the conception of justice in the minds of the majority of the citizens. During the period for which there is failure to correspond, jurisprudence makes it its business, as best it may, to reduce to a minimum the disadvantages due to the inevitable slowness of the legislative power.

Can justice conflict with law? Is there an unjust law? The question can be put in this way only if no account is taken of the distinction we have established between formal justice and concrete justice. Indeed, an attempt to judge law in the name of justice is possible only by means of a confusion. Law will be judged by means, not of formal justice, but of concrete justice, that is of a particular conception of justice which assumes a settled scale of values. In effect, we shall not condemn or reform in the name of justice, but in the name of a vision of the universe—sublime perhaps, but in any case regarded arbitrarily as the only just one. Whereas one conception of the world is condemned by means of another, we must not say that law is condemned in the name of justice, unless, that is, we want to create confusions advantageous only to the sophists. Indeed, positive law can never enter into conflict with formal justice, seeing that all it does is to establish the categories of which formal justice speaks, and without whose establishment the administration of justice is quite impossible.

We have now reviewed the principal conceptions of concrete justice and have seen how all of them can be regarded as determinations of formal justice. We can, then, affirm the existence of an element common to the more usual formulas of justice—an element making it possible to define the formal part of any conception of justice.

The application of formal justice calls for the prior establishment of the categories regarded as essential. Now, we cannot say which are the essential characteristics—those, that is, which must be taken into account for the application of justice—without positing a certain scale of values, a determination of what is important and what is not, of what is essential and what is secondary. It is our view of the world, the way we distinguish what has value from what has none, that will bring us to a given conception of concrete justice.

Any moral, social or political evolution leading to a modification in the scale of values will at the same time modify the characteristics regarded as essential for the application of justice. By the same token, it brings about a reclassification of mankind into fresh essential categories.

For the distinction between fellow-countryman and barbarian, free man and slave, Christianity substitutes the distinction between believer and unbeliever, and this alone counts in the last resort for divine justice. The French revolution regrouped the members of the nation into one single essential category and recognised only citizens equal before the law, whereas the *ancien régime* had recognised nobles, clergy, bourgeoisie and serfs, each subject to a different juridical system.

The humanitarian conception of the nineteenth century sought to reduce national and religious distinctions to the minimum, and to extend to the maximum the civil rights accorded to all the inhabitants of a state, even to make of these rights attributes flowing, by virtue of natural law, from the simple quality of being man.

Whereas the liberal conception of the state determined the status of citizenship by means of purely formal criteria, the national-socialist conception sought to envisage the state under the guise of a people's community (*Volksstaat*) to which only the members of one and the same race, one and the same ethnic group, could belong. The administration of justice had to take this distinction as its essential basis, and had to treat in radically different ways those who, by virtue of their origin, were subjects in law and those who could be treated only as within the jurisdiction, no more than objects at law.

It is clear from these different examples how modifications in the scale of values bring about modifications in the administration of justice. But, whatever the differences between the conceptions of concrete justice, all assume the same definition of formal justice, which requires beings forming part of the same essential category to be treated in the same way.

If the idea of justice is confused it is because each of us, in speaking of justice, feels obliged to define concrete justice. The result is that the definition of justice carries with it also the determination of the categories regarded as essential. Now this, as we have seen, implies a given scale of values. In seeking to define concrete justice, we include in the same formula the definition of formal justice and a particular view of the world. Hence flow such divergencies, misunderstandings and confusions that, in fastening on the differences that set the various formulas apart, we do not even notice that they have an element in common—the same conception of formal justice. Yet we have shown that there is no reason why disagreement on the application of justice—the result of the various conceptions of concrete justice—should stand in the way of agreement on the definition of the formal part of justice.

Be it noted that the confusion between formal justice and concrete justice is the reason why every conception of justice has seemed to comprise a conception of the world: in effect, every definition of concrete justice implies a particular view of the universe. Hence the attraction of the idea of justice and the importance attached to its definition. But from the very fact that the definition of formal justice does not in the least prejudge our judgments of value, we shall find all the less difficulty in reaching agreement on this definition, since, when it is presented in this way, the idea of justice loses at once much of its attraction and nearly the whole of its emotive meaning.

The idea of formal justice is clear and precise, and its purely rational character stands out sharply. The problem of justice is thus partially clarified. Indeed, the difficulties raised by concrete justice cease to exist when we are preoccupied with formal justice alone.

We see how formal justice can be reconciled with the most varied philosophies and codes of law, how we can be just in attributing the same rights to all men, and just in attributing different rights to different categories of men, just in accordance with Roman law and just in accordance with Germanic law.

True, all the difficulties raised by the idea of justice are still far from being smoothed out, and formal justice cannot burden itself with all the contradictory usages of the idea of justice. On the contrary, every time we speak of justice we must put to ourselves the question—are we concerned with formal justice or with one of the innumerable conceptions of concrete justice? Not but what the introduction of this latter distinction offers a double advantage. First, there is the advantage of not importing into the examination of formal justice the difficulties inherent in employing a formula of concrete justice. Secondly, there is the advantage of being enabled to elucidate the difficulties proper to the employment of formal justice, in particular those that derive from the relations between formal justice and concrete justice. It is to the examination of these latter difficulties that our next section will be devoted.

(iii) THE CONTRADICTIONS OF JUSTICE AND EQUITY

If the distinction between formal justice and the different formulas of concrete justice had served merely to obviate certain regrettable confusions, it would already have constituted a step forward in the understanding of the idea of justice.[1] But the distinction can claim even greater usefulness, for it will enable us to throw light on, and perhaps to resolve, problems which without it might have appeared insoluble. One of these problems consists in establishing the meaning and usage of an idea allied to that of justice, the idea of *equity*.

Formal justice has been defined as the principle of action according to which the persons who belong to one and the same essential category ought to be treated in the same way.

It follows from this that the administration of justice assumes a classification or ordering of persons in accordance with the essential characteristic that serves as its basis.

[1] This can be realised, for example, if one looks into the proceedings of the third session of the International Institute of Law and Juridical Sociology: *Le but du droit : Bien Commun, Justice, Sécurité*. Paris, Sirey, 1938.

The persons under consideration can be divided into two categories according as the sole characteristic taken into account is present or absent. They can be divided into further categories if each essential category is determined by another species of the same genus or by the degree to which a characteristic of variable intensity presents itself. In this latter case, we shall be in a position not only to divide the field under discussion into classes: we shall even be able to set these classes in order in accordance with the degree of intensity to which their members possess the essential characteristic.

Let us clarify our thinking by taking an example. Let us assume that the field under discussion—all those to whom it is desired to administer justice—consists of all the heads of family in a given town. We wish to give different treatment to those who follow a profession and to those who have none: at once we get two essential categories. If we wish to treat the heads of family differently according to the nature of their main profession we get quite a number of essential categories. Ask each head of a family to declare his annual income, and you get categories which can easily be placed in order in accordance with the size of the amount declared.

Every time justice has to be administered the field under discussion must necessarily first be subdivided in this way. Such a task has its technical difficulties. Nevertheless, the administration of justice would be relatively simple if one had to be content with one single essential characteristic, however complex. The administration of formal justice would be within the bounds of possibility.

Unfortunately, reality is far more complicated than that. What happens is, in fact, that our feeling for justice takes account at one and the same time of several independent essential characteristics, and these give rise to essential categories which are by no means always consistent with one another.

Let us take the case of a humanitarian employer desirous of fixing his workers' remuneration with due regard both to their work and to their needs. Only too often he will be in a quandary. This will happen every time two workers form part of the same essential category having regard to their work, and of different categories having regard to their needs, or *vice versa*. Which is the appropriate way to deal with them? Either way, the action taken will be formally unjust. Put the case of two workers doing the same job. One is a bachelor, the other is the father of a large family. Treat them alike, and there is injustice because by the principle 'to each according to his needs' more ought to be given to the man burdened with a family than to the man whose only obligation is his own support. Treat them unequally, and injustice again arises, because the same treatment is not given to two persons forming part of the same essential category from the standpoint of the formula 'to each according to his works'.

Here we are faced with one of the numberless contradictions of justice. These contradictions occur so often that we might even regard them as the normal thing. They drive us, almost irresistibly one might say, to affirm that perfect justice is something out of this world. Indeed, we can never declare that we have been perfectly just, that we have taken into account all the conceptions of justice that combine within us to form that confused amalgam we call the feeling for justice, that we have given the same treatment to people forming part of one and the same category which we regard as essential. On the other hand, we can always affirm that formally injustice has been done if regard has not been had to a classification considered as essential by the very man who has failed to take it into account. Moreover, the ordinary run of life is there to prove that justice is usually spoken of only in generalities, whereas, whenever specific cases come up, injustice is what we almost always hear about.

There is one way of getting out of the troubles caused by juridical contradictions. This is deliberately to give priority to one essential characteristic at the expense of all the others, to settle on the characteristic that is to be given the first consideration, the rest being allowed to exert their influence only in so far as the primary one is not thereby disturbed.

The most effective way of reaching this point consists in bringing out this essential characteristic by means of outward indications, natural or artificial.

For long those who demanded the abolition of slavery were met with the final and conclusive argument that divided mankind into essential categories based on the colour of their skins. It seemed quite normal that white men should not be treated as slaves—but why reserve such treatment for creatures in a quite different category, the negroes? Negroes are not human, it used to be said, that is, they do not form part of the same essential category as white men, so one could treat them inhumanly. Similarly, the idea of regarding the Jews as beings of a different race, marked by clear and obvious outward signs, was supposed to justify the quite special treatment it was intended to give them.

But much more common than the use of natural indications, is that of artificial ones to mark the distinction, the characteristic, to which the most importance is attached and which is regarded as essential. The most usual of these indications is *uniform*. The wearing of uniform testifies that the wearer regards himself as, above all, forming part of a given group. It is this belonging to a group, or to one of its subdivisions, that will be taken into consideration when it comes to administering justice. All who form part of the same group, or of the same subdivision, are equal: they must be treated alike regardless of any other characteristic that might conflict with the primary characteristic. In rendering the administration of justice more difficult and less clear-cut, juridical contradictions by that very fact blunt the feeling for justice. On the other hand, the wearing of uniform in the army gives especial encouragement there to the feeling for justice because it lays down, so to speak, one single essential category—rank. Those dressed alike must be treated alike, and soldiers dressed differently must be treated differently. In the army the hierarchy established by rank and manifesting itself by outward indications outweighs all others. For that very reason juridical contradictions are less frequent and the feeling for justice is keener and displays itself more vigorously.

Where the contradictions of justice become apparent and the administration of justice drives us to flout formal justice, we have recourse to *equity*. This—it might be regarded as the crutch of justice—is the indispensable complement of formal justice whenever the administration of formal justice becomes admittedly impossible. It consists in a *tendency not to treat with excessive inequality beings forming part of the same essential category*. Equity tends to diminish inequality where the establishment of perfect equality—of formal justice—is rendered impossible by the fact that simultaneous account is taken of two or more essential characteristics which come into conflict in certain cases of application.

Whereas the requirements of formal justice are quite precise, equity, on the contrary, constitutes merely a tendency opposed to all formalism, to which it should be complementary. It steps in where two kinds of formalism come into conflict: if, then, it is to play its equitable part, it cannot but be non-formal.

Suppose that in the administration of justice we wish to have regard to two essential characteristics, and to give identical treatment to two beings forming part of the same essential category. If, in doing so, we are led into giving excessively different treatment to two beings forming part of one and the same essential category, as determined by the second of the two characteristics, equity will move us not to have regard solely to the first of the two characteristics in arriving at justice.

Let us again take the case of two workers doing the same job, one a bachelor and the other the father of a large family. Like treatment in pursuance of the formula 'to each according to his works' will mean excessively different treatment if it is desired to have regard to the formula 'to each according to his needs'. Equity will move us to reduce this difference. But suppose it is desired to raise the wages of the father of a large family. The same treatment will then no longer be given to two workers forming part of the same essential category in respect of their work. Whatever the attitude adopted, whatever the extent to which the one or the other formula of justice is taken into account, the outcome will be a contravention of formal justice.

But how far should account be taken of the one essential characteristic or the other? *A priori* there is no rule to give the answer. Once equity is invoked, there is nothing for it but pure compromise. Equity can be achieved only by throwing over juridical formalism in cases where this entails contradictions.

Recourse to equity may be indispensable where the contradictions arising are unforeseen. But there is a possibility of resolving these in less arbitrary fashion whenever these difficulties have been foreseen and a decision has been taken in advance as to the degree of importance it is desired to attach to each of the characteristics whose application led to the conflict. This decision at once replaces the conflicting essential characteristics with one more complex characteristic having several variables and taking account of each of the preceding characteristics.

Rationing, enforced in all countries in time of war, furnishes an excellent example how, in the attempt to achieve justice by having regard to the various conceptions of it, the formula of concrete justice that had to be applied has been progressively made more complex. It being the concern of the state to distribute as justly as possible the small quantity of goods made available to the population, the formula that secured acceptance in the first place was 'to each the same thing'. But at once it was realised that there were classes of persons whose needs were greater and who, for various reasons, could not be ignored if one wished to take account of the formula 'to each according to his needs'. The authorities were led to make special provision for children, the aged and various categories of the sick. Then it was decided to grant supplementary coupons to several categories of workers, not only because their needs were greater but also because their work was useful to the community and it was desired to reward those who were engaged in it. Accordingly, this standpoint took into consideration the formula 'to each according to his works'. Finally, account was even taken of the formula 'to each according to his rank'. For not only farmers, who constituted the first line in a community which depended on their efforts, but also the members of their families, were granted quite special privileges. It goes without saying that this same formula enabled the *Herrenvolk* to award themselves double rations in all the occupied countries. Thus it is that in the example of rationing we catch on the wing a particularly striking example of the administration of concrete justice by the state and of the degree of complexity such a formula of justice can arrive at.

In the case of two workers doing the same job, one of them a bachelor and the other with family responsibilities, there is a way of resolving the conflict resulting from the application of two differing conceptions of concrete justice. This is to replace them with a more complex formula of justice to take account at one and the same time of the men's work and of their needs. The determination of the new essential characteristic will to a large extent be arbitrary. In effect, how far should regard be had to the one formula of concrete justice or to the other? Everything depends on the importance accorded to them. A purely capitalist conception, which considers labour as an article of sale, can assign only a quite secondary importance to the needs of the worker, still less to those of his family. This conception would like to have regard essentially to the labour which he renders. For it, this last factor will be decisive in determining the complex characteristic. In any circumstances the capitalist employer would try so to arrange things as not himself to carry the difference between the wages granted to the single worker and those of the worker having family responsibilities. If he were forced to carry the difference he would for preference try to take on bachelor workers. On the other hand, the state, to the extent that it favours large families, will attach more importance to the satisfaction of their needs. It will manifest this attachment by means of family allowances and, above all, in imposing differential income tax.

Whatever the relative importance assigned to either of the two formulas of justice, in establishing a more complex formula to take account in some degree of them both, the result is to resolve the contradictions which previously appeared. The new formula of justice, whose application involves no further contradictions, also makes it possible to avoid resorting to equity.

Let us note, by way of conclusion to these observations, that the transition from the preceding formulas to a more complex formula is not determined solely by them: in effect there must exist reasons foreign to these formulas if it is to be possible to fix the coefficient of importance allotted to either one of them.

Social life offers the spectacle of a continual oscillation between justice and equity. We have recourse to the latter whenever, in the working out of a law or regulation, no account has been taken of essential characteristics to which importance is attached by considerable sections of the population—what we call public opinion. Indeed, we shall be offended by too great a difference in the treatment laid down by the law or the formula of justice which is applied to persons forming part, in respect of this neglected characteristic, of the same essential category. We shall want to appeal to equity to reduce this excessive difference. On the other hand, we shall prefer to keep to the letter of the law for as long as this expresses public feeling adequately enough.

We see at once that the appeal to equity, conditioned by the introduction of new essential categories, will be more frequent in periods of transition, when one scale of values is being replaced by another.

Equally, the appeal to equity will be made in periods of economic and monetary disturbance, when the conditions that existed when the rules were laid down have changed so much that too great a gap is obvious between the rules formerly adopted and those that would in current circumstances have been accepted.

Suppose we live in a period of inflation. A worker has undertaken to deliver a job requiring three months' work in return for wages equivalent to those of a skilled workman. If, by the day when the work was due to be paid for, the wages of a skilled workman had gone up one hundred times we should be upset by the inconsistent treatment received by the worker imprudent enough to have made his bargain on the basis of the old scale. Equity will call for a reduction in this inconsistency. The day may come when legislation will bring about obligatory revaluation of earlier contracts. Equity will then give way to formal justice. Meanwhile, during the period of transition, we shall have to be satisfied with resorting to equity.

To conclude, we appeal to equity whenever the simultaneous application of more than one formula of concrete justice, or the application of the same formula in different circumstances, produces contradictions which make it impossible for the requirements of formal justice to be complied with. Equity is used as the crutch of justice. If justice is not to be lame, if we are to be able to do without equity, we must wish to apply only one formula of concrete justice, without having to take account of changes capable of producing unforeseen modifications in the situation. This is possible only if our conception of justice is very narrow or if the formula of justice employed is complex enough to take account of all the characteristics regarded as essential.

(iv) EQUALITY AND REGULARITY

Let us resume the analysis of our idea of formal justice.

Formal justice prescribes that persons forming part of the same essential category ought to be treated alike. It is the formula of concrete justice that will furnish the criterion that makes it possible to say when two persons form part of the same essential category: it is this formula that will indicate how in principle each member of that category ought to be treated.

It is possible for the rule of justice to lay down precisely and incontrovertibly the treatment due to the members of an essential category only when it is a case of allocating something that is available in unlimited quantity. More often than not, this is not the case. Where it is not, the rule will have to limit itself to indicating treatment that will take in one or more indeterminate factors, the determination of which will depend on external circumstances.

Thus it is that the criminal law to be administered by the judge can provide for the penalty to be imposed on, say, every housebreaker: years of imprisonment are normally always available. But suppose it is a case of a distribution of property. The formula of concrete justice can never indicate precisely which items go to each beneficiary. All it can say is what fraction of the property to be distributed each is entitled to; and the denominator of the fraction might in any case depend on the number of beneficiaries. The formula providing for an equal distribution contains two variables, the determination of which is governed by circumstances independent of the rule. One depends on the size of the property to be distributed, the other on the number of persons sharing in the distribution. Where x indicates the property to be distributed and n the number of beneficiaries, each person will receive $\frac{x}{n}$.

In the same way, when it is a case of rewarding a group of competitors in accordance with the formula 'to each according to his merits', there is agreement that the prize awarded to each shall be proportional to his merit. But the real value of each prize will depend on the total amount which it had been decided beforehand to distribute.

However that may be, good administration of justice in any case requires equal treatment for the members of the same essential category. Now, what is the basis of this requirement of equal treatment? Simply the determination of the way in which any one member of the category is to be treated. It is because any member whatever of the category falls under the rule that, in applying the rule, we are led to treat them all in the same way. If every child in the school is to get a bun, Peter, Paul and James, who are children in the school, will each get a bun. The fact that they get the same thing flows quite naturally from the fact that they form part of the same essential category. The equality of treatment is purely and simply the logical consequence of having to do with members of the same category. Thence flows the fact that we do not discriminate, or make any difference, between them—that, in observing formal justice, we treat them in the same way. Action in accordance with the rule is equivalent to giving equal treatment to all those between whom the rule does not discriminate.

D   37

It follows that equality of treatment in formal justice is nothing more nor less than the correct application of a rule of concrete justice which determines how all the members of each essential category ought to be treated. When the fact of belonging to the same essential category coincides with the equality of treatment provided for its members our feeling of formal justice is satisfied. And conversely, once equal treatment is regarded as just, there exists an essential category to which belong all those to whom the treatment is applied.

Our analysis shows that, contrary to current opinion, it is not the idea of equality that constitutes the basis of justice, even of formal justice, but the fact of applying one rule to all the members of an essential category. Equality of treatment is merely a logical consequence of the fact of keeping to the rule.

If, however, equality seems to play so large a part in practice, it is because the rule of justice very often includes elements whose determination depends on the number of persons to whom the rule is applicable. The rule itself thus appears to be founded on a relation between the members of the same category, that is, their equality.

Let us suppose that it is a question of judging people according to their merit. If we are, like God, free to mete out our rewards and punishments, in full assurance that their number is inexhaustible, we can define a precise and determined rule and be satisfied to apply it. This rule will not have to pay any regard to the number of persons to be rewarded or punished, because we know there is enough for everybody. In such a case, we see at once that equality is merely a consequence, that it flows from the fact that two beings to whom we have applied the rule are placed in the same essential category.

Similarly, the judge, when it comes to sentencing a criminal, usually has no other consideration in mind than applying the law. He tells himself there will always be plenty of room in the prisons. But if the prison becomes too small for the number of prisoners to be kept in custody, if the judge is obliged to have regard to this new factor in administering the penalty, he will be led to apportion this in relation to the number of persons liable to share in it.

This hypothesis may appear singular, because the conditions of its application are abnormal, but it becomes much more plausible when it comes to distributing rewards. In effect, whereas we may assume that the number of places in Paradise is unlimited, the greater part of the rewards made on earth, and all sharings out, permit the distribution of goods only in limited quantities, and so must take account of the number of beneficiaries in order to establish the share of each individual.

Let us assume that in a case of inheritance the share of the sons has to be twice that of the daughters. Then, if there are two sons and two daughters, we must assume that each son will receive the same, and the elder daughter the same as her sister, in order to arrive at the fraction to be allotted to the one or the other.

The use made of equality in the computation may lead to no practical error, since equality is a consequence of following the rule. It can, however, produce errors of perspective when the nature of justice is in question. It may cause to be regarded as essential what is simply the consequence of following a rule.

Formal justice, then, simply comes down to the correct application of a rule.

From this conclusion we can at once understand how far formal justice constitutes the element common to all the conceptions of concrete justice. Each of these favours a different rule, but they all affirm that to be just is to apply *a* rule—their own.

On the other hand, we see how formal justice is linked with logic. Indeed, the application of the rule must be correct and logically impeccable: the just act must be in conformity with the conclusion of a specific syllogism. We will call this the deontic syllogism because its major term and its conclusion are norms of conduct.

Let us assume that it is a question of just treatment to be applied to m_1. If m_1 is an A, and if all A's must be B, then m_1 must be B. If through our action m_1 has become B, then our action has been just. Similarly, if m_2, m_3, m_4 are A's, our action, in order to be just, must make them all B's. The equality of treatment results from a syllogism being applied in our action to the members of one and the same essential category.

This reasoning enables us to clarify our thinking about formal justice. To be just does not consist in applying correctly any rule whatever. One is not being just when applying, for example, the rule 'you must not lie'. For the rule to be applied should have a certain logical structure. It must enunciate, or imply, the major term of a deontic syllogism having the form:

> All M's ought to be P
> or   No M ought to be P.

The rule to be applied will be a universal, affirmative or negative, containing an obligation to treat all the persons in a given category in a certain way. The universality of the rule is no more than a consequence of the fact that it applies to all the persons in a category. The rule will be affirmative or negative according as it has to do with an obligation to act or to refrain from action.

These clarifications make it possible to furnish a third definition of formal justice. It consists in *observing a rule which lays down the obligation to treat in a certain way all persons who belong to a given category.*

This definition is equivalent to the two preceding ones. In effect, we have seen that equality of treatment is linked to the fact of observing a rule. On the other hand, the category in question in the definition is the essential category, for it is the category that is taken into account in the application of justice.

The conditions for the application of formal justice reduce themselves to the three components of a deontic syllogism:

(*a*) the rule to be applied, which provides the major term of the syllogism;
(*b*) the quality of the person—the fact of regarding him as a member of a given category—which provides the minor term of the syllogism;
(*c*) the just act, which must be consistent with the conclusion of the syllogism.

The foregoing thoughts bring to light the kinship existing between justice and the requirements of our reason. Justice is in conformity with a chain of reasoning. To use the language of Kant, we might say that it is a manifestation of practical reason. It is in this respect, indeed, that justice stands in contrast to the other virtues. These, with their greater spontaneity, bear directly on the real, whereas justice postulates the insertion of the real into categories regarded as essential.

Charity is the virtue most directly opposed to justice. It can be exercised spontaneously, without calculation or preliminary reflection. Its aim is to relieve suffering, whatever it may be, regardless of any other circumstances. Charity is symbolised by the white-veiled sister moving from one wounded man to another and finding for each the soothing remedy, the comforting word. She is not concerned with the merits of any of them nor with the severity of their injuries. Men are in pain and they must be helped, without restriction and without reservation. The ideal of charity is unconditional and constitutes a categorical imperative. It is universal and is limited neither by rules, nor by conditions, nor by words. Charity is instinctive, direct, not open to discussion. There is no agreement on formulas of charity, because charity has no need of formulas to express itself. It is a stranger not only to any conception of system, but even to any form of reasoning. It dispenses with any discursive element.

Justice, on the contrary, is inconceivable without rules. Justice is fidelity to rule, obedience to system. It can do without emotion or enthusiasm. We think of it as of a cold and severe old man, weighing, calculating, measuring. Nothing can be less spontaneous than justice. The individual is nothing for it: it must see only a member of a class. All that is individual, spontaneous, emotional, the administration of justice should do its best to disregard. It cannot love, for to it favouritism is forbidden. Its attachment can be the result only of esteem, of careful evaluation. It must be strictly calculated, measured, proportioned. Justice cannot be instinctive: it is subject to rules, conditions, qualifications. The obligation it imposes is conditional, hypothetical, for the way one will act depends on the category to which the subject of action belongs. The administration of justice postulates reflection, discernment, judgment, reasoning. In this sense, justice is a rational virtue, the manifestation of reason in action.

Be it noted in this connection that the administration of formal justice demands in the practical field the same steps of reasoning as are necessitated in the theoretical field by the administration of a law.

An act, to be just, must give effect to the conclusion of a syllogism in which the major term is constituted by a formula of concrete justice or by one of its consequences, and the minor by a qualification which incorporates a being in an essential category.

The application of a theoretical law to particular facts presents exactly the same structure. The major is constituted by a universal law, the minor by a qualification and the conclusion will be an assertion about reality.

Take the classic example of the theoretical syllogism:

> All men are mortal,
> Now Socrates is a man,
> Therefore Socrates is mortal.

The structure of this syllogism differs from that of a deontic syllogism solely in the fact that its major term and its conclusion assert, not what ought to be, but what is. This difference has by way of consequence the establishment of other relations between the fact and the rule, in the theoretical as in the practical field.

Theoretical law admits of no exception: it is universally or necessarily true. A single fact contrary to the law is enough to invalidate it. In this sense it can be affirmed that fact takes precedence over law, for it is the former that disqualifies the latter; it is facts that put laws to the proof. In the theoretical field it is the facts that establish the standard. This conception is the very condition of induction.

Per contra, practical, normative law can be neither universally nor necessarily followed. Where there is necessity, there can be no obligation. On the contrary, obligation postulates liberty. Constraint can be applied only to the free. Regulation can be applied only to what is not necessitated. Accordingly, the conception of a normative law assumes the existence of facts not in conformity with it. But the existence of a fact of this kind does not invalidate the law. On the contrary, it is the law that imposes itself on the facts and is the judge, not of their reality, but of their value. It follows that normative laws as prescribing standards cannot have an inductive basis.

It is most important to know whether a field of reality is subject to theoretical or to normative laws, the former stating what is, the latter determining what has value. In effect, everything subject to theoretical laws is outside the scope of human will no less than of human evaluation, which is to be regarded as one of the ways of acting on a will that is free. When we affirm that a field of human activity is subject to theoretical laws our aim is to remove it from the action of the human will and from that of normative laws. The consequence of affirming that the law of supply and demand rules economic life is to remove economic phenomena from the normative rules that would attempt to control economic life. On the contrary, regulation of economic life (fixed prices and wages, rationing) prove that the law of supply and demand is no more than a tendency which mankind can canalise like the course of a river.

If we speak of the injustice of nature or of destiny we are positing that they are not ruled by universal laws but by normative laws. We are positing that the unfolding of natural phenomena depends on a will capable of subjecting itself to laws, but capable also of freeing itself from them. As the necessary is not susceptible to a value judgment, making such a judgment is equivalent to assuming that what is evaluated is not necessary, that the fact depends on a will which could modify it. The necessary is that which it is not possible to negate. Assuming the possibility of such a negation comes to the same thing as denying the opposite necessity: it is making the occurrence of a phenomenon dependent on a will, on an arbitrary factor. The intervention of the divine will, by eliminating necessity, subjects the universe to normative laws and makes possible appreciations of its value.

If we set aside the difference we have just brought out—between theoretical and normative laws—we shall note the existence of a like scheme of reasoning which is used to explain a phenomenon as well as to justify an act.

To explain a phenomenon is to show how it is deduced from the accepted rules. The explanation is relative to those rules. If it conforms to the conclusion of a chain of reasoning which invokes accepted premises the phenomenon is explained.

The same thing applies when it comes to justifying an act. The act is just if it conforms to the conclusion of a chain of reasoning of which the premises have been granted, one of these constituting a deontic judgment flowing from a formula of concrete justice.

Explanation and justification make use of the same procedures of reasoning. They differ only in the nature of one of the premises of the argument.

Formal justice consists in observing a rule containing an obligation to treat all the members of a given category in a certain way.

This definition reminds us strongly of the conception put forward by Professor Dupréel under the name of static justice.

'*Static justice,*' he says,[1] '*consists in observing an established rule, whatever that rule may be.* The duty of justice is to apply the recognised rule. The *just* or upright man is he who obeys this duty. Such a man is a judge who administers the law scrupulously. The teacher shows himself to be just by giving each pupil the marks and the form-order he deserves: it is because he respects the rule and the conditions of the examination.

'Static justice, then, or justice in the strict sense (integrity) appears as a rule superimposed on the other rules, and ensuring their observance by making that observance a moral duty. Not that all the rules or conventions we find established in a society are in themselves moral rules. This quality could not be claimed by all the provisions of regulations which are based on opportunist reasons or reasons of specific convenience, as for example the proportion the state will levy on inheritances or the side of the road vehicles are to keep to. It was no moral law that inspired the inventor of the game of piquet to fix the relative values of the king and the ace. But once these conventions are established it becomes unjust to infringe them. At every moment consent to the advantages of being a member of a society implies the commitment to observe all its rules, and it is to this implied commitment that the *rule of justice* corresponds.

'Justice (static justice) is, then, the *rule of rules* of a society. It is what gives a moral value to respect for regulations of every kind, even when these are not in themselves specifically moral. Justice is, then, *par excellence*, the moral rule guaranteeing the very existence of the social group, because it is justice that entails moral demerit in the perpetrator of any infraction of the rules of the group, no matter what the nature of those rules.'

Static justice, then, is based on the established rules, on the rules recognised by the group. This conception is in one sense narrower than that of formal justice, which is based on the rules accepted by the one who applies them, whether or not they are imposed by the group.

In another sense formal justice is narrower than static justice in that it calls for the observance of rules of a given nature, and not of just any established rule. Static justice, by sanctioning any rule whatever, juridical or moral, thus coincides with the entire field of morality, whereas formal justice is based on the feeling for equality

[1] *Traité de Morale*, Vol. II, pp. 485–486.

which can be explained only by the application of rules having a well-defined logical nature.

Formal justice tells us that an act is just when it is the result of applying a certain rule. But when can it be said of the rule that *it* is just? Formal justice does not teach us. True, this very silence would enable us without difficulty to manufacture an agreement on the definition of this idea, but many readers will feel by no means satisfied. They will declare that the problem, so far from being solved, has simply been evaded, because we have been content to define a formal justice that is no more than an empty formula.

True justice, these critics will say, consists, not in the correct application of a rule, but in the correct application of a just rule. It is not enough, then, they will say, to rest content with the definition of a just act, independently of the value of the rule. Indeed, neither the analysis of our feeling for justice nor that of the idea of justice is complete if we are content to establish a purely formal justice, and to do so in such a way that our analysis does not allow of choice between a number of formulas of concrete justice, or put us in a position to say when a rule is just and when it is not.

If formal justice is a principle of action enabling us to distinguish just acts from those that are not, it would be highly desirable to find a theoretical criterion which would enable us to distinguish just rules from those that do not deserve that description. In the rest of this study we will try to establish how far it is possible to satisfy this desire.

(v) THE ARBITRARY IN JUSTICE

An act is formally just if it observes a rule which sets out the obligation to treat all the members of a given category in a certain way. Note that the rule itself is not subjected to any ethical criterion: the only condition it must comply with is purely logical in character. Whether it be a case of punishing or rewarding, of applying a law regarding inheritance, a regulation about highway maintenance or a customs duty, if the rule imposes the obligation to treat the members of a given class in a certain way, then observance of the rule results in a formally just act.

We may wonder, not without reason, whether this indefiniteness over the very content of the rule may not lead shrewd minds to evade any accusation of formal injustice, while leaving them almost complete liberty of action and allowing them the fullest possible scope for arbitrary behaviour. Indeed, when we wish not to treat according to the rule a member of a certain essential category, there is nothing to stop us from modifying the rule by means of a supplementary condition causing two categories to emerge where formerly there was only one. This subdivision would at once make it possible to differentiate between the treatment of persons who would thenceforward belong to two different categories. The modification can be of any kind. It can just as well consist in some spatio-temporal restriction as in a limitation afforded by any property whatever of some members of the category. Instead, for example, of saying 'All M's ought to be P', we might say 'All M's born before 1500 ought to be P', or 'All M's born in Europe ought to be P', or, in general terms, 'All M's possessing the quality A ought to be P'. The immediate consequence of this modification of the rule is that all M's born after 1500, born outside Europe, or, in general terms, all M's not having the quality A, ought no longer to be P. Since the old rule no longer applies to them, one is free to elaborate a new rule which will say how they ought to be treated. Here is the whole art of casuistry.

Rather than act in a fashion that is formally unjust, by treating unequally two persons who belong to the same essential category, we shall prefer so to modify the rule that, formally, the action is just and beyond reproach.

Let us take a graphic example of this procedure from contemporary tariff policy.

In these days the tariff policy of states constitutes one of the attributes of their sovereignty. Accordingly, they can, at their own sweet will, levy duty on products of foreign origin which it is desired to introduce into their territory. However, with a view to facilitating international trade, states are led to limit the arbitrary exercise of their powers in the field of tariffs by means of commercial treaties which bind the contracting parties for a stated period of time. Certain of these treaties contain the 'most-favoured-nation clause', which allows the exporters of the state to which this treatment is accorded to benefit from the most favourable customs tariff accorded to any state on any product.

Let us suppose that, in a country A, Denmark benefits from the most-favoured-nation clause. If state A allows Swiss butter to cross its frontiers in consideration of a very low duty, it will be automatically obliged to allow the entry of Danish butter at the same rate of duty: otherwise A infringes its commercial treaty with Denmark and acts in a way that is formally unjust.

State A, notwithstanding the most-favoured-nation clause, does not want to grant the Danish exporters the benefit of its agreement with Switzerland. Neither does it want openly to break its treaty with Denmark. So it gets out of the difficulty by a modification of the rule. Instead of lowering the duty on all butter, it lowers the duty on butter 'originating from cows whose pastures are situated at heights of more than 1,000 metres'. This rule, applying to Swiss butter but not to Danish butter, makes it possible to favour Switzerland without violating the most-favoured-nation clause.

What is the upshot of these thoughts? That it is possible, by means of a modification of the rule, to avoid formal injustice, and this can be done in all cases where the rule itself is not prescribed. In all those cases formal justice can coincide with real inequality due to the arbitrary factor in the rules. The result is that formal justice plays a very minor role in all cases in which there is no question of established rules, imposed on the one who has to observe them.

When there is an established rule to observe, we touch that section of formal justice which coincides with what Professor Dupréel calls static justice, the role of which in practical life is far from negligible, for it constitutes the basis of justice in the administration of positive law.

But if we want formal justice not to be an empty formula outside the field of positive law—whether in ethics or in natural law—it is indispensable to eliminate as far as possible the element of the *arbitrary* in the rules that formal justice has to apply.

The condition imposed by this requirement on the rules will now apply, not to their form, but to their content. Nevertheless, this condition does not exhaust the content of the rule, but imposes on it integration in a system. The consequence of this obligation will be to stress the rational character of the rules of justice.

It is impossible to say what a just rule is without offering a

47

definition—always questionable—of the idea of justice. It does, however, seem possible, without a subjective definition of an idea whose emotive meaning is very pronounced, to complete our thinking about formal justice by analysing the conditions of a rational nature imposed on the rules of concrete justice with a view to obviating the arbitrary element in them.

The formulas of concrete justice lay down or imply essential categories whose members ought to be treated in a certain way, the same for all.

To regard such a formula as unjust amounts to questioning either the classification it lays down or the treatment it provides for the members of the different categories.

Let us assume that the formula prescribes that all the beings we are concerned with are to be divided into three categories A, B, and C, and that the result is that 'All A's ought to be P', 'All B's ought to be R' and 'All C's ought to be S'. In affirming that the rule is unjust, we can either object to the division into three categories, or else, while admitting the soundness of this division, we can regard as unjust the differences in the treatment provided for the members of the three categories. The first criticism will usually come from the advocates of another formula of concrete justice, while the second will be that of a partisan of another interpretation of the same formula.

Let us take a concrete example of controversy about practical questions, presenting it for the sake of clarity as a straightforward application of the formulas of concrete justice.

The system of family allowances, assuming it is regarded as putting into practice the formula 'to each according to his needs', can be attacked on the ground of its being unjust that, in settling the wages of the workers, regard is had to anything but their output. Naturally the supporter of the formula 'to each according to his works' will divide the workers into categories different from those selected by the man who has regard to the formula 'to each according to his needs'. He can accordingly bring a charge of injustice against the classification determined by this latter rule of concrete justice. But someone who finds the system of family allowances fully justified may find it unjust that, for example, the fourth child gets an allowance ten times as big as that granted to the first child, whereas it is the increase in the household expenses due to the first child that is felt the most.

It is at once obvious that this latter criticism is of quite another order than the first. Indeed, it takes its stand on the same ground as the person to whom it is addressed. It already grants a certain common platform in the necessity for family allowances to subsidise the needs of the household. *Per contra*, when a man finds it unjust to have regard to any other formula than that which remunerates the workers in proportion to their output, his criticism does not attach importance to the same value as does the formula 'to each according to his needs'; and it will be infinitely more difficult to find a common ground of understanding between the advocates of these different formulas of justice.

To begin with let us examine the objections of the man who finds it unjust that there should be too great a difference in the treatment of members of various essential categories which he regards as soundly established, and how his objections could be justified.

In criticising French criminal law, which in his view was profoundly unjust, Proudhon wrote: [1]

'A poor devil whose children are crying with hunger, climbs up to a loft at night, breaks in and steals a quartern loaf. The baker gets him sentenced to eight years with hard labour. That is law ... On the other hand, the same baker, charged with putting plaster into his bread instead of flour and vitriol for yeast, is sentenced to a five-pound fine. That is the law. Now, conscience cries out that this trader is a monster and the law itself hateful and absurd. Whence comes this discrepancy?'

Proudhon sees nothing wrong in punishment being meted out to the man who breaks in and burgles as well as to the man who adulterates foodstuffs. What he does find wrong is the disproportion in the two cases between the penalty and the gravity of the crime committed.

What should be the answer to Proudhon to justify the difference in treatment provided for the members of these two categories established by the criminal law? How prove that this is not a matter of measures arbitrarily adopted but of just measures knowingly and advisedly taken? It would be necessary so to define the concept 'gravity of the crime' that the result would, contrary to Proudhon's affirmation, be due proportion between the penalty and the gravity of the act.

[1] PROUDHON, *De La Justice*, Vol. III, p. 169.

In order to show that the rules establishing two different categories, as well as the treatment meted out to their members, are not arbitrary, it is necessary to show that the two rules, and the differences they imply, can be deduced from a broader, more general principle of which they are merely particular cases.

Similarly if we ask, 'Is it just that a labourer should earn five francs an hour, when such and such a doctor earns 50,000 francs a month?' the answer could be that the difference in treatment has nothing to do with justice, being merely an effect of the law of supply and demand. Or, if one wishes to defend the difference as well founded, one will have to find a broader category—such, for instance, as that of the importance of the service rendered—from which it would be possible to deduce the difference in treatment between a labourer and a distinguished doctor.

These two examples are enough to show what is to be understood by an arbitrary rule. A rule is arbitrary in so far as, not being a necessary consequence of a theoretical law, it is not capable of justification.

To speak of other than formal injustice amounts always to a comparison of two different rules. The reasoning with which one could counter it would not prove that the rules are just, because one cannot force the same conception of justice on everybody—but at least it would prove that they are not arbitrary, because they are justified and can be deduced from a more general rule of which they merely constitute particular cases.

In the case of formal justice we are content to compare the treatment meted out to the members of the same essential category, but we have no way of comparing the categories one with another. On the other hand, the criticism directed against a rule of concrete justice leads us to search for a basis of comparison between various essential categories so as to justify the difference in treatment as between those different categories by reference to the relation between each category and the genus on which it depends.

When someone is accused of formulating an unjust rule—unjust because it favours the members of one category as against those of another—his answer can only be to point to the more general rule from which the two rules under comparison can be logically deduced. Justification always consists in showing how a given category fits into a wider category, how a particular rule is deduced from a more general rule.

We have seen the analogy that exists between the explanation of a phenomenon and the justification of an act, how the just act and the phenomenon explained both coincide with the conclusion of a syllogism. We shall not be at all surprised to find the same analogy holds between the fact of explaining a theoretical law and the justification of a normative rule.

Explaining a law amounts to showing that it is deduced from a more general system of which, under given conditions, it constitutes a particular case. Thus, the law of terrestrial attraction constitutes a particular case of the principle of universal gravitation. The need to explain the law of terrestrial attraction made itself felt when the thinker's attention was drawn to an abnormal difference in behaviour. Why does the apple fall to the ground when the moon, subjected to the same attraction, does not crash into the earth by which it is attracted? Why do the apple and the moon behave differently in relation to the earth? The explanation was furnished by the principle of universal gravitation, from which it was possible to deduce both the law of terrestrial attraction and the moon's resistance *vis-à-vis* the earth.

Similarly, the justification of a normative law invokes a more general principle from which can be deduced the different treatment applied to persons who belong to different essential categories.

These considerations show up once again the relativity both of explanation and of justification: every explanation is relative to certain more general laws, and every justification is relative to more abstract principles. But, in view of their arbitrary character, we may also wish to explain those laws, and we may also be under the duty of justifying those principles. Explanation and justification will then have recourse to still more general laws, to still more abstract principles. In the theoretical, as in the practical, field we shall end up by constructing rational systems. The theoretical system of science will be matched by a normative system of justice.

Nevertheless, however far back we go in explanation and justification, there will be a point at which we come to a halt. This halt may be only provisional, and there will be nothing necessary about it. But it will determine the peak of a stage of science, the ceiling of a normative system.

The most general laws of science, which make it possible to

explain all the rest but themselves remain unexplained, fix the most general outlines of reality. It is they which prevent the universe from reducing itself to a tautology, to a mere development of the principle of identity. It is their existence that enables science to look forward to fresh developments, to fresh progress in depth. We will not say, with E. Meyerson, that explanation is no more than the reduction of reality to an identity, but we affirm that it is the fact that this reduction cannot, and never can, be made, that enables us to understand why explanation is always relative and always incomplete and why science will never succeed in exhausting the object of its study.

The laws at the peak of our scientific system may make us accept connections which are logically arbitrary, because unexplained, but there can be no question of casting doubt on them. Indeed, the connections they affirm are universal and define our reality. We can only bow before the facts.

But it is quite otherwise in a normative system. The most general principles of such a system, instead of asserting what is, establish what has value. They lay down a value, the most general value, whence are deduced standards, norms, commandments. Now this value has no basis either in logic or in reality. Since its affirmation results neither from a logical necessity nor from an experiential universality, value is neither universal nor necessary. It is, logically and experientially, arbitrary. It is indeed its arbitrary, and therefore precarious, character that distinguishes value from reality. Just as the norm postulates liberty, so value postulates the arbitrary.

Our attempt to justify rules in order, within the bounds of possibility, to eliminate the arbitrary from them must come to a halt at an unjustified principle, an arbitrary value. A system of justice, no matter how advanced, cannot eliminate all trace of the arbitrary. Otherwise, indeed, it would no longer be a normative system prescribing a standard. It would lay down a logical necessity or an experiential universality, and its normative character would at once disappear.

Any system of justice constitutes no more than the development of one or more values whose arbitrary character is linked to their very nature. This enables us to understand why there is not one single system of justice, and why there can exist as many as there are different values. It follows that if a rule is regarded as unjust by an advocate of another formula of concrete justice—and therefore of a different division into essential categories—all that can be done is to note the antagonism which sets the supporters of the different formulas of justice at odds. In effect, each of them is putting a different value in the foreground. Given the large number of values, the conflict between them, and their arbitrary character, reasoning is unable to decide in favour of either antagonist failing an agreement on such principles as might serve as a starting-point for the argument. For agreement on the rules of justice to be established, it is necessary to be able to justify all the rules under attack, and to refrain from attacking those that cannot be justified, those, that is, which, in the conduct of our action, allot first place to certain values.

If we regard a rule as unjust because it accords pre-eminence to a different value, we can only note the disagreement. No reasoning will be able to show that either one of the opponents is in the wrong. Be it noted that while such a state of affairs occurs most often in discussions of the division of beings into essential categories, it is possible for questions of value to arise even when the subject under discussion is the treatment to be provided for the members of certain categories.

Let us take the criticism directed by Proudhon against French criminal law. We have seen that the opponents could have reached agreement if they had given the same definition to 'the gravity of the crime'. If for one that gravity depends on the disturbance caused to the social order, and for the other on the suffering inflicted on the victim of the crime, we shall find ourselves confronted with two incompatible points of view, each based on a different conception of criminal law, the one concerned primarily with the protection of society, the other putting the individual in the forefront. The result of this difference will in very many cases be a different evaluation of the gravity of the crime. According to the man who is concerned above all with the disturbance caused to society, the theft of a sum of money in the same circumstances will be punishable in the same way, and little weight will be given to the suffering caused by the theft. Contrariwise, the man who is primarily concerned with that suffering will regard the theft of the entire savings of a cripple as infinitely more hateful and grave than the theft of the same amount from the strong-room of a large bank, and will demand a much severer penalty for the first crime.

E

We see how a different conception of the gravity of the crime will make it possible to range in a different order of importance the categories established by criminal law. Thus it is that, in the final reckoning, disagreement about the treatment provided for the members of an essential category, when it flows from disagreement about values, likewise brings about a change in the classification of persons or of acts.

It is only when there is agreement on the values which a normative system develops that we can try to justify the rules and that it is possible to eliminate every factor tending arbitrarily to favour or disfavour the members of a certain essential category. Where agreement on values allows of the rational development of a normative system, the arbitrary will consist in the introduction of rules foreign to the system. It will be possible to attack these rules as unjust, because they are arbitrary and not soundly based.

A rule, then, is not arbitrary in itself. It becomes so only to the extent that it remains unjustified. Since the arbitrary, like justification, is relative to other rules, the entire system is founded on the principles at its base, and its value is linked to that of the arbitrary and unjustified assertions which serve as its foundation. Thus it is that every system of justice will finally depend on values other than the *value of justice*, and its proper moral value will be in function of the arbitrary assertions on the basis of which the system develops.

Professor Dupréel reaches a conclusion of the same kind by means of arguments of a different order.

'There does not exist,' he says,[1] '*an ideal of justice*, unique and capable of being contrasted, when set on the same plane, with some other ideal such as charity or purity. *There are multiple forms of the ideal of justice*, and each one of them has a content which is never *pure justice*, the just in itself, but is *any kind of ideal*, reducible to some other form of disinterested moral aspiration. That is why *the ideal of justice is invariably an aspect which is bestowed on a given ideal, of some variable kind*. Justice is the eulogistic name we give to what we conceive to be good.'

Professor Dupréel proves his assertion not, as we have done, by a purely formal analysis, but by examining three formulas of concrete justice—'to each the same thing', 'to each according to his needs' and 'to each according to his merits'.

By means of an analysis as delicate as it is profound, he shows

[1] *Traité de Morale*, Vol. II, p. 491.

that the egalitarian formula of justice expresses an ideal of respect for persons or of generalised honour.

'The best social order,' he writes,[1] 'would not be that in which each individual could benefit, without any restraint, from all the consequences of his own advantages, his own capacities or the favours of others. Such a situation would constitute a state of inequality indefinitely reinforced, and it will be well to replace it by a convention whereby one and the same fundamental quality or dignity, and one and the same system of prerogatives are acknowledged for every member of society or for all mankind . . .

'For the brute fact of the existence of individuals materially unequal, and unequally capable of taking advantage of such goods as may come their way, the egalitarian proposes to substitute the idea of the person endowed in advance with a minimum of inalienable and identical rights.'

The formula 'to each according to his needs' has value because, 'in applying it, we seem to have the greatest chance of producing, in the circumstances envisaged, the maximum of pleasure and the minimum of pain. But if that be so, this formula corresponds to *an ideal of beneficence*. It is based on the absolute moral value of pain abolished and pleasure promoted. This proportionality is just because it is beneficent. It puts itself forward as the best procedure in the art of well-doing. So that, presented in this form, the ideal of justice is determined only by a content which is not justice in itself, but beneficence.'[2]

As for the formula of distributive justice—'to each according to his merits'—Professor Dupréel notes one thing which is incontestably correct, and that is that to grant the formula is to assume prior agreement on the determining values regarded as merits. 'Now, these merits can only be *virtues of some kind or other*, or rather they will be all the virtues, such as being of service to society or to individuals, respecting rules and conventions, realising the best, and so on . . . From that point this ideal of justice, this alleged nucleus of pure justice, comes down to a *sanction of the other moral values previously acknowledged*! If it is just that the most meritorious should receive the most gratification, it means that justice takes only second place in consecrating values which by itself it suffices neither to engender nor to define.'[3]

[1] *Traité de Morale*, Vol. II, p. 492.
[2] *Ibid.*, Vol. II, pp. 493–494.   [3] *Ibid.*, Vol. II, p. 495.

Basing his case on these three examples, Professor Dupréel shows that any ideal of justice depends on values other than justice itself. His arguments make possible a luminous illustration of the thesis, which we think we have independently demonstrated, that any system of justice depends on the values laid down by its principles.

Nevertheless, justice does possess a proper value of its own, whatever the other values on which it is based. It is the value resulting from the fact that its application satisfies a rational need for coherence and regularity.

Let us take the example of a normative system which has the peculiarity of attaching the highest merit to the stature of individuals. From this system will flow rules imposing the obligation to treat men in a fashion more or less proportional to their height. From this system one can try to eliminate every arbitrary rule, all unequal treatment, all favouritism, all injustice. From the inside of the system, so long as the fundamental principle that serves as its basis is not called in question, justice will have a well-defined meaning—that of avoiding anything arbitrary in the rules, any irregularity in action.

We are thus led to distinguish three elements in justice—the value that is its foundation, the rule that sets it out, the act that gives it effect.

Only the two latter elements—the less important, incidentally—can be subjected to the requirements of reasoning. We can require of the act that it should be in accordance with the rules, that it should give the same treatment to persons who belong to the same essential category. We can require that the rule should be justified, that it should flow logically from the normative system adopted. As for the value that is the foundation of the normative system, we cannot subject it to any rational criterion: it is utterly arbitrary and logically indeterminate. Indeed, while any value whatever can serve as foundation for a system of justice, that value in itself is not just. What we can characterise as just consists of the rules established by the value, and the acts that are in conformity with the rules.

The effect of the arbitrary character of the values on which a normative system is based, their large number and their mutual conflict, is that a necessary and perfect system of justice is unattainable. If we posit the existence of a perfect system of justice we affirm that the value on which it is based imposes itself in an irrepressible way, in short we are affirming the existence of one single value dominating or embracing all the others. The preeminence of that value would not now be arbitrary: it would impose itself logically or experientially, it would be the result of rational necessity or of a fact of experience. Now this hypothesis itself contains an interior contradiction. The idea of value is, in effect, incompatible both with formal necessity and with experiential universality. There is no value which is not logically arbitrary.[1]

Only a very simple-minded rationalism supposes reason capable of discovering self-evident truths and unquestionable values. Since justice has ever been regarded as the manifestation of reason in action, dogmatic rationalism used to believe in the possibility of evolving a system of perfect justice.

Critical rationalism, on the other hand, in diminishing the role of reason and allowing it no power to determine the content of our judgments, is led, by way of reaction, to limit its importance in the establishment of a normative system. Justice, in its capacity as the manifestation of reason in action, has to be content with a formally correct development of one or more values which are determined neither by reason nor by a feeling for justice.

Just as the discussion on formal justice was inconclusive when the aim was to find a simple way of reconciling the different formulas of concrete justice, so the discussion on the rules of justice will be inconclusive if our aim is, finally, to do away with all difference of opinion about values. Our requirement for justice must confine itself to ridding the rules of anything arbitrary which is not the result of an irreducible value judgment. Even as a just act is relative to a rule, the just rule will be relative to the values which serve as basis to the normative system.

All value being arbitrary, there is no absolute justice entirely founded on reason. To be more precise, there is no absolute justice save in respect of identical persons who, whatever the criterion chosen, will always belong to the same essential category. Once the two persons are no longer identical; once the question has to be asked whether the difference separating them must be disregarded or, on the contrary, taken into account; once a

---

[1] Since these lines were written, the author has tried to present, through his theory of argumentation, a way of reasoning about values.

distinction has to be drawn between the qualities that are essential and those that are secondary for the administration of justice; then considerations of value are brought in, and these are necessarily arbitrary.

It is the emotive character of the values at the basis of any normative system that makes the administration of justice appear as an operation from which all trace of the affective is not entirely excluded. A system of justice can throughout reflect the colouring of the fundamental value of which it constitutes a rational development.

With a normative system based on the ideal of beneficence, we may even be led to put obstacles in the way of the strict administration of justice, if such irregularity results in diminishing suffering. We shall not think too badly of the judge who does not administer the law in its full rigour if he does this solely in consideration of an exceptionally unhappy situation. Similarly, the prerogative of mercy with which sovereigns are endowed enables them to soften the severities of the law by taking into account special circumstances which the judge did not have to take into consideration.

Moreover, the real inequalities taken into account in applying a formula of justice raise a fresh problem for the conscience. Is it just that people or their acts should be naturally unequal? Is it just that one man should be born straight and another crooked, one good-looking and one deformed? Two different ways of answering this question are possible. It can be said that inequality is an effect of natural law, of destiny, and that justice is a stranger to all that is necessary. On the other hand, a believer will answer that these inequalities are the result of the divine will, whose decrees are inscrutable. But either of these answers will have, as a consequence, some tempering of the administration of justice. The first will bring in the idea of irresponsibility, in such fashion that only those acts will be punished which appear to be the doing of a free, and therefore responsible, will. The other will have as consequence that the administration of justice will be mitigated by charity, for those from whom God withholds his benefits ought to be able at least to look to the compassion of men for some compensation.

The effect of the arbitrary foundations of justice is that it does not force itself on us directly as do other more spontaneous virtues, so that last-ditch intransigence in its administration can even lead to consequences which a noble soul will feel to be unjust—*summum jus, summa injuria.* That is why a person with a passion for justice will not be content with blind and rigid application of the rules flowing from his normative system: he will always have in mind the arbitrary basis of his system, which is not, and never can be, a perfect one. He will not forget that, beside the values he recognises, there exist other values for which men will be led by their devotion to sacrifice themselves, and that a revision of values is always possible.

Thus, while justice has the appearance of being the sole rational virtue, in contrast with the irregularity of our acts and the arbitrary character of our rules, we must not forget that its own action is itself based on arbitrary and irrational values, in contrast to which stand other values to which a refined feeling for justice cannot remain altogether insensible.

(vi) CONCLUSION

Justice is a prestige-laden and confused idea. A clear and precise definition of the term cannot exhaust the conceptual content, variable and diverse as it is, to be found in its daily usage. In defining it we can emphasise only one aspect of justice, and to this we try to transfer all the prestige of justice taking all its usages as a whole. This way of proceeding has the drawback of effecting, by means of a logical subterfuge, the transfer of an emotion from a term to the meaning we desire arbitrarily to give it. In order to avoid this drawback, the analysis of justice will be limited to seeking out the factor common to various conceptions of justice: this factor obviously does not exhaust the full meaning of the idea, but it can be defined clearly and precisely.

This common factor, called formal justice, enables us to say when an *act* is regarded as just. The justice of an act consists in the equality of treatment it provides for all the members of one and the same essential category. This equality itself results from the conformity of the act to rule, from the fact that it coincides with a consequence of a given rule of justice. Proceeding from this point, we have been able to define the notion of equity which makes it possible to escape the contradictions of justice in which we become involved through desiring to apply several incompatible rules of justice simultaneously.

It is a much more delicate matter to define an idea enabling us to say when a *rule* is just. The only requirement we can formulate in respect of a rule is that it should not be arbitrary, but should justify itself, should flow from a normative system.

But a normative system, of whatever kind, always contains an arbitrary element—the value affirmed by its basic principles which themselves are not justified. This latter touch of the arbitrary it is logically impossible to avoid. The only claim one could rightfully make would consist in eliminating everything arbitrary save what is implied in affirming the values at the basis of the system. Since, on the other hand, the arbitrary element in any normative system serves to sanction natural inequalities, which also are not susceptible of justification, it follows that, for this double reason, there is no necessary and perfect justice.

This imperfection of any system of justice, the inevitable element of the arbitrary that it contains, should always be present to the mind of the man who would apply the system's extreme consequences. Only in the name of a perfect justice would it be morally right to affirm *pereat mundus, fiat justitia*. But any imperfect normative system, if it is to be ethically beyond reproach, should draw fresh inspiration from contact with the more immediate and more spontaneous values. No system of justice should lose sight of its own imperfection. Every system should thence conclude that an imperfect justice, without charity, is no justice.

II

THE THREE ASPECTS OF JUSTICE[1]

1. IN all the normative disciplines which directly or indirectly govern action in regard to others—whether it be law or political philosophy, ethics or religion—justice constitutes a central value. No other can be invoked that is so full of associations when it comes to characterising an act (such as a judicial decision), a rule or a reasonable agent. The search for the conditions which make it possible to attribute the quality of being *just* to an act, a rule or an agent amounts to determining the criteria of what has value, of what deserves approval, in the field of social action. Since, however, every world-view fashions in its own way the criteria of value with respect to conduct, there will not be the slightest cause for surprise in the conclusion which emerges from a study of writings concerning justice.[2] This is that the idea of justice is plunged in ambiguity and confusion, at first sight all the more hopelessly incurable for resulting both from the variety of ideologies which affect the character of the idea and from the diversity of levels at which a theory of justice is developed. In Book V of the Nicomachean Ethics, which so far as we are aware constitutes the first analytic study of the idea, Aristotle was already drawing

---

[1] Extract from *Annales de l'Institut International de Philosophie Politique*. Vol. III: Natural Law. Appeared also in *Revue Internationale de Philosophie*, No. 41, 1957.

[2] In this connection reference may be made to the bibliographic guidance in Professor G. DEL VECCHIO's remarkable study *La Giustizia*, Roma, Studium, 4th ed. 1951; and to the English translation of the work, edited by A. H. Campbell, Edinburgh University Press, 1952.

attention to its ambiguity and to the multiplicity of its aspects.[1]
To facilitate analysis there is, it seems to us, good ground for
treating successively the just act, the just rule and the just man.
Specific requirements are involved in this task, which should precede the examination of the interactions that can occur between
the various levels at which the ideal of justice is appealed to.

2. If we remain exclusively at the level of the act, of the manifestation of a will, we shall characterise the act as just if it is in conformity with the correct application of a rule. At this level the
ideal of justice tends to be modelled on the more elementary
operations of arithmetic and physics: it is desired that decisions
should conform to weighing, measuring or calculating. The judge
apportioning to each his due in accordance with the law can be
assimilated to those advanced machines which indicate the total
the customer is to pay by multiplying the quantity of goods delivered by the price per unit. The total is just because the account
is correct and no one questions either the accuracy of the machine
or the price per unit. On this view the perfect judge would be like
an infallible machine, giving the answer when furnished with the
elements of the problem, without being concerned to know what
is at stake or who might benefit from any possible error. The
bandage covering the eyes of the statue of Justice symbolises this
disinterested attitude: it is not persons—and they are not seen as
such—who are judged, but beings falling into one or another legal
category. The judge is impartial because he pays no respect to
persons. The judgment will be the same whether friends or
enemies are involved, the powerful or the wretched, rich or poor.
All those to whom the same rule applies are to be treated alike,
whatever the consequences. The machine is without passions: it
cannot be intimidated, or corrupted, or, for that matter, moved to
pity. *Dura lex, sed lex.* The rule is equality, that is, interchangeability of those who are subject to justice: their personal particularities will be taken into account only to the extent that doing so
is a legal condition of the application of the law. This is the view
of formal justice,[2] the very formalism of which confers on it a
logical structure encouraging correct deduction and more particularly the use of the syllogism: what is valid for all the members
of a category applies to any particular member of that category.

[1] ARISTOTLE, *Nicomachean Ethics*, 1129.   [2] Cf. *Concerning Justice.*

Nothing should be allowed to interfere with the strict development of the train of reasoning: this is the condition on which it
will be possible to maintain a legal system giving a feeling of
security and certainty to all those who come under it. The ideal of
juridical positivism would be a legal system so well worked out,
laws so clear and complete, that ultimately law could be administered by an automaton. Such an attempt at clarifying and improv-
ing the legal system is the object to which the exegetic school has
devoted itself.

At the level of the act the role of the judge is to apply the law,
such as it is, without any other consideration: it is not to modify
the law in the name of conceptions which pass judgment on the
rules themselves. His justice is static, not dynamic.[1] The just, for
him, is that which conforms to the law. He has not to ask himself, as a judge, if the law conforms to justice. This involves,
obviously, a heteronomous conception of justice, insufficient for
the moralist or the philosopher. Its justification lies in the doctrine
of the separation of powers, which allots the exclusive right of
law-making to the legislature and the power of administering the
law to the judiciary; and sees in the supreme court the policeman
charged by the legislature with the duty of ensuring that the
judges do not violate the law in their judgments and decrees.

Whatever the origin of the rule applied—whether it spring from
an act of the legislative power, from custom or from legal precedent—a decision in accordance with the rules is satisfying to the
mind by reason of that mental inertia which finds it normal and
rational that the decision taken in one case should likewise be
taken in similar cases (*stare decisis*). Whether the decision results
from the application to a specific case of a previously established
rule or of precedents furnished by earlier judgments which constitute a scheme of reasoning applicable to the current case, justice
and reason require that the same attitude should be adopted in
face of essentially identical situations. Change, and change alone,
needs to be justified. In the sphere of thought, as in that of action,
the rule of justice presents as normal the repetition of one and the
same procedure of conduct.[2] This explains the rationality of
formulas of justice which vary greatly—because their starting-

[1] Cf. E. DUPRÉEL, *Traité de Morale*, Brussels, 1932, Vol. II, pp. 485–496.
[2] Cf. C. PERELMAN and L. OLBRECHTS-TYTECA, *Traité de l'Argumentation*,
Paris, 1958, § 52, 'La Règle de Justice'.

points are different—but which all constitute applications of the rule of justice in the field of conduct:

Do not do unto your like what you would not wish him to do to you.
Act towards your like as you would wish him to act towards you.
Require of your like only what you are prepared to carry out yourself.
Agree that you should be treated as you treat your like.
Act in such a way as you would wish all those like you to act.

Like in all these maxims designates him to whom the same categories apply as to the agent.

Defining the just act or decision by reference to the correctly applied rule assumes that no problem is presented either by the choice or by the interpretation of the rule. The rule in accordance with which judgment is to be given should be beyond dispute and clear in all the cases in which it is applied. Failing this, the personal intervention of the judge becomes indispensable, and it will no longer be possible to rest content either with formal justice or with formal logic in order to arrive at a just judgment. Sometimes the decision of the judge in choosing the rule may be determined by strict rules governing the procedure in such cases, but it will not always be so: the law may reveal itself insufficient, and recourse to equity may then appear inevitable.

For Aristotle the equitable is just: it is not the legally just but a correction of legal justice. For, as he makes clear, whereas law is universal, it is not possible to deal with some situations by means of pronouncements that are both universal and just. The judge's equity will mitigate the imperfection of the law, which holds for usual cases but not for those that deviate from the norm. He will be just in taking the decision that the legislator would have taken if he had been present and had known the case in question.[1] Saint Thomas similarly advises that, when the law is defective, judgment should not be given according to the letter of the law, but recourse should be had to equity, according to the intention of the legislator. He takes up the counsel formulated in the *Digest* (I, iii, de Leg. Senatusque consult. 25) according to which 'there is no principle of law or favourable rule of equity that permits a provision benignly introduced for the benefit of mankind to be turned

[1] ARISTOTLE, *Nicomachean Ethics*, 1137b.

to harshness by a stricter interpretation, to the prejudice of those for whose sake it was devised'.[1]

Though the law be incomplete, obscure or insufficient, the judge must deliver judgment (Article 4 of the Code Napoléon). The judge's equity must supplement the law, but his decision will no longer be just on purely formal grounds: the rule applied must itself be just. A perfect machine may possibly be capable of administering formally correct justice: it could never judge in equity.[2]

3. When for one reason or another there is disagreement about the application of the law, the question of the just rule arises. It does so in various circumstances. We may be trying, within the totality of the law in force, to isolate the precise rule applicable in the particular circumstances. Or it may be a question of supplementing the law's silence and of judging in equity. Or again we may be utterly in opposition to the positive law, and invoke provisions of another order—moral rules, religious precepts or Natural Law.

In the event of either the rule to be applied or its interpretation being contested, the judge, taking his decision within the limits of a given legal system, will concern himself with the *ratio juris*, with the purpose either of some particular law or with that of the legal system taken as a whole. According as these questions are envisaged broadly or narrowly, the answer to them will depend either on the techniques of exegesis or on the philosophy of law. The legislator's intention is often ambiguous. Its determination will in certain cases be limited to the examination of the preamble; in others it will be the outcome of a general theory of law or even of a political philosophy. In this eventuality the judge's decision will be just if it is consistent with the spirit of the legal system as that is conceived.

For some people this method of proceeding will in turn depend, not on the level at which the just rule is dealt with, but on that at which the just act is under consideration. In effect, they say, the act is just when it results from the correct application, not of an isolated rule of law, but of the legal system taken as a whole. The role of the jurists who develop doctrine is to enable the judge to

---

[1] St. THOMAS, *Summa Theologica*, Secunda Secundae, 60, 5.
[2] With regard to equity, cf. M. RÜMELIN, *Die Billigkeit im Recht*, 1921.

have a clear view of the system of law he is charged with administering. The system and its elements are elucidated, but not judged: we are still entirely at the level of positive law, which remains the sole norm of the just decision.

For others, who are against this legal formalism and positivism, law is a technique at the service of the ideal of justice.[1] The role of the judge is but rarely limited to a formal deduction: the judge is the embodiment of the living law and should, in carrying out his mission, draw inspiration from the Roman praetor, for whom the law was *ars aequi et boni*.[2] Rules of law and precedents are indispensable for making it possible to institute a stable legal order, to ensure the security of transactions. But this is by no means enough. The good judge is he who makes use of the full legal armament in order to ensure the reign of justice. And it is just in so far as they have succeeded in this task that courts and tribunals will be respected. The judge cannot rest content with administering the law in conformity with the will of the legislator: he must use the law in order to give reasons for his decisions, but these must above all be equitable. The judge is not in the service of the power that has appointed him: he is in the service of justice. The supreme court is not the policeman of the legislature: it is the legal conscience which must keep watch in order that law should be just.

On this view the judge does not limit himself to administering the law, but uses it in order to buttress his feeling for equity, to which he will give ear particularly when the law is obscure or incomplete. But whence comes this feeling which ought to guide him in the exercise of his judicial functions? How are we to bring it to a fine point? How, in terms of this feeling for equity, are we to form a conception of what a just rule is? We are on the verge of dropping the juridical view of justice—conformity with the law—in favour of a different view which aims at imposing itself on the law and governing it. Few people will dispute the legitimacy of the point of view which transcends positive law: but many jurists, arguing from the doctrine of the separation of

---

[1] Cf. B. CARDOZO, *The Paradoxes of Legal Science*, New York, 1928, p. 10, taken up and developed by E. N. GARLAN, *Legal Realism and Justice*, New York, 1941, pp. 75-97.

[2] For the role of equity in Roman Law, and the influence exercised in this direction by Greek rhetoric, see J. STROUX, *Summum Jus Summa Injuria*, Leipzig, 1926.

powers, will forbid the judge to appeal to this feeling, save in exceptional cases, and will demand that the responsibility for passing laws which conform to the spirit of justice be left to the legislator. Normally it is the legislator, not the judge, who is the elected representative of the people: it is the legislator, in a democracy, who is the nation's spokesman. Allowing the judge to decide on the just rule amounts to assuming that there are standards other than those of the legal system from which he should draw inspiration in making his decisions, it amounts to subordinating positive law to the individual conscience of the judge, to his political philosophy, to his religious convictions, to some kind of Natural Law. Opposition to the positive law in force is perfectly admissible, but not on the part of the judge in the exercise of his functions. Any man may have the most respectable reasons for rebelling against the established order: the legislator alone has the legal power to change it.

The dream of a juster society has inspired the works of a great number of thinkers; and the study of the conditions for, and the consequences of, establishing a just order constitutes the central object of the philosophy of law and of moral, social and political philosophy. The Plato of the *Republic* and the *Laws* is the model whose ascendancy sways the minds of western thinkers. Instead of justice conceived of as conformity with the customary standards of behaviour, he prefers justice as conformity with ideal rules. Against the numerous definitions of justice, which he discards one after another,[1] he sets the one which he considers to be based on reason, namely that 'the possession of one's own property and the doing of one's own business constitute justice'.[2] Justice is not conformity to a system of customary or legal rules adopted by men, but the conformity of these rules themselves to a pre-existing order. The problem of justice is in this case subordinated to the philosophical problem of establishing that fundamental order which will have as its outcome a theory of rational or Natural Law which ought to guide the legislator desirous of developing a just positive law. It is only when the matter has not been regulated by this prior fundamental order that the legislator may determine with full sovereignty the norms of the just and the unjust. St.

[1] PLATO, *Republic*, 331d, 331e, 332c, 333d, 334d, 338c, 339a, 433a.
[2] *Ibid.*, 434a; cf. also 441d and e.

Thomas expresses himself very clearly on this point. 'The human will,' he says, 'is able by common consent to declare a thing just if it belongs to the category of things which have no inherent repugnance to natural justice. It is here that positive law has its place. Hence the definition of the Philosopher concerning positive law, namely, "That before being established it did not matter if it were this way or that, but, once established, it does matter." But if anything is inherently repugnant to natural law, it cannot be made just by human will, as for instance if a law were enacted permitting robbery or adultery. Hence the saying in Isaiah,[1] "*Vae qui condunt leges iniquas*".' [2]

Natural Law, to which St. Thomas alludes, is pre-existent to positive law. But it is not always so.

In certain theocratic societies the divine commandments do not exist prior to positive law, but *constitute* it. After proclaiming the Decalogue, Moses enjoins his people to observe it out of fear and love for Yahwe: 'Ye shall diligently keep the commandments of the Lord, your God, and his testimonies, and his statutes, which he hath commanded thee. And thou shalt do that which is right and good in the sight of the Lord' (Deuteronomy, vi, 17–18). Religious, moral and juridical commands are not distinguished one from another, or, if they are, it is by means of rules of competence and procedure of only secondary importance. We have here a conception of justice which is not philosophical but prophetic, and we will deal with it later. Meanwhile let us return to the philosophical point of view.

The classic schools of Natural Law assimilate the activity of the jurist to that of the scientist. According to these schools, the role both of jurist and of scientist is to bring out into the open structures already prefigured in the nature of things. We recall in this connection the celebrated remarks of Montesquieu: 'Before there were laws made, there were potential relations of justice. To say that there is nothing just or unjust save what positive laws command or forbid is to say that before the circle had been drawn all the radii were not equal. We must, then, admit relations of equity existing before the positive law which establishes them.' [3] Just

---

[1] ISAIAH, x, 1. 'Woe unto them that decree unrighteous decrees.'

[2] ST. THOMAS, *Summa Theologica*, Secunda Secundae, 57, 2.

[3] MONTESQUIEU, *L'Esprit des Lois*, Book I, Chapter 1. Cf. CICERO, *De Legibus*, I, 6–10.

laws are those which, by bringing out and formulating the potential relations of justice, give them their actuality and positivity.
We are not concerned here with a creative invention, but with the
legal recognition and sanction of objective and pre-existing
relations.

On the other hand, the supporters of a rational law put it forward as a purely human creation directed to the realisation of
ends, whether utilitarian or ideal.

Hume does not hesitate to say that the rules of justice are not
natural, but artificial, though this does not mean that they are
baseless,[1] for they are essentially useful. They 'are intended as a
remedy for some inconveniences which proceed from the concurrence of certain *qualities* of the human mind with the *situation*
of external objects'.[2] Jeremy Bentham, unlike Hume, did not limit
justice to the regulation of questions of private property; he was
accordingly to establish a complete utilitarian legislative system to
serve as the legislator's inspiration in developing a just scheme
of law.

For the supporters of an ideal rational law—and indeed from
Kant to del Vecchio—justice is essentially based on respect for
the autonomy of each human person. This is how del Vecchio
puts it: 'Justice desires every subject to be recognised and treated
by every other as an absolute principle of his own actions. Justice
desires that in reciprocal treatment this meta-empiric identity of
nature should be taken into consideration, with the consequent
exclusion of any disparity not founded on the effective manner of
being and operation of each individual: for these purposes all
behaviour should be objectively referred to the same absolute
standard.'[3] This formulation, inspired by a universalist human-
ism, gives precise form to the rule of justice, 'Act in such a way
as you would wish those like you to act,' in the sense of Kant's
categorical imperative. Those like oneself might have been
limited to the men of the same tribe or race, or have embraced all
living beings: in practical conditions they comprise all those
human beings who are assumed to be endowed with a measure of
independence and whose personality commands respect. A positive law will be considered as just in so far as it constitutes 'a

---

[1] D. HUME, *Treatise of Human Nature*, Book III, Part II, Section I.
[2] *Ibid.*, Book III, Part II, Section II.
[3] DEL VECCHIO, *op. cit.*, pp. 119–120.

satisfaction—partial and imperfect, but indispensable—for that "thirst for justice", that need for adjustment and balance between individuals, which is our innate possession and which still must, in some fashion, be translated into experience and there given validity'.[1]

The standpoints adopted by philosophers in order to determine whether a rule is just are—as witness the few samples here offered —variable in the extreme. They all, however, seek in their own way to limit that factor of the arbitrary favoured by those who would impose laws solely in the name of the force at their disposal. Laws, it is felt, should conform either to a pre-existing reality or to a rational system designed with a view to giving effects to an ideal end. For a just rule is not arbitrary: it must have the justification of a basis in reason, even if that basis does not command unanimous agreement.[2]

Taking as a basis the idea that like beings must be treated alike —a formulation of the rule of justice wide enough to arouse no objection—each philosophy will seek, in accordance with its own system, to justify the fact that certain differences make it impossible to consider as alike beings distinguished by characteristics judged to be essential—their merits, needs, works, rank, origin or any combination of such characteristics. Each philosophy will indicate how the treatment of beings belonging to different categories ought to be proportioned to the *value* thus made clear. It is on such considerations that Aristotle bases the proportionality— not the equality—presiding over the rational determination of distributive justice.[3]

That proportionality must, moreover, govern all the forms of justice of which the categories can be organised in a system making possible their comparison from a given point of view. Thus, in criminal law, the gravity of the penalty ought to be proportional to the seriousness of the offence in order to ensure that the penal provisions are just, that is, devoid of any arbitrary element, because rationally justifiable. Naturally, however, even rationally developed systems of criminal law may differ one from another if they admit differing criteria for establishing the seriousness of a crime or if they are more or less severe in fixing penalties.

[1] DEL VECCHIO, *op cit.*, p. 160.
[2] Cf. *Concerning Justice*, Section v, 'The Arbitrary in Justice'.
[3] ARISTOTLE, *Nicomachean Ethics*, 1131.

A perfectly just system, of which no one would have cause to complain, could be realised only by a legislator of such a degree of rationality that none of his decisions presented an aspect open to question. In other words, all his decisions would have to conform to universally valid criteria. But even that would not be enough to bring about the reign of absolute justice. For the distinctions of fact, which form the basis for the division into different categories differently treated, would equally have to be not merely given, but also founded on reason. Why should one man be a coward and another brave, one an imbecile and another intelligent, one hasty and another thoughtful? Whether the distribution of good and ill, of virtue and vice, be made at random or be the effect of divine grace, the system, however rational, can only sanction situations containing an element of the arbitrary giving ground for complaint to the victims. It is in answer to this objection that the philosophies of the East have developed the theory of *karma*, in which the advantages and disadvantages of one's life on earth are the reward or punishment of an earlier life—a theory by which Plato seems to have been inspired.[1]

Since the attempt to eliminate the arbitrary entirely from a human scheme of justice seems to be hopeless, the mind is forced to accept the insufficient character, in the absolute, of a purely rational justice. Just as equity is called in to supplement the regulation of just action, so charity is the necessary and indispensable supplement of any system justifying the rules themselves in a human justice concerned to do harm to no one and to afford no one a valid motive for complaint.

4. The just agent, human or divine, is often defined as he who sets himself to deliver just decisions or to know and recognise just rules. In this case the justness of the agent constitutes a derived virtue and not the source of all justice.

The traditional definition of justice among the Romans—'constans et perpetua voluntas jus suum cuique tribuendi' (*Digest*, I, 1, 10)—shows the just man in the guise of an upright judge ever doing his best to arrive at a just decision. The quality of the agent is a function of the justice of the act—the various aspects of which we have examined earlier—and does not enrich the idea itself of justice. The same is the case if, conceiving the justness of the

---

[1] Cf. PLATO, *Timaeus*, 41c *et seq. Laws*, X, 903d *et seq.*

agent as a function of the just rule, we characterise as just the man who conforms to rational or Natural Law because he accepts its teachings and subordinates his conduct thereto. An excellent example of this point of view is afforded by Montesquieu's well-known letter on justice.

'If, my dear Rhédi,' he says, 'there is a God, he must necessarily be just. For if he were not, he would be the worst and most imperfect of beings.

'Justice is a relation of conformity really existing between two things. That relation is always the same, whatever the being considering it—whether God, or angel, or indeed a man.

'It is true that men do not always see these relations. Often, even when they do see them they depart from them, and their own interest is always what they see best. . . . Men may do injustice because it is to their interest to commit it. . . . But it is not possible that God should ever do anything unjust. . . .

'Thus, were there no God, it would still be our duty to love justice, that is to say, to do our best to be like that being of whom we have such a wonderful idea and who, if he did exist, would necessarily be just.' [1]

The epithet of *just* applied to the agent seems to us to supply an original contribution when, contrary to the conceptions of Ulpian and Montesquieu, the just agent becomes the source and standard of all justice.

In primitive societies taboos, prohibitions and positive instructions are religious in nature or origin, and obedience to divine commandments is the foundation of all justice. Piety includes justice, and in ancient Greek tragedy, for example, injustice was confused with impiety.[2] Plato's aim, and more particularly that of Aristotle, was to mark off justice as a specific virtue with the effect of distinguishing it from virtue in general.[3] He who applies himself to virtue is wise; he is just only in the exercise of certain functions. Now what makes the specific quality of our western civilisation is the way in which to the stream formed by the rationalist Graeco-Roman tradition is added the Judaeo-Christian religious

[1] MONTESQUIEU, *Lettres Persanes*, letter 83.
[2] Cf. W. NESTLÉ, *Vom Mythos zum Logos*, Stuttgart, 1940; D. LOENEN *Diké*, Amsterdam, 1948.
[3] ARISTOTLE, *Nicomachean Ethics*, 1130.

tradition, which draws its spirituality from the primacy accorded to the just God, the model of perfect conduct, and to the just man inspired by that divine model both in his thought and in his action.[1] In contrast to the juridical view of the Romans and the philosophical view of the Greeks, the Judaeo-Christian view of justice is essentially prophetic, for it is through the prophets as intermediaries that God reveals himself to men.

God is Righteousness and Justice (Deuteronomy xxxii, 4; Isaiah xlv, 21), but his justice is charity and clemency. An appeal to his justice is at the same time an appeal to his mercy (Psalm cxliii, 1) for in him they coincide. 'The Lord is justice in all his ways, mercy in all his works' (Psalm cxlv, 17). Similarly, in the Christian tradition, the First Epistle of St. John sees God indifferently as justice (ii, 1; ii, 25) and as love (iv, 8).

Yahwe is just, he loves justice (Psalm xi, 7). All those that seek after justice must listen to him and follow his commandments (Isaiah li, 1). Similarly, for the Christian, Christ is the model from whom the faithful should draw inspiration. 'He that saith he abideth in him ought himself also so to walk, even as he walked' (1 John ii, 6). The teaching of St. Paul, which, in his controversy with the Doctors, asserts the primacy of charity over the strict observance of the law ('For he that loveth another hath fulfilled the law', Romans xiii, 8; cf. Galatians v, 14) makes no opposition whatever between charity and justice. According to St. Paul, God in his justice shows mercy and is compassionate (Romans ix, 14–16). In Christianity, as in Judaism, 'the just shall live by his faith' (Habakkuk ii, 4; Romans i, 17).

The just is he who rests in God, is inspired by him and observes his commandments, but he is *above all* he who is upright in heart (Psalm xxxii, 11). In Leviticus, in the midst of the many ritual and cult instructions to be observed by the just man, there shines out the famous precept, 'Thou shalt love thy neighbour as thyself' (Leviticus xix, 18); and this is extended to the stranger a few verses farther on—'the stranger that dwelleth with you shall be unto you as one born among you, and thou shalt love him as thyself' (Leviticus xix, 34). The idea of justice incarnate in the ideal of the just man expands and flowers in the Judaeo-Christian tradition,

[1] Cf. L. DIESTEL, 'Die Idee der Gerechtigkeit, vorzüglich im Alten Testament' (*Jahrbuch für Deutsche Theologie*, Vol. V, Gotha, 1860), and A. DESCAMPS *Les Justes et la Justice dans les Evangiles et le Christianisme Primitif*, Louvain, 1950.

and its development can be followed in the Psalms and in the Proverbs, in the Prophets assailing religious hypocrisy and calling for more uprightness and human solidarity (Isaiah i, 10–17), in the Book of Job describing the conduct of the just man (Job xxxi), in the Sermon on the Mount (Matthew v–viii) and in the message of love in the First Epistle of St. John (iv, 7–21; v, 1–4). In this evolution ritual observance is progressively subordinated to conscience: the just is he whose heart is pure and whose will is upright. It was in the line of this tradition that St. Anselm, a forerunner of Kant, was to define justice as 'uprightness of will observed for its own sake'.[1]

From St. Augustine to Malebranche, Christian doctrine was scarcely to distinguish between charity, or the love of God, and justice, or the love of order, 'because the idea of God, as sovereign justice is more appropriate for governing our love than any other'.[2] 'Those who have charity,' said Malebranche in his *Entretiens* (viii, 13), 'are just in the disposition of their heart but are not just in full strictness because they have not precise knowledge of all the relations of perfection that ought to govern their esteem and their love.'[3]

The just man is he who imitates divine justice.[4] For Leibniz, God is 'the essential or substantial justice which the most virtuous man imitates'.[5] In order to be just it is not enough to have charity because 'in justice are comprised both charity and the rule of reason'.[6] By way of conclusion to his numerous reflections on universal jurisprudence, Leibniz defined justice, human and divine, as 'a charity conformable to wisdom: thus when we are moved to justice, we endeavour to secure good for all, so far as that can reasonably be done, but in proportion to the needs and merits of each; and if we are sometimes obliged to punish the wicked, it is for the general good'.[7]

The rationalism which affirms that 'we have reason in common with God' provided the transition from religious and hetero-

---

[1] ST. ANSELM, *De Veritate*, Chapter XII.

[2] MALEBRANCHE, *Traité de l'Amour de Dieu*, Roustan, 1922, p. 76, quoted by G. GRUA, *Jurisprudence Universelle et Theodicée selon Leibniz*, Paris, 1953, p. 194.

[3] Cf. G. GRUA, *op. cit.*, p. 194.

[4] Cf. BOSSUET, *Sermons*, Paris, Garnier, 1928, Vol. III, *Sermon sur la Justice*, p. 7.

[5] G. GRUA, *op. cit.*, p. 401. [6] *Ibid.*, p. 212. [7] *Ibid.*, p. 507.

nomous conceptions of justice to moral autonomy, without, how-ever, abandoning reference to an ideal model. According to Kant, it is not necessary, in order to judge our actions, to move outside ourselves. It is sufficient to adopt as our rule 'the conduct of this divine man within us, with which we compare and judge our-selves, and so reform ourselves, although we can never attain to the perfection thereby prescribed'.[1] The just man will act in such a way as to conform to the duty laid upon him by the categorical imperative.[2] The religious imperative is replaced by the impera-tive of our own conscience.

The benefit of this transition from the transcendent to the immanent, from religious commandments to the imperative of the practical reason, is the result of the moral autonomy thus realised. Indeed, so long as our conceptions of the just were de-pendent on our religious faith, as revealed by the prophets speak-ing in the name of the Absolute, our faith had only to be shaken and morality was deprived of all basis: if God does not exist, everything becomes permitted. But things are quite different if it is our own conscience that constitutes the ultimate criterion.

Ultimate criterion does not mean absolute criterion. For if our conscience is our final resort, that conscience is by no means the same thing as an unchanging pattern all of whose teachings could here and now be codified *ne varietur*. We must grant to the con-science of the just man an indefinite possibility of moral per-fectibility.

The Judaeo-Christian prophetic contribution, with its absolute pattern of the Just transcending rules and systems, enabled western culture to make the transition from closed to open justice, from formulas of justice that were always relative to the ideal of absolute justice.[3] It is only in this latter form that justice comes to the same thing as the moral conscience of which it synthesises all the aspirations.[4]

---

[1] KANT, *Critique of Pure Reason*, tr. Norman Kemp Smith, Macmillan, London, 1958, p. 486.

[2] KANT, *Die Metaphysik der Sitten, Einleitung in die Rechtslehre*, Academy of Prussia, Berlin, 1914, Vol. VI, p. 236.

[3] H. BERGSON, *Les deux Sources de la Morale et de la Religion*, Paris, 1932, pp. 75-78.

[4] Cf. the studies of Dr. BARUK in *Psychiatrie Morale Expérimentale*, 2nd edition, Paris, 1950, p. XIII, and (with Dr. M. BACHET), *Le Test 'Tsedek', le Jugement Moral et la Délinquance*, Paris, 1950, pp. 79-82.

5. The three levels at which we have placed ourselves in order to analyse the idea of justice have each in turn given us a wider view. The just act is correctness, the rejection of inequality. The just rule is reason, the rejection of the arbitrary. The just man is conscience, the rejection of inhumanity. The ideal of justice, as a living force in the western tradition, combines all these points of view, giving priority to one or another in accordance with the world-views and the disciplines by which it is developed.

The level of the act—at which the just is defined by correctness relatively to the rule—has the advantage of furnishing a criterion on which there will be universal agreement when conduct is characterised as just for reasons other than the holiness and absolute perfection of the agent. Only a perfect God—of whom it is granted *a priori* that, whatever he does, he will act justly—can dispense with following the rules. We are free, in such an eventuality, to submit to divine justice, but we are incapable of understanding it, for it cannot be justified by reason. It cannot serve as a guide to human action, and it cannot be made use of in social life.

All human justice assumes rules of conduct, for it has a duty to justify acts by their conformity with rules. But is it permissible for it to remain indifferent to the content of the rules themselves, like the mathematician who, as such, is not called on to concern himself with the consequences of his calculations? There are legists who defend this point of view—out of scepticism, out of respect for the force which has imposed the public order of which they are the guardians or, more simply, out of professional scruple. Let us, indeed, not forget that the ideal of a stable legal order, fixing the rights and obligations of each individual and guaranteeing certainty together with clarity, is difficult of realisation if the judge allows himself to be diverted from his technical reasoning by considerations of equity. But how far does the legal system constitute a given order for the judge? Or how far, on the contrary, is it an order which he himself has developed? The passage to and fro between certainty and equity, between equity and certainty, is the very life of jurisprudence and determines more particularly the idea we form of the role in the legal system of the supreme court.

For philosopher or prophet alike, correct application of the rules may be important; but that is only a secondary aspect of their concern. What matters to them is not only that the rules should be correctly applied but that the rules followed should also be just.

The practical philosopher sets before himself the task of working out a human order justifiable by reason: confidence in the possibility of that enterprise coincides with confidence in the powers of autonomous human reason. To accept the revelations of the prophets as the basis of justice is to acknowledge the powerlessness of our rational faculties.

Two criticisms can be formulated against the prophetic conception of justice. On the one hand, regarding the divine commandments as an external order which we must obey, without putting it to the proof of our reason and our conscience, amounts to foundering in a theological formalism comparable to the formalism of the jurists: it is the triumph of the letter and the abdication of the spirit. On the other hand, if the prophets must be granted a special grace which is denied to the rest of mankind, and which supplements our natural lights with a supernatural illumination, must not those deprived of that grace nevertheless be able to test its authenticity? For is it not true that there have ever been false prophets in Israel? Are there rational criteria that will enable us to discern the true prophets? We fall back to the level of systems and philosophical controversies. Is it the nature of the message that will enable us to recognise the true prophet? We find ourselves referred back to the moral conscience and to its immanent criteria.

The supporters of a prophetic conception of justice, based on the imitation of a Living God, Righteousness and Love, will see the essence of justice in uprightness of heart and good will. Justice, for them, cannot be reduced to rules or to systems, but dwells in the enlightened intention to work for the best on the inspiration of a perfect model. This intention finds expression according to the period, in the piety of the faithful or the charity of the sage. Reason alone is insufficient to guide us in action and, even if it were possible to work out a rationally satisfying human order, why should our conduct conform to it? What renders rational conclusions respectable, if not the divine model from which they seem to be inspired? There is nothing just save the upright heart in pursuit of the Absolute.

The three precepts of Ulpian—'honeste vivere, alterum non laedere, suum cuique tribuere' (*Digest*, 1, i, 10)—seem to me, properly interpreted, to sum up our analysis of the idea of justice. These precepts have been understood in the most varied ways. Leibniz sees in them formulas of universal justice, commutative justice and distributive justice.[1] For Kant they sum up our legal duties, which comprise a *lex justi*, a *lex juridica* and a *lex justitiae*.[2] As for ourselves, interpreting as we do the third precept in a purely legal sense (allot to each that to which he is entitled in accordance with the law), we see in these three formulas the three complementary aspects of the idea of justice—the prophetic, the philosophic and the juridical—corresponding to the levels of the agent, the rule and the act which we have been distinguishing in our analysis.

The complex idea of justice thus presents itself in the west as a field of encounter to which come for their mutual enrichment the well-tried formulas of the Roman jurists, the rational systems of the Greek philosophers and the impassioned invocations of the Jewish prophets. All have contributed to that great tradition—Christian, rationalist and, later, secular—by which our thought is enriched and our conscience informed with life.

[1] Leibniz, *Textes Inédits*, by G. Grua, Paris, 1948, Vol. II, p. 607.
[2] Kant, *Die Metaphysik der Sitten*, pp. 236–237.

III

THE RULE OF JUSTICE[1]

TO the extent that the role of practical reason is confined to the adjustment of means to unquestioned ends, its action manifests itself in the virtue of prudence. But when the totality of a course of conduct, and not merely its instrumental or technical aspects, is critically analysed by reason, the concept we have recourse to in order to qualify approved behaviour is that of justice. In the philosophic tradition of the west, it is justice, in effect, that is regarded as *the* rational virtue. The wise man is not content to follow his impulses, his interests and his passions, nor for that matter his leanings towards pity and sympathy. It is not enough, for the wise man, to be good and charitable: his conduct must be just. Justice, Leibniz tells us, is the charity of the wise man, and according to him it embraces, over and above the tendency to do good by relieving suffering, *the rule of reason*.[2] That is why, if there exists any practical employment of reason, it must manifest itself in just action bearing witness to a rationality which unjust behaviour would not display. Now, if we follow the incessant controversies about the just and the unjust, in private as in public life, without being in a position to provide a rule or a criterion binding on everybody, we may well wonder whether we should not give up all hope of seeing our action guided by reason. But before we resign ourselves to this conclusion of despair, it is worth inquiring whether the rule of reason, referred to by Leibniz, although not making possible the automatic solution of all conflicts, might not

---

[1] From *Dialectica*, Vol. 14, No. 2/3–15/6–15/9, 1960.
[2] Cf. G. GRUA, *Jurisprudence Universelle et Théodicée selon Leibniz*, Paris, 1953, p. 212.

be able, after the manner of the Kantian imperative, to furnish a scheme of action of a formal character which would not be entirely devoid of scope and usefulness. It is to the working out of such a scheme, and to some philosophical reflection upon it, that this account of the rule of justice will be devoted.

The idea of justice has always been compared with that of equality, and I think it may be useful to seek a first approximation to the rule of justice by starting with an analysis of what the relation of equality implies.

Two objects a and b are equal if they are interchangeable, if, that is, every property of one of these objects is also a property of the other. In normative terms it follows that, if a and b are equal, everything that is said of one of these objects must be able to be said of the other, for these two affirmations are equivalent and have the same truth value. In saying that it is just to treat equal beings alike—since every property of one of these beings is also a property of the other and there consequently exists no reason which would make it possible to justify treating them unequally— just treatment puts itself forward as the treatment based on reason because in conformity with the principle of sufficient reason. The normative consequences with respect to assertions about two equal objects might even be regarded as a particular case of just treatment: if all just treatment of two equal objects ought to be equal, then the same must be the case with assertions about them, for saying is a particular case of doing.

The rule of justice calling for equal treatment of equal beings seems difficult to question, but its field of application is very narrow, if indeed it exists at all. Indeed, since Leibniz and his principle of indiscernibles, above all since Frege and his distinction between the meaning and designation of a name, logicians are more and more inclined to deny the existence of things which would be identical in all their properties. The assertion that a is equal to b, conceived as their complete identity, seems simply to signify that the nouns 'a' and 'b' designate one and the same object, even if their meaning—that is, the way in which this object is designated—differs in the two cases. If, then, we want the rule of justice to be able to guide us effectively, we must formulate it in such a way that it will tell us not how to treat persons who do not differ from one another, but how to treat persons who are not identical, that is, equal, from every point of view. That is the only real problem touching the rule of justice.

When people are heard complaining of having been unjustly treated—because they have not been treated like their neighbour or competitor, or because they have been treated in the same way although deserving to be treated better—nobody will suppose that these people were identical with those to whom they compare themselves or that no matter what difference between them would have sufficed to justify unequal treatment. On the contrary, these people will expressly specify all sorts of differences. They will say that the other party is richer or more influential, that he is a relative or friend of such and such an official, that he is a member of a clique or of a political or religious group close to the centre of power. But if they complain, it is because they claim that the differences ought not to have exercised any influence on the decision taken or that essential differences, which should have operated in their favour, have been without effect. The fact is, they claim that *certain* elements, regarded as *essential*, and nothing else, ought to have been taken into consideration. The decision is said to be unjust because it has failed to take account of them or because it was taken by reference to irrelevant factors having nothing to do with the case. Injustice, it seems, does not result here from the unequal treatment of identical persons, but from the unequal treatment of different persons the differences between whom were irrelevant in the instance. From the point of view of the criteria which ought to have been applied, the persons were similar, and that is why they should have received the same treatment. Injustice will also be attributed to the equal treatment of persons who, according to the criteria in question, ought to be assigned to different categories for which unequal treatment was provided.

But what are the differences that matter, and what are those that do not, in each given situation? On this, divergencies can manifest themselves, and they do so in fact. Let us characterise the differences that matter as essential and let us say that persons between whom these essential differences do not exist are essentially similar. In this case *the rule of justice requires that those who are essentially similar should be treated alike.* But the rule of justice, as it is formulated, has been called elsewhere the rule of *formal justice*,[1] because it does not tell us *when* beings are essentially similar nor *how* they must be treated. Now the application of this rule in concrete cases makes it necessary to specify these two conditions. If it is positive law that is supposed to furnish the criteria of application the rule of justice comes to a precise point and becomes the rule of law, demanding that all who are similar in the eyes of the law should be treated in a way laid down by the law. In conforming to the rule of law we conform to the rule of justice, made precise in accordance with the will of the legislator. Justice is defined in this case as the correct application of the law.

What meaning should be given to the rule of justice as long as its conditions of application have not been laid down? It simply means that in one's action it is necessary to be faithful to a regular line of conduct. If a person has been treated in a certain way *qua* member of a certain class, every other member of that same class will have to be treated in the same way. This conception, characterised by Professor Dupréel as static justice,[2] calls for the observance of an established rule, whatever it may be. Just action is that which conforms to an accepted rule or at least to an established precedent. When an authoritative decision has resulted in a case belonging to a given category being treated in a certain way, it is just and rational to apply the same treatment to a case essentially similar. The establishment of a reasonable order quite naturally presupposes conformity with precedent (*stare decisis*). The rule of justice invites us in effect to transform into precedent, that is, into an instance of applying an implicit rule, every earlier decision emanating from a recognised authority.

If a first formulation of the rule of justice made it possible to compare it to equality, conceived of as complete interchangeability, the formulation now adopted makes it possible to compare it to the idea of legality, which would be presupposed by every induction based on experiment. Is it necessary, in order to make an induction—that is, to pass from a particular case to the general rule—to assume that events are governed by objective laws? It

[1] Cf. *Concerning Justice.*
[2] E. DUPRÉEL, *Traité de Morale*, Brussels, 1932, Vol. II, p. 485.

would be enough, it seems to me, to see in induction nothing more than the application of the same tendency that has led us to the rule of justice. Each phenomenon would be treated as a precedent, that is, as the manifestation of an implicit rule according to which essentially similar phenomena manifest the same properties. Mill's canons, or any other technique of the methodology of induction, would serve only as a means of applying a check. Every time a phenomenon does not conform to expectations, there is occasion for modifying one way or the other the category of essentially similar phenomena of which the particular phenomenon constitutes a sample. There is no question in this context of speaking of justice or injustice. For, unless we grant a miracle, we assume that phenomena always unfold in conformity with the rules. Our sole business is, by means of experiment, to check the rules that have been worked out. It is impossible in this connection to overestimate the importance of the invalidating case, which is something essential to the progress of research.[1]

Our suggestion, as regards the basis of induction, presents some analogy with the views of Kant as well as with those of Kelsen. As with these two, it is our mind which, in my theory, imposes on phenomena its requirements of rationality. But whereas with Kant it is, in the analogies of experience, a case of showing that experience is possible only by the representation of a necessary connection of perceptions in conformity with the categories, my view, which equally presupposes a regulating principle, carefully avoids being unduly precise about its terms. Nothing but this flexibility of formulation makes it possible to safeguard its universality in application. Kelsen, for his part, in his detailed and stimulating studies,[2] compares the principle of causality with that of immanent justice. But whereas he believes that the methodology of the natural sciences is emancipating itself from this conception with its origin in theology, the connection which I establish between the rule of justice and the basis of

---

[1] Cf. K. POPPER, *Logik der Forschung*, Vienna, Springer, 1935, pp. 12–14, and P. GRÉCO, *L'apprentissage dans une situation à structure opératoire concrète*, in P. GRÉCO and J. PIAGET, *Apprentissage et connaissance*, Paris, Presses Universitaires de France, 1959, p. 116.

[2] Cf. H. KELSEN, *Society and Nature*, Chicago University Press, 1943, and the article 'Causality and Retribution', *Philosophy of Science*, 1941, reproduced in *What is Justice?*, University of California Press, 1957.

induction has no recourse to any explanation of a transcendental order, and its outlook, at once rational and formal, enables it to adapt itself to all the variations of scientific methodology.

The comparison between the rule of justice and the assertion of the regularity of phenomena will enable us to point out what distinguishes the one from the other, and will give us a better understanding of the role of the rule of justice as a directing principle of our thought. When a phenomenon under study fails to turn out according to expectations we may ask ourselves whether the experiment has been properly carried out, whether its course was not falsified by the intrusion of factors not taken into account or whether finally the observation of it was not tainted with error. But when our doubts on all these points have been quieted there is nothing for it but to modify at least one of the rules which has played a part in our arriving at the prediction now shown by the experiment to be wrong. An aspect of the formula which had not previously attracted attention will have to be incorporated in the totality of essential characteristics, that is to say, of those that ought to be taken into account in the formulation of the rule. If we exclude the hypothesis of lawless behaviour—of a miracle, that is—everything contrary to the predictions formed by reference to the accepted rules will have to be explained by the imperfections of those rules. The advance of the natural sciences will consist in the progressive extension of the network—conformable with experiment—of regularities in the universe. On the other hand, when the behaviour of a responsible agent does not conform to that which is prescribed by an accepted rule of law our first reaction is not to modify the rule but to condemn the agent's conduct, which will be characterised as unjust. It will indeed often happen that not only third parties but also the delinquent agent himself will agree on this characterisation of the act. But it is not always so. It is possible for the agent who is condemned in virtue of given legislation to have a perfectly clear conscience and to regard his conduct as reasonable and just, because in conformity with rules other than those promulgated by the established order. This situation raises a problem different from that of static justice or of the conformity of action to a recognised rule. It raises the problem of the just rule which ought to serve as a criterion in action.

Can the rule of justice be of any help to us in this field? At any rate it enables us to set a boundary to the problem. According to it, it is just to treat alike those who are essentially similar. It does not specify when two beings or two situations are essentially similar, neither does it tell us how they should be treated. Now in every concrete case, if we are to be able to declare that an act is just or unjust, we must find an answer to these two questions. This answer is usually sought in two orders of considerations, sometimes combined. Quite often the justice of the rule will be based on the authentic character of the source from which it emanates. This will sometimes be the deity, whose sacred character guarantees that the commandments revealed are just. Sometimes it will be the king, whose power is based on his being the representative of God on earth. Sometimes it will be parliament because it is the authentic representative of the national will. Finally, it will sometimes be the mind and will of the people themselves as displayed in custom and tradition. It happens, on the other hand—especially when a draft law is under discussion—that every effort is made to show that its provisions are in conformity with our need for justice, that equal treatment is given to situations that appear to be essentially similar and that that treatment itself is justified.

Be it noted in this connection that neither the first nor the second order of considerations can be deduced from the rule of justice, whose formal character does not permit of conclusions of this kind. It is, on the contrary, these considerations that furnish precise indications without which the rule could not guide us in concrete cases. They will have to resort to techniques of reasoning which imply evaluations and which we have studied at length in our treatise on argumentation.[1]

Let us assume that a new draft criminal code is being discussed. The code may differ from the existing code or from the local customs it is intended to replace, either by classifying offences differently or by fixing different sanctions. In principle, it will modify the provisions in force only if there are grave reasons for departing from the established order, for every arbitrary modification will appear unjust in so far as it results in baseless differences in treatment. There will be no failure, in effect, to compare the

[1] Cf. C. PERELMAN and L. OLBRECHTS-TYTECA, *Traité de l'argumentation. La nouvelle rhétorique*, Paris, Presses Universitaires de France, 1958.

new rules and their consequences with earlier situations regarded as essentially similar. If differences in treatment are manifest, injustice will be seen in them unless it is possible sufficiently to justify either the new classification or the difference in treatment. That is the reason for the traditionalist character of any juridical order, which only a revolution is capable of overthrowing, and even then leaves in being a vast number of elements of the past.

The fact is, the rule of justice results from a tendency, natural to the human mind,[1] to regard as normal and rational, and so as requiring no supplementary justification, a course of behaviour in conformity with precedent. In any social order, then, everything that is traditional will appear to be a matter of course. *Per contra* every deviation, every change, will have to be justified. This situation, which results from the application of the principle of inertia in the life of the mind,[2] explains the role played by tradition. It is tradition that is taken as a starting-point, it is tradition that is criticised and it is tradition that is maintained in so far as no reason is seen for departing from it. And this holds good in the most diverse fields—ethics or law, science or philosophy.

If there is to be a departure from tradition there must be reasons, which will vary with the field in view. But whenever the question arises of specifying or modifying the conditions for applying the rule of justice those reasons will lead us finally to an ideal vision of man or society which will provide the ultimate basis of the recognised criteria. Let it be granted that a just criminal code ought to establish a due proportion between the gravity of the crime and the severity of the penalty, that a just social and political system ought to establish a due proportion between merit and reward, or between need and satisfaction; then the application of these general principles will always necessitate a conception of the ideal —human, individual and social—in virtue of which the legal provision is justified and for the realisation of which the provision has been worked out.

If we assume it to be possible without recourse to violence to reach agreement on all the problems implied in the employment of the idea of justice we are granting the possibility of formulating an ideal of man and society, valid for all beings endowed with

[1] Cf. J. PIAGET, *Apprentissage et connaissance*, p. 42.
[2] Cf. C. PERELMAN and L. OLBRECHTS-TYTECA, *op. cit.*, pp. 142–144.

reason and accepted by what we have called elsewhere the universal audience.[1] I think that the only discursive methods available to us in the matter stem from techniques that are not demonstrative—that is, conclusive and *rational* in the narrow sense of the term—but from argumentative techniques which are not conclusive but which may tend to demonstrate the *reasonable* character of the conceptions put forward. It is this recourse to the rational and the reasonable for the realisation of the ideal of universal communion that characterises the age-long endeavour of all philosophies in their aspiration for a city of man in which violence may progressively give way to wisdom.

[1] C. PERELMAN and L. OLBRECHTS-TYTECA, *op. cit.*, § 7.

IV

THE ROLE OF DECISION
IN THE
THEORY OF KNOWLEDGE[1]

HOW far the structure of our knowledge is determined by the fact of deciding in favour of a particular thesis or the obligation to take a decision, by the desire or obligation to connect a proposition with a systematised field of knowledge—here is a question which theoreticians should carefully investigate.

In the classical view, both rationalist and empiricist, every human decision which does not consist in yielding to rational evidence or to sensible intuition is a cause of error. For all Pascal's protestations, his assertion that we have put out to sea, that we have to choose and wager, his ideas, though they may have contributed to the development of the probability calculus, have had scarcely any influence on the theoreticians of knowledge.

Not that the problem has escaped them. For Descartes, 'the actions of life do not often brook delay, and so it is a very certain truth that, when it is not in our power to discern the truest opinions, we must follow the most probable' (*Discourse on Method*, Part III). But this rule of conduct, good as it is in practice, has nothing in common with scientific method. When there is no question of acting, but merely of meditating and knowing, Descartes tells us, we cannot make too much allowance for scepticism. When it came to science he took the firm and constant

[1] Report presented to the Second International Congress of the International Union for the Philosophy of Sciences. Zurich, 1954.

resolution 'never to receive anything for true which he did not know self-evidently to be such'.

This distinction drawn between the method advocated for the sciences and that which is to be recommended in 'the actions of life' assumes a quite clear separation between theory and practice and a difference in kind between the truths of science and the opinions that guide our action. The truths, guaranteed by evidence, are eternally and universally valid; they are the result of a solitary meditation independent of all scientific tradition and all linguistic elaboration as well as of the needs of practical life. Seen in this light, the history of the sciences would consist in the growth in the number of their truths. It is only when scientific method is so conceived that it would be worthy of being integrated in a theory of knowledge.

Such a conception of scientific activity might seem very strange to all who take part in it: it is that activity, nevertheless, which has provided the framework for the classical theory of knowledge in which the scientist is viewed as standing on his own in face of nature. It is true that the work of Whewell, Brunschvicg, Enriques, Bachelard, Piaget and above all Gonseth, as well as the whole pragmatist movement, have set scientific activity in a different perspective, but no one, so far as we know, has concerned himself with our problem, which is that of the role of decision in the structure of knowledge.

In order to make clear our point of view let us take two systematised fields offering us the extreme cases—that in which the scholar's decision has no influence whatever on knowledge, and that in which decision plays an essential part—the two cases being furnished one by formal logic and the other by law.

A system of formalised logic contains rules for constructing properly framed expressions, axioms and rules for deduction. All these rules must be quite free of ambiguity, and every existent (man or machine) capable of distinguishing signs and of arranging them in accordance with a given order ought to be able to recognise whether the expression is properly framed and the deduction correct. It is the examination of the structure of the system which makes it possible to determine whether the system is coherent, what the expressions are that can be deduced from it, whether a properly framed expression is independent of it—so that either the expression or its negation could be adapted to the system without the system's becoming incoherent. The will of the investigator can in no way modify the conclusions to which the examination of the system has led: the only way of avoiding an unwelcome conclusion is to replace the system by another in which it would no longer be possible to obtain the result that one wishes to avoid.

Things are quite different in a juridical system. The judge is bound by the system of law he has to administer: in modern states he has no legislative power. But, on the other hand, there is laid on him the obligation to judge: all modern systems contain provisions regarding the offence of the denial of justice. A prosecution for denial of justice may be brought against 'the judge who refuses to judge on the pretext that the law is silent, obscure or insufficient' (Article 4 of the Code Napoléon; cf. Article 258 of the Belgian Penal Code). This presupposes that the judge, whose competence in the matter is established by the law, should be able to answer whether the law is or is not applicable to the case, whatever its nature may be; he should, furthermore, give a reasoned judgment, that is, indicate how he connects his decision with the legislation he is administering. By this double obligation the legislator has decided in advance that for the judge the juridical system is deemed to be coherent and categorical, and juridical technique ought to adapt itself to this double requirement. If a given situation appears to be governed in a confused fashion by several texts the judge should say what the reasons are for which he applies the text that has his preference; if there is no text enabling him at first sight to decide one way rather than the other he should find a technique of interpretation which will permit him nevertheless to discover a solution. He is helped in his task by the scholars who elaborate juridical doctrine and study the difficulties which are capable of arising. The techniques peculiar to the reasoning of jurists, the problems posed by the interpretation of the law, the arguments that justify its application—all go hand in hand with the obligation laid on the judge to decide and to give reasons for his decision. His business is to draw up a judgment as consistent as possible with the provisions of the law, and such consistency cannot be determined by the criteria of formal logic alone. The obligation to take a reasoned decision is an essential element in the constitution of juridical knowledge.

For the classical rationalists the obligation to decide can play a part in practice, but not at all in the constitution of science, whose true propositions coincide with the ideas of divinity. Now in the divine mind, and in the nature of things, everything is determined (Leibniz) or even necessary (Spinoza): the truths of science rediscover the ideas of divinity which form a coherent and categorical system. In the mind of God, and from the point of view of the rational knowledge which ought to take its inspiration from it, the obligation to decide creates no problem, since the system of divine ideas is categorical and makes it possible to supply an answer to any question. This assumes, by the way, that the questions are formulated in a language corresponding exactly to the divine ideas, and that any language deviating from them can engender nothing but confusion and error.

The extrapolation which consists in conceiving the divine thought on the pattern of a system of geometry is based on the preconceived idea, now recognised as false, that it is possible to enrich a system's means of expression *ad infinitum* without removing its categoricalness. Now it is in this case alone that the role of decision would count for nothing in the development of knowledge. Contrariwise, the decision alone would be important in the absence of any system which enabled reasons to be given for it, but then decisions, being based on nothing and devoid of all rationality, would be entirely arbitrary and would make no contribution whatever to the development of knowledge. In fact, our real knowledge lies between these extreme cases. Formal systems which make it possible to demonstrate any proposition that can be formulated in them, or its negation, are exceptional, and their syntax is poor. In all other cases the decision of the investigator can play a part in the development of knowledge.

If the structure of the juridical disciplines is dominated by the obligation to decide, the role of decision is far from negligible in philosophy, in the natural sciences and in the human sciences. It can show itself in varied circumstances.

A question having been put, we can ask ourselves whether the known facts and the methods accepted in a given discipline enable an answer to be given. If it cannot, the investigator, unlike the judge on the bench, is under no obligation to furnish a reasoned answer: he can abstain, and his decision can be that the data available to him are insufficient. But he can also contrive new methods or amend the old ones in search of a solution to the problem put to him. For example, the tried and tested techniques of modern history do not make possible the solution of a great many historical problems of Greek antiquity. Accordingly, if we lack the evidence of a number of authorities who are mutually in agreement we may be satisfied with less certain sources of information. Thus the requirements of historical criticism vary with the questions about the past which are under study. The methods applied depend very largely on the nature of the questions put; and anyone demanding the same degree of precision and strictness in every case would more often than not have to abstain from giving any answer and would often be regarded as lacking in good sense. This conclusion—which holds good for all the sciences—is *a fortiori* applicable to philosophy. Indeed, when it comes to philosophy, the desire to impose on the investigator the obligation to apply only certain methods in solving the problems posed in philosophy is all the more arbitrary in that there is nothing more the subject of controversy than philosophical methodology.

Another epistemological situation in which the structure of knowledge depends on the decision of the scholar is that in which, a fact being known and its independence of a field of systematised knowledge being unquestioned, we ask ourselves whether we are going to modify that field in order to adapt it to the fact we wish to attach to it. The problem would be quite different if experiment had furnished us with results incompatible with the theoretical expectations: as the results contradict the theory, this latter must be amended, and the discussion can then relate only to the modifications proposed. On the other hand, in the situation envisaged, the discussion can bear on the advantage of considering the new facts—whose establishment is the object of research of an empirical kind—as relative to a field of knowledge of which they are formally independent. Unlike law, the sciences know nothing of rules of competence, and it is for the scientist to accept the responsibility for the decision to integrate the facts in question in the field of his research. This extension of theory, with the unification it introduces into our knowledge, constitutes one of the main elements of scientific progress, the other element consisting in the elimination of the incompatibilities that appear both within the theory itself and between the theory and the data of experience. This decision to integrate the new facts with the theory gives direction, in a way that is essential, to the discovery of new and appropriate hypotheses, and encourages the modification of principles and of accepted classifications, as also of the meaning of technical terms. The logic of discovery obeys neither the formal schemes of deduction nor the canons of Mill: it is governed by requirements that can be expressed only by means of such ideas as simplicity, economy of thought, fertility, regularity, generality, none of which are susceptible of unambiguous definition.

If the desire to answer precise questions is the spur of any technique, the desire to connect facts independent of it with a field of knowledge produces, along with the anxiety to eliminate the contradictions between theory and experience, the tension expressed by what F. Gonseth has called the principle of duality, which is essential to the dialectical conception of science. The consequence of the tension between theory and experience will sometimes be that certain results will be criticised, even condemned as not consistent with sound scientific method. Sometimes, when the facts are beyond argument, the tension may give rise to a recasting of principles and methods. In this latter case the accommodation effected by the man of science between facts and methods does not take place under the aegis of evidence, but consists in searching for the solution which is most appropriate and seems most consistent with reality, the reasons for the preference given to a particular solution being in any case rarely determined entirely by experiment and calculation.

In allowing the principle of duality, and also the responsible decisions entailed by its application, a decisive role in the evolution of sciences and techniques, as also of political and philosophical ideas, we shall be in a position to understand both the interior development they present and the reasons why they become diversified.

If scientific opinion in every branch of knowledge departs from common sense, and if scientific methods can vary from one branch to another, even—within the same discipline—from one question to another, the reason is that ideas, starting probably from a common stock of knowledge, have become differentiated by contact with special problems proposed for solution, and that certain methods have been adapted to them. So that nowadays the practice of each discipline necessitates a prior initiation both into the corpus of doctrine and into the methods regarded as valid. Obviously this does not mean that the various sciences develop in a vacuum, without influencing each other. It does mean that their development does not solely depend—as certain positivists thought and perhaps still think—on such factors as simplicity or generality: that would incidentally assume a classification of the sciences which is carried out from a unitary point of view. The ideal of the unity of science, which proposes to unify the sciences under the banner of a scientific method borrowed from one of them—or rather from a scientific method constituting an idealisation and schematisation of reality—neglects the concrete historical situation in which the various disciplines have developed. The ideal of the unity of science seems rather to follow the line of a Cartesian conception of knowledge.

Science, according to the Cartesian conception of it, is composed of self-evident truths fixed *ne varietur*, whatever the further development of knowledge: this assumes that the language in which these truths are enunciated, and the ideas that serve to express them, will be subjected to no future reversal in consequence of the progress that science might make. Indeed, this is also the opinion of all positivist men of learning. For them all science consists in the facts that have been established and definitively remain so, regardless of the theories—transitory and secondary as these are in the evolution of the sciences—in which the facts have been integrated.

But if we assume that the sciences develop on the basis of opinions previously accepted—and replaced by others either when difficulty results from some contradiction or in order to allow of new elements of knowledge being integrated in the theory—then the understanding of scientific methodology requires us to be concerned not with building the scientific edifice on the foundation of self-evident truths, but with indicating why and how certain accepted opinions come to be no longer regarded as the most probable and the most suitable to express our beliefs, and are replaced by others. The history of the evolution of scientific ideas would be highly revealing in this regard. If Whewell's theories on induction are still superior to anything done in this field they owe their superiority to a prior historical investigation of the inductive sciences. Whewell had the great merit of drawing attention to the importance of language for scientific theory and to the way in which the progress of thought is a concomitant of the evolution of concepts. A careful study of the reasoning employed by the creative and original thinkers, both in science and in philosophy, would reveal that that reasoning is infinitely more varied than anything to be found in the manuals of logic or scientific methodology. This result will perhaps move the logicians to concede more importance to the study of the theory of argumentation, which has been utterly neglected for the past three centuries, on account both of rationalist and Cartesian conceptions and also of positivist and empiricist ideas regarding the methodology of the sciences.

In this new way of looking at things, which we offer in opposition to the classical views of scientific activity, neither the self-evident principles of the rationalists nor the irrefragable facts of the empiricists constitute clear and distinct elements of knowledge which no subsequent progress would later modify or make more specific.

If in the most varied disciplines we find principles which every effort is made to preserve untouched, and if certain statements seem to withstand the evolution of knowledge, it is because the ideas contained in these apparently universally valid propositions do become more specific or are modified in order that the principles may continue to maintain their validity. The assertion that every proposition is either true or false can be kept, provided we are allowed to redefine accordingly the ideas of 'proposition' and of 'truth'. In order to claim that every phenomenon has a cause, it is necessary to take one at least of these terms in a sense different from that given to it by Kant. 'It is necessary always to act in conformity with justice' is a universally valid ethical rule, if one is allowed to take a different view of the conception of justice. We can grant that the study of history is based on the postulate that human nature does not change, provided we do not enumerate with precision the human traits that we assume to be unchanging.

A claim that the facts, once established, can be considered as a definitive and permanent acquisition amounts to an assumption that no progress—theoretical or experimental—will modify any of their constituent elements or even the way in which they have been stated. This standpoint may seem defensible for a Platonist who believes that the conceptual structures by means of which the facts have been expressed constitute an adequate reflection of a rational reality. The scholar who does not share this point of view will limit himself to claiming that what he calls a fact constitutes a kind of residuum which is handed on from one theory to another, and which no evolution of knowledge can fail to take into account. This attitude again is perfectly tenable, provided no attempt is made to specify once and for all just what constitutes the irreducible residuum.

Analogous considerations would be in order so far as concerns the methods and criteria which have made it possible to establish the untouchable principles and the irreducible facts. The invariable character of these latter assumes methods and criteria of such perfection as to guarantee the immutable character of the results: scientific progress would then be purely quantitative. But that is not how scientific activity turns out in practice: it is not based on a collection of methods *ne varietur* established prior to our research and given us for all purposes. The methods have been adapted to the solution of particular problems, and fresh problems may well oblige us to conceive fresh forms of thought and fresh techniques. If we try to transfer methods tested in mathematics and physics—still more, idealised and frozen conceptions of those methods—into the most varied fields of knowledge, we are often condemning ourselves to sterility. A psychology whose techniques did not go beyond measuring and calculation would have to give up for a long time—perhaps for ever—any attempt to answer essential questions concerning the knowledge of man. This way of proceeding, moreover, leads us to set up everything that is science, and is treated in a manner conformable to a unique model of knowledge, in opposition to the intellectual developments due to the decisions that have to be taken but which are neglected from the theoretical point of view by being regarded as irrational. This amounts to treating as irrational not only all reasoning about values but also philosophy and the human sciences, which by being subjected to such requirements for 'rationality' would inevitably be reduced to triviality. Fidelity to certain methods may not make it possible to answer certain questions; but that is not necessarily because the questions are devoid of significance. It may equally be that the methods it is desired to use are inappropriate.

Our point of view should not in any way be taken as favouring irrationality. It is only when the techniques regarded as rational are reduced to their simplest expression that the field of the irrational is enlarged beyond all bounds.

In fact, however, the answer we give to questions put to us by practical life, the way in which we attach the new facts—often themselves answers to questions we put to reality—to theoretical systems of which they were logically independent, all our behaviour in so far as it is not based on strict deduction—all these are only very rarely the result of an arbitrary decision.

The reasons on which our decisions are based consist more often than not of opinions which we consider the most probable, probability in this case being in any case rarely susceptible of quantitative determination. These opinions are worked out by means of reasonings which depend neither on self-evidence, nor on an analytic logic, but on presumptions whose investigation depends on a theory of argumentation. Not all opinions and all argumentations merit equal consideration. This does not prevent the existence of a rational argumentation, an argumentation which, like Kant's categorical imperative, claims to be valid for the community of reasonable minds.

The role of decision in the working out of our ideas has been far too much neglected in the theory of knowledge. By taking account of the reasons we have for deciding in a particular way, or of the techniques of reasoning by which the decisions or the facts are linked to theoretical systems, we hope to be able to reintegrate in a theory of knowledge aiming at being rationalist the whole of the vast field now outside it, a field which includes among other things the very methods by which the theory of knowledge is developed.

V

THE SPECIFIC NATURE OF
JURIDICAL PROOF[1]

THE reason for my being asked to present a report at the discussion of the thirteenth session of the Société Jean Bodin devoted to the question of proof [2] was no doubt the desire to put before historians of law and professional jurists the point of view of a logician who is concerned with the study of reasoning in its various forms. The organisers who were kind enough to invite me doubtless hoped that my observations would produce a feeling of unfamiliarity which would be favourable to keen discussion. To produce that feeling, it will suffice if I spend a few minutes in recalling the conception of proof formulated by the logicians and the mathematicians.

For them, proof is normally constituted by a demonstration which makes it possible to deduce a proposition from premises which are either axioms or propositions themselves already proved. According to the classical conception of deductive method—as expressed, for example, in Pascal's short treatise 'Concerning the Geometric Spirit and the Art of Persuasion'—axioms should be propositions which are perfectly self-evident in themselves. True, Pascal adds that, however clear and self-evident these propositions may be, it is still necessary to ask whether they are granted. However, he corrects himself a few lines later when he affirms that this latter principle can be ignored without risk of error.

[1] From the *Journal des Tribunaux*, Brussels, 1959, No. 4255.
[2] This study was the subject of a report made by the author on 3 October 1959 at the Faculté de Droit de Paris on the occasion of the thirteenth session of the Société Jean Bodin.

Recourse to self-evidence, on the one hand, and recourse to the agreement of the interlocutor, on the other, seem to derive from two different traditions, as much opposed to each other as law and fact. What is self-evident ought to be granted, but what is to be done if that which is characterised as self-evident is called in question? On the other hand, what is granted might be neither self-evident nor even—in an extreme case—true. Analogously, is it necessary in law to regard as not requiring proof well-known facts, or those which are explicitly or implicitly acknowledged and admitted by the parties?

In the modern conception of deductive method, in its axiomatic form, the mathematician neglects this problem of the truth of principles. He will say that his role is solely to demonstrate what consequences can be drawn from a collection of axioms which furnish the starting-point—hypothetical if you like—of his system. As for the truth of these axioms, its establishment is the duty of the person who wishes to apply the axiomatic system, or, possibly, of the philosopher of science.

Similarly, we could require of the rules of deduction which enable us to link theorems with axioms that they should be unquestionable (or unquestioned?) and that they should furnish a proof that appears conclusive to any normally constituted mind. But modern logicians are content to require that these rules should be at once explicit and devoid of ambiguity, so that the operations of proof can, if necessary, be checked by the use of machines. But this is feasible only if the rules of deduction make no appeal to any intuition based on the meaning of the propositions, and relate only to signs and to operations carried out on signs. When these conditions are realised we can say that the axiomatic system and the proofs it furnishes are formalised. A theorem will be a proposition based on axioms and proved by the correct application of the system's rules of deduction.

It is essential that an axiomatic system should be *coherent*, that is, that it should not be possible within it to demonstrate a proposition *and* its negation. It is not indispensable, on the other hand, that an axiomatic system should be complete, that is, that it should be possible within it to demonstrate every proposition whose formulation the system permits of *or* its negation.

These brief observations are enough to enable us to understand why demonstrative proof is impersonal: it is binding on any normally constituted mind, it can even be furnished mechanic-ally, and its correctness cannot depend on the assent of one particular person or another. Furthermore, in such a system it is not possible to prove the pro and the con, that is, a proposition and its negation, unless the system is to be incoherent and therefore unworkable. On the other hand, in every incomplete system—and that is the usual case—there exist insoluble pro-blems, propositions of which neither the truth nor the falsity can be proved.

Let us compare what we have just said about axiomatic systems with the characteristics of a modern legal system. The latter puts the judge under the obligation both to give a judgment, under pain of denial of justice (cf. Article 4 of the Code Napoléon and Article 258 of the Belgian Penal Code), and to give a motivated judgment. Because of these obligations, the legal system is treated as a complete system in which every claim of the parties ought to be susceptible of being adjudged as consistent with or contrary to the law. The system may be considered complete in itself or, as under the Swiss Civil Code, it may become so only by the avowed intervention of the judge: in either case it is important to note that the obligation to give a judgment takes priority over fidelity to any particular rules of proof, deduction or interpretation. If the judge is to be able to give judgment in any circumstances he must be left a certain liberty in this field, on condition that the use he makes of it is subject to check.

The role of writers who interpret a living law which is still being administered is to facilitate the judge's task and to provide solutions to all cases that appear to be open to dispute. The obliga-tion to find a workable solution thus rests equally on the writers who wish to guide the judge. Their obligation is, in point of fact, less absolute, for the intrepreter, faced with a situation which to him appears insoluble, need do no more than appeal to the legis-lator for an amendment of the law. The historian of law is *a fortiori* free to stress the difficulties presented by an ancient legal system without seeking means for resolving them. It remains true, however, that in most instances the primary and no less admitted duty of the teacher will be to provide solutions for cases in which the law is applied, on condition of thinking out new techniques of interpretation for the purpose of achieving that end. The way in which such interpretation is justified and grounded will not consist in a conclusive *demonstration*, applying rules enumerated beforehand, but in an *argumentation* which is more or less effective in character. The arguments employed will be characterised not as correct or incorrect, but as strong or weak. Every argumentation is addressed to an audience, large or small, competent or less competent, which the speaker seeks to persuade. It is never conclusive: by means of it the speaker tries to gain the adherence of a free being, employing reasons which that being should find better than those advanced on behalf of the competing thesis. Now we can understand how, before a tribunal, it is possible to plead for and against. The judge who takes a decision after hearing both parties does not behave like a machine, but like a person whose power of evaluation, free but not arbitrary, is more often than not decisive for the outcome of the argument.[1]

These considerations explain the peculiarities of legal reasoning in so far as it consists in an *interpretation* of the law. They are especially noteworthy when compared with mathematical reasoning. They throw light for us on the mechanism of proof which, in its capacity as the basis of an assertion, consists of a demonstration in a mathematical system and of an argumentation in a legal system.

The foregoing observations explain why my statement concerns the specific nature not of judicial, but of juridical, proof. I know that, in our law, judicial proof is concerned only with fact, the law being deemed to be known, particularly by the judge. The legal problems regarding proof are essentially those which arise with respect to the law of a foreign country or, as the case may be, a local custom. But the important thing is always to prove the existence of a legal norm, not its scope: the reasons that can be advanced in favour of one interpretation or another of the law do not depend on the techniques of proof but on the techniques of interpretation, regarded as having no connection with the field of proof.[2] This way of seeing things is perfectly justified in our legal organisation, which implies both the separation of powers and the

[1] Cf. C. PERELMAN and L. OLBRECHTS-TYTECA, 'La Nouvelle Rhétorique', *Traité de l'Argumentation*, Paris, Presses Universitaires de France, 1958, p. 682.
[2] Cf. H. DE PAGE, *Traité Élémentaire de Droit Civil Belge*, second edition, Brussels, 1942, Vol. III, pp. 662-663.

distinction between fact and law which is essential for determining the limits of the control exercised by the supreme court; but it needs itself to be situated in its institutional context.

If proof before a tribunal consists in founding a claim by establishing 'the fact which gives rise to it and the legal consequences flowing therefrom having regard to the system of law in force',[1] it is important to stress that technically judicial proof concerns fact only. Ought we to see in this tradition the influence of classical Roman Law and of the division of the proceedings into two stages, first before the magistrate and subsequently before the judge, a division which inevitably limited the pleadings before the judge to questions of fact? I am not qualified to answer this question.

I would like, however, to point out that in the *Rhetoric* (Book I, 1375a, 24) Aristotle, in dealing with extra-technical proofs, that is those which do not depend on the speaker's art, enumerates five kinds, namely laws, witnesses, contracts, torture and the oath. Be it noted in this connection that his examination of the laws covers not only specific laws—'those that are written and govern the city'—but also common laws—'all those which, without being written, seem to be recognised by universal consent' (*Rhetoric*, Book I, 1368b, 7–8). In Aristotle's time, then, judicial proof was not confined to establishing the facts, but had equally for its object the justification of 'the legal consequences flowing therefrom'. The possibility, indicated by Aristotle, of pleading against the written law on the basis of natural law and equity (*Rhetoric*, Book I, 1375) would appear to show that the separation of powers was not as rigid in his time as it is in ours. Besides, can it be claimed that the proof constituted in mediaeval procedure by the ordeal or the judicial duel is a proof of fact, whereas its effect is to give a total decision on the issue of the dispute? It is true that with us proof of fact is clearly separated from pleadings in law. Nevertheless, we have thought it worth while first to emphasise the peculiarities of this debate, and more especially the fact that legal interpretation is based on an argumentation that must convince the judge and not on an impersonal and conclusive demonstration.

[1] Cf. H. DE PAGE, *Traité Élémentaire de Droit Civil Belge*, second edition, Brussels, 1942, Vol. III, p. 661.

In what does judicial proof of fact consist? How is it distinguished from historical proof? What is it that determines its specific nature?

The historian is free in principle to study the facts that interest him and to choose his subject with due regard to the effective or presumed existence of means of proof which he judges to be sufficient. Often indeed the subject will be marked out for him by virtue of the availability of relevant documents or the possibility of subjecting them to a profitable method of investigation. As for facts already acknowledged, the historian may regard them as authenticated, himself doing no more than refer to the documents by which they are attested or to the studies by which they have been established. Usually, apart from educational purposes, he will call them in question only if he can throw new light on them by furnishing fresh factors or a new interpretation of old ones.

It is quite exceptional in the scientific field for a decision formally to carry the authority of *res judicata*. Who would have the competence, the right or the power in this field to ban the consideration of any particular question? Only a learned body, an institute or an academy could conceivably take up such a standpoint, and that only in circumstances quite out of the ordinary: thus it was that the Paris Academy of Sciences decided one day to cease examining works whose object was to demonstrate the squaring of the circle. But normally the way in which a man of learning employs the time available to him on researches which he judges to be interesting and fruitful is something left entirely to his own unfettered evaluation.

The judge does not possess the same liberty. He does not choose the causes which he will have to judge. Litigation is brought before him and, in giving his decision, he performs an act of sovereignty with the object of maintaining law and order, by declaring what is in conformity with the law. He must give judgment within a reasonable time, and his decisions will be authoritative as *res judicata*, after the lapse of the time allowed for lodging an appeal and for taking the case to the supreme court. The decision of a case is deemed to be correct, and the parties must abide by the court's conclusions. In any case, more often than not it is these conclusions that matter to the parties, far more than the facts themselves, which are little more than a basis from which legal consequences flow.

The role of the judge is not that of an arbitrator, for the procedure is not settled by mutual agreement between the parties. It is the plaintiff or the public prosecutor who has the initiative: the defendant or the accused has been summoned before the court and every precaution has been taken to prevent him from impeding the due process of law. In this situation the judge's business is to apply the law, together with, when appropriate, any matter agreed on by the parties, and to take his decision in conformity with the relevant legal presumptions.

These presumptions safeguard the *status quo*, which cannot legally be modified, when counter-proof is admitted, without a judicial decision. It is for the person putting forward a claim tending to modify the *status quo* to establish that that claim is well founded. The attitude of the defendant—the person to whose detriment the plaint has been brought—will be an essential factor in all cases in which public order is not at stake. When it is a case of facts alleged by the plaintiff which seem conclusive or simply relevant, proof of them need be furnished only if they are denied by the defendant. The latter's admission, although not constituting a proof of the acknowledged facts—and that is why it is not admitted, or at least is not sufficient, when public order is concerned—is fully credited against its maker when his private interests alone are at stake. By reason of these consequences, the person who makes an admission is required to have the capacity of enjoying the rights whose loss he risks by his admission.

What are the admissible facts which there is good ground for proving? The answer to this question depends essentially, in civil cases, on the attitude of the parties, though the judge may nevertheless exercise the right officially to require proof of facts which may seem to him conclusive (Article 254 of the Belgian Code of Civil Procedure). But 'he is not authorised to declare a fact established simply because he has gained positive knowledge of it outside the proceedings'.[1] In effect, it is for the parties, not the judge, to provide in debate evidence of the disputed facts in so far as they result from the judicial contract. If he ceases to be passive, the judge risks finding himself reproached for his lack of impartiality.

No limitation is placed on the forms of judicial proof when the parties can resort to all means capable of producing conviction in

[1] AUBRY and RAU, *Cours de Droit Civil Français*, 5th edition, Paris, 1922, Vol. XII, pp. 73–74.

the mind of the judge. But most frequently there are rules governing the admissibility of evidence: the methods of proof admitted
are limited and legally graded. Sometimes even their probative
value is precisely fixed, each degree authorising some procedural
step or other. In that case the judge's sovereign evaluation of the
worth of the evidence admitted is exercised only within the limits
of legal provisions.

Legal presumptions which forbid counter-proof, or which lay
the burden of it on the party who claims to oppose them, do not
put the arguments for and against on a footing of equality, for by
them the party for whose benefit they exist is dispensed from all
proof (Article 1352 of the Civil Code).

The presumptions *juris et de jure*, which forbid counter-proof,
are aimed at providing a guarantee against the calling into question of certain situations which the legislator does not wish to see
disturbed. They form a dike against the assaults of inveterate
litigants. For the most part the rights protected by these presumptions will be founded on unquestioned facts, but it is essential
that they should be capable of being protected against any possible
questioning. The security resulting from this protection has been
judged to be more important for the social order than an occasional and exceptional failure of these presumptions to conform
to objective reality—a failure which it is in any case almost always
difficult to be certain of beyond all shadow of doubt. If unlimited
questioning of a judicial decision, on the ground of inconsistency
with justice or with the will of the legislator, were possible, cases
could drag on interminably, with all the resulting disturbance,
weariness and expense. If prescription could not protect existing
situations the peaceable enjoyment of real property would depend
on a *probatio diabolica* which it would be quite impossible to furnish. In the final analysis, every order assumes the existence of
unquestionable facts: they may be guaranteed by self-evidence or
by common knowledge; they may equally be guaranteed by the
power which prevents their being questioned.

The presumptions *juris tantum*, which admit counter-proof,
govern the whole field of judicial procedure. Ordinarily they are
limited to presuming what in practice most frequently occurs in
the society governed by the system of law which prescribes them.
But they may equally be aimed at giving, though in less radical
fashion, protection to established situations, which they do by

laying the burden of proof—which is always a proof counter to the presumption—on the party claiming to upset them. The course of the proceedings may, according to the way they go forward, bring into play presumptions alternately in favour of one party or the other. The responsibility of counter-proof will always rest on the one who, at a given moment in the judicial proceedings, does not benefit from the presumption adopted—the party 'who claims to deprive the other of the advantages of his current position'.[1] The proceedings can conclude only with a judgment cast in the form of a decision which is settled, and to challenge which no further evidence will be admitted.

With such a conception of proof nothing could contrast more strongly than the method advocated by Descartes for making sure of our knowledge. The first rule of that method implies a corresponding obligation to reject, without according them the least belief, things that are not entirely certain and indubitable, no less than those that appear to be manifestly false (First Meditation). By holding aloof, therefore, from everything in which he could imagine the least doubt, Descartes was obliged to discard everything which is no more than opinion, conjecture or presumption, everything susceptible of being questioned being equally uncertain.

This requirement of self-evidence would render impossible not only judicial decisions but even any activity depending on a process of deliberation. Descartes indeed fully realised this and did not fail to allow that 'the actions of life do not often brook delay, and so it is a very certain truth that, when it is not in our power to discern the truest opinion, we must follow the most probable' (*Discourse on Method*, Part III). His method should be applied only to scientific knowledge. But is it truly applied in the sciences? Since the paradoxes of logic and of the theory of sets shook mathematics to its foundations, we have been witnesses, in the deductive sciences, of the triumph of formalism which, without asserting the self-evident character of axioms and rules of demonstration, is content to stress our capacity to distinguish signs and to carry out on them operations devoid of ambiguity. Whereas, for Descartes, the geometric method, with the self-evident character of its axioms and deductions, was to serve as a universal

[1] AUBRY and RAU, *op. cit.*, p. 83, note 19.

model for all the sciences, the scope of that self-evidence has today been diminished even in the formal sciences. As for the natural sciences, the widespread employment of the calculus of probabilities has profoundly modified their methodology. Less than ever can they dispense with assumptions and hypotheses and, as in law, when proof is not a simple didactic exercise but aims at establishing the truth of a doubtful proposition, it will be a counter-proof to certain accepted assumptions.

The characteristic of scientific proof is that it knows nothing of the separation of powers, more particularly of the legislative and judicial powers. In it all presumptions are human, not legal; presumptions in respect of which counter-proof is inadmissible are foreign to it. The facts established by the scientist will have their repercussions on the system of laws and assumptions if they seem to run counter to the predictions which are drawn from them. The modifications proposed by the investigator in order to restore coherence will be submitted to the specialists in the discipline, and they will evaluate them in accordance with criteria developed within that discipline and proper to it.

In law, on the other hand, the manner of contesting legal assumptions by the administration of counter-proof is rarely left entirely to the evaluation of the judge. The rules of evidence established by the law furnish assumptions of which the judge must take account, whatever his inner conviction. These rules are normally founded on what, in a given environment and at a given period, seems to provide the maximum in the way of guarantees of justice. It can be understood how in an age of illiteracy acceptance was given to the rule 'witnesses are more credible than written documents'; and how in another age of widespread education the opposite rule should be applied, namely 'written documents are more credible than witnesses'. In an epoch which is highly hierarchic it is understandable that the credibility—even the admissibility—of witnesses should be governed by assumptions motivated more perhaps by anxiety to favour the privileged than by the desire to establish objective truth. But it can be allowed that in the eyes of the mediaeval legislator these two concerns may have appeared to coincide.

Why did Roman law permit torture in certain cases and on certain persons, and not in other cases and on other persons? Why, in some legal systems, is the innocence of the accused presumed, the burden of proof being always incumbent on the prosecutor; whereas in others the mere fact of accusation suffices to create a presumption of guilt of which the accused must clear himself? Why, in certain systems, are rules of evidence relatively non-existent and in others strict? Does the answer lie in the greater or lesser degree of confidence reposed in the discernment and integrity of the judges?

All these questions, in which theoretical concerns, such as the search for objective truth, are mixed with practical concerns, such as the safeguarding of a given social order, are of great interest no less from the point of view of epistemology than from the historical and sociological side. For the problem of judicial proof, like that of juridical proof, constitutes only one aspect of the general problem of proof. It is important to understand that proof, aimed as it ultimately is at providing a basis for convictions, does not present a uniform face to the world, but varies according to the fields and the cases in which it is applied. A thorough investigation of proof in law, of its variations and evolution, can, more than any other study, acquaint us with the relations existing between thought and action.

VI

SELF-EVIDENCE
AND PROOF[1]

THERE is an argument, well known in the history of philosophy, which makes all knowledge ultimately depend on some kind of intuitive or sensory immediacy. According to this argument, either the proposition itself is self-evident:[2] or else it can be shown to follow, with the help of a chain of intermediate links, from other propositions which are self-evident. Moreover, it is this self-evidence of immediate knowledge and only this which, again speaking traditionally, sufficiently guarantees the truth of the affirmations of a *science*, as opposed to those of various and fluctuating *opinions*. It is these opinions which, clashing against one another interminably, produce nothing but the endless sterilities of philosophical controversy, which no form of traditional proof or demonstration can ever bring satisfactorily to an end. Whereas in science, on this view, agreement can be produced through self-evident knowledge, as soon as one moves within the realm of opinion one can only, in the end, subscribe to the view of La Fontaine that the argument of the strongest is always the best.

Following the Augustinian train of thought, Duns Scotus asserts that anything which is 'evident' must not only be present

[1] The first of two Special University Lectures delivered at University College in the University of London in March 1957. The lecture was translated from the French by Mrs. R. B. BRAITHWAITE. It has appeared in French in *Dialectica* (June 1957) and, in this translation, in *Philosophy*, Vol. XXXIII, No. 127, October 1958.

[2] The French word 'évidence' is difficult to translate into English and in this article is rendered, in accordance with the context, by 'self-evidence', 'evidentness', 'immediacy' and 'evidence'.

but also be distinctly perceived. Thus this necessary and fundamental immediacy was ascribed, on Scotus's view, neither to our knowledge of the past nor to our knowledge of religious dogmas. In both of these fields, either reliable witnesses or reliable authorities were indispensable to make good the lack of immediate 'evidence', this same immediate 'evidence', moreover, being required in any testimony produced by intermediaries to guarantee, for the recipients, the testimony's truth.[1] During the whole period, of course, before religious conflicts started tearing apart the whole western world, propositions guaranteed by faith, founded, as it was held to be, upon supernatural revelation, were considered to convey certainty of knowledge in a manner parallel to and also comparable with the certainty conveyed by the propositions of science. But the theological dissensions of the sixteenth century, which were followed by the Wars of Religion and by the period characterised by that formula of resignation, *Cuius regio, eius religio*, incited seventeenth-century and eighteenth-century thinkers to extract from these propositions about matters of faith, some smaller but solid kernel of self-evident and immediate knowledge.

What, then, is 'evidence' used in this wide sense?

A proposition is 'evident', or, as is more often said in English 'self-evident', when anybody who can grasp the meaning of its terms is certain of its truth. On this view the assent of the intellect, in contrast to that of the will, is a direct function of the entity which is grasped. It is not in the power of the intellect to control or determine the degree of this assent, for the simple reason that this is strictly proportional to the evidentness and also to the intelligibility of the apprehended object,[2] 'object' being used here in the widest possible sense. This same distinction between intellectual and voluntary assent can be retraced in the thought of the seventeenth-century philosophers; it is present both in the work of Descartes and of Locke. For both of these philosophers the intuition of a connection between simples, whether these simples are simple natures or simple ideas, produces an infallible conviction that the connections indeed are thus.

[1] Cf. PETER C. VIER, O.F.M.: *Evidence and its Function according to John Duns Scotus*, Franciscan Institute Publications, St. Bonaventure, N.Y. 1951, pp. 48–51.
[2] *Ibid.*, p. 55.

Moreover, this intuition of certainty must be sharply distinguished from that purely subjective feeling of conviction which is by no means incompatible either with error or with illusion. For this evident certainty of knowledge does not consist in any absence of doubt in the mind of the knower as to the truth of what is known. It is something objective, a positive property: the absence of all falseness in what is known.[1]

In his recent study of the problem of knowledge,[2] A. J. Ayer summarised the interesting analysis given in the first chapter by listing the necessary and sufficient conditions for the presence of knowledge. For a statement to be called knowledge, he said, first, it must be true, secondly one must be sure of it, and thirdly one must have the right to be sure of it. But whereas, for him, this right to be sure of it can be justified in various ways, too complex to be themselves included in a definition of knowledge, for the classical epistemologists, this right was only justifiable, in the last analysis, by the self-evidence of the propositions which formed the ultimate foundations of all knowledge.

The 'evidence' *ex terminis* of a necessary proposition is that property which, according to rationalists, consists in its truth being the direct result of a clear understanding of its terms. According to empiricists, this same 'evidence' results either from some necessary connection or from some necessary incompatibility between ideas. The immediate 'evidence' of a contingent proposition, on the other hand, is gained from an intuition of the presence of an immediate object; the best example of such immediate contact is provided by introspection. That we are alive; that we are conscious—such facts are certainties which not only have no need of proof, but without the prior assumption of which, no proof is possible.[3]

For the classical epistemologists, 'evidence' is not simply a particular state of mind in the person who is aware of it—and which of course, taken alone, could not possibly guarantee the truth of its object. A proposition is evident, if it is evident at all, before it is entertained, and it keeps this quality of evidence even when the mind is not struck by it as self-evident, through

---

[1] SPINOZA: *Ethics*, II, XLIX, scholium.

[2] A. J. AYER: *The Problem of Knowledge*, London, Macmillan, 1956, p. 34.

[3] Cf. VIER, *op. cit.*, pp. 121 à 125. So too ARISTOTLE, *Metaphysics*. 1011a, ST. AUGUSTIN: *De Trinitate*, XV, Patrologia latina, 42, col. 1073.

incomplete comprehension either of its terms or of their inter-relations. In actual fact, to come to perceive the self-evidence of such a proposition, it will quite possibly be necessary for the mind to have known beforehand the definition of one or other of its terms, since it is this definition which will serve as a con-necting link in the demonstation of its truth. But in this case, the original proposition will no longer be self-evident when taken on its own (*per se nota*); its self-evidence will be indirect and mediate. It will be *nota per aliud*, known because of the know-ledge of something else.

Thus it comes about that, as soon as one discusses this im-mediate evidence, and, in particular, as soon as one discusses self-evidence, either as a criterion of truth or as the foundation of knowledge, one is immediately brought up against two problems, firstly that of the nature of definition, and secondly, even more generally, that of the nature of language. If one wants to avoid the difficulties that result from facing this fact—if, in particular, one wants to avoid the obligation to define, one after another, the terms which are used in any argument—the only way of doing this is to place the foundations of all self-evidence in some kind of intuition; in terms of an intuition of connection between simples, simple natures, simple ideas and simple terms, all these being con-sidered as indefinable, and as existing in a universe in which sign and signified exactly correspond without any possibility of error or ambiguity.

Now, in contrast to Descartes and Locke, who believed neither in the utility nor in the possibility of proving 'evident' proposi-tions, Leibniz refused to trust himself to the idea that all know-ledge of axioms had to be founded on intuition alone.[1] He required that these axioms should be shown to be reducible to primitive axioms which he called *identicals*.[2] Having less con-fidence, apparently, in our intuition of simple terms than in the ultimacy of the subject-predicate relation, he wanted to make every primitive proposition consist in an identity affirming that this relation was analytic.

These two requirements, moreover, that of requiring simplicity of terms and that requiring self-evident propositions to be

[1] LEIBNIZ: *Nouveaux essais sur l'entendement*, in *die Philosophischen Schriften*, ed. GERHARDT, Vol. V, p. 67.
[2] *Ibid.*, p. 388.

analytic, have been regularly laid down as essential, either as alternatives or in conjunction, by authors who were investigating the logical conditions for self-evidence. We are bound to ask ourselves therefore what we are to make of them.

The first requirement presupposes both an atomic conception of reality, and the existence of a language the structure of which conforms to that of reality. It assumes, further, that this reality is perfectly known. It also presupposes that immediate knowledge of it is possessed by all rational users of this language, which, to satisfy the requirement I have just given, must be logically prior to all human usage. In fact, I need hardly say that the very enumeration of these preconditions is enough, nowadays, to give pause to the most fanatical defenders of the establishment of criteria for self-evidence.

The second requirement, namely that laying down the analytic character of self-evident propositions, seems, at first sight, considerably more reasonable. Indeed examples are frequently quoted of such self-evident analytic propositions, pre-eminent among these being the assertion 'that a whole is greater than any one of its parts', and the differing applications of the Identity Principle, 'A is A'. But since the development of the theory of groups has established such truths as that the group of whole numbers has the same power as that formed by certain of its sub-groups, such as the sub-groups of even numbers, there being as many even numbers as there are numbers—it has become a truism that the principle of the whole being greater than its parts does not hold for the domain of the infinite. Thus it has now become customary to call in question the 'evidentness' of what had once seemed the very paradigm of a self-evidently true proposition. And although it seems at first sight as though the Principle of Identity was exempt from this form of attack—although it seemed indeed that the self-evidence of this principle was the one thing which could never be called in question—yet we only have to take a glance at natural language in order to be able to quote statements which at first sight could be considered as applications of this principle, and yet which also could be equally well considered as asserting contingent and indeed contestible truths: 'Money is money': 'Business is business': 'War is war'. What are we to make of these? Moreover the form is a natural one and alive in language. I remember the spontaneous remark of a woman who, coming upon her husband and finding him in tears at the return of their son after a long period away, said: "Now I see that it is not only the case that mothers are mothers; it is also the case that fathers are fathers."

It is obvious that, for logicians, the possibility of making any application of the Identity Principle presupposes that the same signs always keep the same meanings. But do they? To what extent is one in fact assured of this complete identity of meaning? Only when constructing an artificial language which postulates this identity, in the use of its symbols. And even then the only real way to avoid awkward discussions of significance is just to manipulate signs without even asking how they signify, let alone whether the propositions obtained by combining them are true. But, under such conditions, what becomes of the criterion of self-evidence? It is reduced to a general feeling of confidence that the process of manipulation of the signs is controllable, by mechanical means, from starting points which are beyond dispute because they are explicitly arbitrary. Thus a linguistic principle of tolerance is substituted for a criterion of self-evidence, since the consequences of adopting the criterion were such that contemporary thinkers were unable to contemplate them.

It comes to this: modern logicians, though inheritors of the classical tradition, practically never try to establish the first principles which they use as self-evident. What they are concerned with is to stress the necessary nature of the connection between the premises and the consequences obtained from them by operating the rules of the system and this necessity of connection is seen by them as correlative to the analytic nature—which in its turn is agreed to be due to the linguistic nature—of these conclusions. Now, it is true that the Polish logician Jaskowski has been able to prove the equivalence between a certain number of axiomatised logical systems and systems of natural logic having no axioms.[1] But he does not present his rules of supposition as self-evident, for the simple reason that, not being propositions, they cannot be true or false. Are these rules then purely arbitrary? And if they are, why call them rules of logic? If they differ from the rules for manipulating the pieces of a game, such as chess, on this view this is only because they can be interpreted with the help

[1] Cf. St. JASKOWSKI: *On the rules of suppositions in formal logic*, Studia Logica I, Warsaw, 1934.

of models, acquaintance with which guarantees for us the truth of the propositions obtained by using the models to interpret the signs. But, in that case, what criterion guarantees our knowledge of the models? Do we have to fall back, after all, on an unacknowledged criterion for establishing infallible self-evidence, a criterion which applies to simples, which can be apprehended by any rational being, which is unaffected by any change of culture or technology, and which takes the same form equally for a mathematical specialist and a small child? Is it not the case that, unless we have recourse to some such criterion, we find ourselves plunged into a complete scepticism which involves in one fell swoop the repudiation of all possibility of certainty, an insistence on the arbitrariness of all opinion, and the ultimate denial both of the existence of any logic whatever and of the existence, too, of any rationality?

I just do not believe in reducing the problem to these two naked alternatives. In the rest of this lecture, therefore, I shall try briefly to present a conception of proof which, without deriving from the classical theory of self-evidence, does not immediately land those who hold it in a scepticism so complete as to extend to all departments of knowledge.

Now, what were the presuppositions which forced the classical theorists of knowledge to posit the sheer alternative, which seems to me so disastrous, between complete scepticism and knowledge founded on infallible self-evidence?

It seems to me that these presuppositions were two in number:

1. The principle that a conclusion is never more strongly established than the least certain of its premises:
2. The principle that assured knowledge can only be founded on intuitive self-evidence.

We shall examine each of these in turn, beginning with the second. And we shall begin by asking what the idea of a self-evident intuition can mean; what theory of knowledge, what methodology of science, what conception of reality and what conception of action, too, go with it. In order to develop this train of thought, we shall have recourse to examining Descartes' philosophy. For he, of all men, seems to have had the gift of bringing a strict rigour, together with a quite admirable native sense of what followed from what, to the problem of elucidating the consequences of taking seriously the rationalist criterion of self-evidence.

For Descartes, and throughout the whole domain of knowledge, the slightest doubt was, at once, a sign of the presence of error.[1] Before any knowledge could be certain, as opposed to being just plausible, it had to have as its objects the simples; and these simples had to have the property of being known by themselves; and knowledge of them, being clear and distinct, could not contain any element of falsity.[2] Now knowledge, thus conceived, cannot be progressive. Either it is perfect, right from the start, or it cannot exist at all. On this view also, those who desire to take the shortest path for arriving at truth will occupy themselves uniquely with objects of knowledge which are capable of having certitude. And this certitude must be comparable with that which can be achieved by the demonstrations of arithmetic and geometry.[3]

The essential, for Descartes, is not to develop this or that particular science but to strengthen the basic power of reasoning. For him, human wisdom always remains one and the same, however different may be the objects to which it is applied. It can no more be changed in its operation by its relation to these objects than a ray of sunlight by the variety of the things which it lights up.[4] This is why the whole object of Descartes' method is to increase the strength of the natural light of reason; and this is why this light can be obtained in a manner which is quite independent of the study of any special science.[5] This method, founding all knowledge as it does on self-evident intuitions, will obviously be the same for all branches of knowledge. It will proceed by establishing an order going from simple to complex. According to this conception, every man must begin afresh for himself the work of building the structure of all knowledge; and in doing this he must set on one side those problems which he is incapable of treating by the method which, before starting to treat any of them, he has pre-selected.

Two consequences in particular of this theory of knowledge deserve to be chosen for special emphasis. The first of these is the asocial and unhistoric character which is ascribed by the theory to what is known. The Cartesian theory of knowledge is, in the end,

---

[1] DESCARTES: *Oeuvres*, éd. de la Pléiade, *Méditations*, p. 161.
[2] *Ibid.*, *Regulae*, p. 50.   [3] *Ibid.*, *Regulae*, p. 10.
[4] *Ibid.*, *Regulae*, p. 5.   [5] *Ibid.*, *Regulae*, p. 6.

a theory of knowledge which is not human, but divine; of knowledge as acquired by a unique and perfect Being, without initiation, training, tradition or need to learn. On this view, the history of knowledge, on its positive side, becomes uniquely that of additions, not that of successive modifications. Even if it be granted that in order to achieve such knowledge a man must first divest himself of his prejudices and his errors, yet it is assumed also that these will leave no trace to sully the purity of ultimately reached truths. In sharp contradistinction to the point of view in which all progress and knowledge consists in successfully battling with some error—according to which, in fact, every advance is defined in terms of the error which it eliminates,[1] Cartesian knowledge is given, in one instant, after a complete break has been made not only with error, but also with opinion and probability, for science must be purged of these before it can achieve genuine knowledge.

The second consequence of the Cartesian method is that it produces a complete separation between theory and practice. Descartes himself insists, in several passages, on the inapplicability of his method in two spheres: that of matters of faith, and that of daily life.[2]

Thus when it is a question not of the contemplation of truth but of living a life the needs of which require rapid action, his method is of no use to him at all.

The position which I desire to maintain could be said to be the antithesis of the Cartesian view. Whereas self-evident intuition, for a Descartes or a Locke, is something which by its nature has no need of proof, something indeed which is susceptible of no kind of demonstration, I shall grant the status of knowledge to a tested opinion, to an opinion, that is, which has survived all objections and criticisms and with regard to which we have a certain confidence, though no certainty, that it will resist all such future attacks.[3] I do not believe in the existence of any absolute criterion which would have to be itself the guarantee of its own infallibility. I do believe, on the other hand, as we all do, in intuitions and convictions in which we place confidence, until there is reason to think that this confidence has been misplaced.

---

[1] Cf. G. BACHELARD: *La philosophie du non*, Paris, P. Univ. France, 1940.

[2] DESCARTES: *Op. cit., Méditations*, p. 165. *Secondes réponses*, p. 273.

[3] Cf. HUME: *Treatise of Human Nature*. Book I, Section VII, *in fine*.

In order that any such actual process of proof may be applicable it is essential to realise that a judgment, though it can be supported by intuition, must be different from it in kind. For otherwise, not being significant, it could not be true; moreover, since it was not significant, no proof of it would be possible. A statement can only be verified by means of the predictions which it makes possible and the attitudes which it causes to be approved; and these, in their turn, are again imagined as being subjected to the further controls of experience and of our moral conscience.

Those conceptions of proof which present the proved proposition as the final product of a totality of operations, starting with those defined by the axioms of the system, are only defensible if axioms and rules of operation are alike considered to be self-evidently true. If one falls back on a formalist conception of deductive proof, if one insists on the arbitrary character of a developed axiomatic system, one never gets to the point of being able to see what the totality of proposed transformations has in common either with truth or with any grounds for it. If the whole deductive apparatus is to be able to fulfil its role, both its axioms and its rules of operation must be interpreted. Moreover, a sufficiently high value must be placed on such an interpretation for any lack of agreement between the results of the calculation and the results of measurement to be considered as a reason for rectifying something in the system. In general the theory will be rectified in a way which will primarily lead to certain modifications of the interpreting principle. But the possibility cannot be ruled out that the actual mechanics of calculation may also, at some point or other, have to be rectified.

The general history of the art of achieving deductive rigour which the evolution of logic in the twentieth century so remarkably exemplifies, does not encourage the conviction that, in this field it is at all likely that perfection has as yet been achieved. But even someone who, unlike the present writer, considers that the advances already made do constitute sufficient reason for having unbounded confidence in our present formal techniques, would hesitate to ascribe to an *interpreted* system—the only kind of system to which it could sensibly be ascribed—an evidentness sufficient to render redundant all further proof. This refusal to ascribe evidentness leads to scepticism only in the case of those philosophers who argue that, were there no truths sheltered from all demands for proof it would not be permissible to regard any truths as proven.

But the life of the mind does not, in actual fact, oscillate thus between an absolute certainty and an absolute doubt. We should tend to think, on the contrary, that the very fact of being faced with such a choice would of itself destroy the very possibility of our having any intellectual life. For this life requires the assumption that there are reasons which can be found for undertaking to believe something without these reasons being so dazzlingly self-evident that the propositions believed in stamp themselves as truths on the mind of any rational being who attentively studies them.

In order for us to have reasonable knowledge of anything, it is quite enough that the premises on which the piece of knowledge in question is founded should be such that it can provisionally be accepted without discussion. But this does not mean that at some other time or in another historical or methodological context these same premises could not be brought into question. But in order to question them the method of universal doubt will be of no avail. For, to borrow a rule from Leibniz[1], we will assume that no change must ever be made without a reason being given. In order, therefore, to entertain a doubt, it must be possible to give a justification for so entertaining it. As against Descartes, who, as I say, in the realms equally of theory of knowledge and of ontology, would have nothing to do with opinions or contigent entities, but insisted on a foundation of absoluteness consisting of self-evident truths and necessary Being,[2] lack of which he thought would throw him into unrelieved doubt and uncertainty, I think that, when the criterion of evidentness is rejected, all opinions do not become plunged in an equal degree of uncertainty. For not only can some still be preferred to others. It is also the case that reasons for having such preferences, and for maintaining them, can be given, that is, once we decide to regulate our mental life according to an initial principle of inertia which is the counterpart of Leibniz's rule.[3] It is just because, having once adopted an opinion

[1] LEIBNIZ: *Op. cit.*, p. 500.

[2] Cf. DESCARTES: *Op. cit., Discours de la Méthode*, p. 103. *Premières réponses*, p. 243.

[3] Cf. C. PERELMAN and L. OLBRECHTS-TYTECA: *Traité de l'argumentation*, paragraph 27, Paris, Presses Universitaires de France, 1958.

it seems to us reasonable in general to hold to it, that it is not reasonable to abandon it without having some grounds for doing so. And it is precisely this principle which accounts for the importance given in every society to those traditions which it is the task of education to hand on. Those rules and techniques which our system of initiation forces us to acquire are precisely those which later experience will enable us to improve by causing us to adapt them as the situations to which they have to be applied may change. It is just because, before being adults, we have all been children, subject to a slow formation by parents and masters, that we can now lay claim to be called reasonable beings. What illusion, what presumption too, there is in the attitude of a Descartes, resolutely walking along the path of knowledge like a man walking completely alone, and in the dark.[1] If we must think of the process of gaining knowledge in terms of the metaphor of following a path, I prefer the Leibnizian analogy, according to which it is a whole body of men, not a solitary wanderer, who do the walking. This whole body, the human race, considered as practitioners of 'those sciences which lead to happiness', are recommended to walk in a concerted and orderly way, to share out the possible avenues of advance, to make the highways easily recognisable and to keep them in repair.[2] The Cartesian conception of the gaining of knowledge presupposes reason, fully armed, to spring innate from each one of us, needing only to be liberated from the constraints of education in order to become straightway apt for contemplation of self-evident truths. But the fact of the matter is that this same faculty of reason is slowly constituted and consolidated within us by means of a long apprenticeship which both guides the course of our discernment, and also forms our judgment, both because of the rules which are taught us and because of the changes we bring to them as a result of their use.

If philosophical activity is the highest form which intellectual activity can take, this is just because philosophy subjects to reflection and to criticism the very instruments by which knowledge is obtained. Now these have been made to assume their present form by receiving the impact both of the problems to which they have been applied and of the techniques which man has adopted to solve them. And to conceive the process of the increase of know-

[1] DESCARTES: *Op. cit.*, *Discours de la Méthode*, p. 102.
[2] LEIBNIZ: *Die Philosophischen Schriften*, ed. Gerhardt, Vol. VII, p. 157.

ledge as essentially connected with the statement and solution of special problems, automatically involves refusing to connect knowledge with any kind of antecedent infallibility—as well as refusing also to separate theory from practice. When the primordial role of special problems in determining theory of knowledge, is recognised, one can no longer refuse to examine as relevant those further problems which have no solution found for them by any single infallible method. As soon as one conceives of the development of method—any method—as part of a search for a procedure which will have to be adapted to the problem to be solved, one deprives oneself thereby of the *a priori* right to claim uniqueness for any method independent of the choice of field to which it is to be applied. On the contrary, it is precisely the man who holds this point of view who will come also to understand the relative and regional character of all knowledge, linked as this is to particular cultures, temperaments, fields of research. Moreover, it is this very specificity or individuality of knowledge which gives to it its character, which makes of it a know-how, which in part can be historically explained. Such knowledge will have taken the form it has, above all because of the part which it has played in correcting, or at least palliating the errors which went before it. And the end-product of this evolution is human knowledge itself, imperfect, but perfectible, a sphere in which the achievement of each creating mind becomes embedded in a tradition which the thinker learns and accepts before he gets to the point of rectifying it at some point or other at which it is already acknowledged to have been defective.[1]

And there is more to be said. For is the first pre-supposition behind the classical theory of evidentness true? This pre-supposition asserts that no conclusion of any argument can be more certain than the least certain of its premises. This assertion follows from the reduction of all proof to analytic proof, analytic proof being conceived either as syllogistic or as any technique which enables conclusions to be reached from premises, by means of operations which only work on the signs of a language. But why envisage proof always in terms of a single model? The convergence of a great number of indications, each susceptible of interpretation,

[1] C. PERELMAN: *Education et Rhétorique*, Revue belge de Psychologie et de Pédagogie; No. 60, Bruxelles, 1952.

which differ from each other, and also which vary in their degree of reasonableness, this final convergence can lead to conclusions so sure that only a lunatic would ever think of doubting them. Must one refuse, for instance, to believe in the possibility of knowing the past, or of foreseeing the future, just because this belief can only be founded on a chain of reasoning, one or more of the links of which is not quite solid: and anyway, must one always conceive of reasoning in terms of a chain which is only, by definition, as strong as its weakest link? When we have to reconstruct the past, the arguments which we use seem to me very much more like a piece of cloth, the total strength of which will always be vastly superior to that of any single thread which enters into its warp and woof.[1]

Hume very thoroughly recognised that all the arguments which he could pile up to produce doubt about the principle of causality did not in the least shake his spontaneous confidence in it, and in the law-bound character of phenomena. Can we not use this same affirmation of his, to produce as it were, a counter-pressure, by submitting to the same kind of destructive criticism his reasons for piling up doubt? When any given analysis of knowledge leads to obviously paradoxical conclusions, one is clearly free, either to accept the conclusions or to revise one's techniques of analysis. Kant, for instance, found salvation from scepticism by being able to place confidence in synthetic *a priori* judgments. But is his answer the only possible answer to Hume's criticism? I think, myself, that the answer is best found by developing an epistemology founded on what a theory of the nature of argumentation, as it actually is, can teach us. Such a theory of argumentation has been far too much neglected both by contemporary logicians and by contemporary philosophers. Its importance, nevertheless, emerges clearly in the greater and greater importance which modern critical thought accords to the study of language. Every proof is concerned with some one proposition, or, speaking more generally, with some one thesis or hypothesis. This cannot have its foundation exclusively in an intuition, no matter of what nature. Before any hypothesis whatever can be stated, some language must be used for stating it in. Contrary to the opinion both of realists and nominalists this language is neither a simple copy of pre-

[1] C. PERELMAN and L. OLBRECHTS-TYTECA: *Rhétorique et Philosophie*, Paris, P. Univ. France. 1952.

established structures, nor an arbitrary creation of man. Although language is a human artefact, it is not produced by any irrational decision of a single individual. It develops, normally, in the midst of a community, the members of which can modify it by the use they make of it as soon as they consider there are any reasons for promoting any change. Whereas realism and nominalism present us with a theory of language which precludes any appeal to reasoning or argumentation as justifying the use which is in fact made of it, either because language is treated as part of an external reality, or because the choice of a language is held to be undiscussable because purely arbitrary, my view is that the reasons which determine the choice of any language, and, above all, of those which bear on the form of its extension and development, ought themselves to become the object of argument. And this assertion alone, once granted, enables us to understand why any philosophy which refuses to allow any importance to a study of argumentation, is bound to oscillate between dogmatism and doubt. It will veer between a conception of reason which eliminates the reasoning individual altogether, and a conception of the nature of voluntary action which never provides the acting agent with any reason for taking decisions.

The choice of language is part and parcel of a theory. It is also a logically indispensable element in any description of reality. Such a description is a human product in which considerations of formal structure combine with cultural motivations which are as much emotive as practical. Since language is thus neither logically necessary, nor wholly arbitrary, its actual use is subsequent to some kind of argument, sometimes explicit, more often implicit, when the usage appears traditional. In such a case, only historical research can disinter the forms of reasoning which justify the use of language which has in fact been made and the direction in which it has since developed. And this justification will now seem to us to be reasonable when the strands of reasoning of which it is made up, without compelling our agreement, commend themselves nevertheless as having within them what I can only call an intention of universality, of claiming to hold good for the whole community of reasonable men, and that we participate in this point of view.

Thus, in the domain of proof, instead of separating evidentness from the subject who perceives it, and reason from all other human faculties, we propose a conception of the nature of rational argument such that, just because it engages the assent of the man who develops it as well as of the man who admits it, can for this very reason be subjected to Kant's categorical imperative: we should only propose, as instruments for convincing others, statements and methods of supporting them which both pass the test of our self-constituted judgment, and at the same time will hold good for the whole intellectual community.[1] We are the judges of the force, value and relevance of arguments, and in passing judgment we ourselves are guided by the forms of argument which have seemed convincing to us in the past. We are also guided by that general rule of justice which requires from us that we treat in the same manner situations which seem essentially of the same kind.[2]

These rules which thus guide our decision in permitting forms of reasoning are, for the most part, not enough to eliminate all discussions and all disagreements. But in default of an impersonal and absolute criterion of validity, furnished by self-evidence and providing a method of proof founded on self-evidence, we can still justify our decisions in the fields of action and of thought by forms of argument which are neither constraining nor mechanical. The guarantee of these, in the last analysis, is supplied by the solidarity which their use and their evaluation establishes between the person who constructs them and the person who adopts them. The responsibility of the man who thus engages himself, is, as ever, a corollary of his freedom.[3]

[1] Cf. C. Perelman: *La quête du rationnel*, in *Etudes de Philosophie des Sciences*, en hommage à F. Gonseth, Editions du Griffon, Neuchâtel, 1950.
[2] Cf. Chapter III and *Traité de l'Argumentation*, paragraph 52.
[3] Cf. Chapter IV.

VII

OPINIONS AND TRUTH[1]

IT is traditional—and not only in philosophy—to contrast truth with various opinions, reality with diverse appearances, objectivity with fleeting impressions. Truth, reality and objectivity ought to make it possible to cut short debate, to distinguish the false from the true, illusion from what conforms to the real, hallucination from what conforms to the object. Truth, reality and objectivity mark out the straight road of knowledge and put us on our guard against all deviations. They provide the norm to which it is proper to submit opinions, appearances and impressions whose status is equivocal and whose basis uncertain, since they are the source at once of knowledge and of error. Let us make no mistake about it: without opinions, appearances and impressions our access to truth, reality and objectivity is closed. Truth must be believed, reality must manifest itself, objectivity must be perceived. Nay more. For the confiding and credulous child opinion and truth, appearance and reality, impression and objectivity are indistinguishable. It is we who, having to hand the material worked out by a critical tradition, speak in this context of confusion, whereas the unawakened mind is still at a prior stage. The moment of distinguishing comes only when, in respect to the same single object, opinions clash, appearances are in opposition and impressions cease to agree. It is because not all opinions, appearances and impressions are compatible that there is ground for dissociating truth from opinions, reality from appearances and objectivity from impressions. Thenceforward we know that there

---

[1] From *Les Etudes Philosophiques*, 1959, No. 2, La Vérité, Presses Universitaires de France.

are false opinions, illusory appearances and deceptive impressions, but not all of them are of this kind. We need a criterion to save what is worth saving.

This criterion is not immediately given at the same time as opinions, appearances and impressions, for, if it were, error would be quite inexplicable. Descartes, in order to find it, took the course of submitting to the test of methodic doubt everything we had accepted uncritically, and of eliminating what did not stand up to examination. Let us see what survives and what its characteristics are. We know the result of the test: the self-evident is what is indubitable; it forces itself upon us, whatever our efforts to resist it or to shake it; it is the most solid of our certitudes. All our opinions will be brought to the touchstone of self-evidence. Those in respect of which the smallest doubt is left will be rejected: the rest will furnish the irreducible nucleus and the model of all knowledge, for they are at once given and guaranteed. That which is self-evident forces itself on our thought as true, self-evidence being merely the subjective aspect of an objective truth. At once we have found the method for the right conduct of our reasoning. By trusting only what is self-evident or reducible to self-evidence, we shall be in possession of an objectively valid science, 'the true propositions which constitute it being the same thing as being'.

A counterpart to the conditions that must be observed in order to constitute a science is to be found in the conditions that enable us to preserve ourselves from error and to forearm ourselves against it. We must be on the alert for preconceptions and prejudices, fruits of imagination and haste propagated by 'education, habit, example and authority'.[1] And Rousseau was to do his best to apply these rules in his new educational system. 'Let him (your pupil) know nothing because you have told him, but because he has understood it himself; let him not learn science, let him discover it. If ever you replace reason in his mind by authority, he will reason no more: thenceforward he will merely be the plaything of the opinion of others.' [2]

On what conditions will self-evidence be an indication of truth and a criterion of the value of opinions? To begin with, the very idea of deceptive self-evidence or false self-evidence must con-

[1] DUMARSAIS, 'Essai sur les préjugés', Œuvres, Paris, 1797, Vol. VI, p. 135.
[2] Émile, Paris, Firmin-Didot, 1898, p. 181.

stitute a logical impossibility. For otherwise there would at once arise in respect of it the problem of the criterion which makes it possible to distinguish the truly from the falsely self-evident, and we should merely have pushed the difficulty back a stage. Self-evidence, to play its part, ought not only to guarantee the truth of its object, but ought itself to be indisputable: the dissociations opinion–truth, appearance–reality, impression–objectivity are not conceivable so far as it is concerned. Self-evidence, by nature indubitable, will refer back to a veritable knowledge which describes the real as it objectively is.

In self-evidence truth is recognised by the real presence of its object.[1] But that object must be sufficiently distinct from all that it is not, sufficiently isolated, to justify the assurance that the self-evident idea does not in any way exceed that which is effectively given to the consciousness. The criterion of self-evidence by no means fits with a global and synthetic view. It must have objects whose simplicity guarantees their distinctness: the self-evident view is analytic, and the world it discloses is an atomised world.

Self-evidence can undergo no variation either in space or in time, and it cannot depend on the individual characteristics of the mind. It will be the same for everyone, whatever his temperament or his education, his age or his native land: all those subjective and variable elements that differentiate mankind constitute obstacles in the way of exercising that invariable faculty, present in every normally constituted human being, which is reason. The right usage of the reason will, then, be preceded by a course of training, by a purification of the subject, by the elimination of everything that could get in the way of the perception of self-evident ideas. These will be in no way a product of history or a creation of the individual or of society, for reason cannot undergo evolution in time, and each man's self-evident ideas reveal eternal and universal truths. These truths will not be formulated in a contingent language, because, for self-evidence to be expressible and communicable without danger of error or ambiguity, the language must follow its object exactly and reflect it without deformation; and the linguistic distinctions and connections must reproduce those of the real. In a realism which is justified in this way, our notions correspond to eternal essences ranged in the world of ideas or thought by a perfect and eternal mind to which they

[1] HUSSERL, *Die Idee der Phänomenologie*, The Hague, Nijhoff, 1950, pp. 59–61.

furnish models for its creative activity. From this latter viewpoint human reason will appear as a faculty illuminated by the divine reason, the source and guarantee of self-evident knowledge. Thus, beginning with Greek metaphysics and continuing through the systems of St. Augustine, Duns Scotus and Descartes, there has been worked out in closer and closer detail a whole absolutist philosophy, with its theory of knowledge, its ontology and its theology—all resting on the criterion of self-evidence, the basis of absolute truths.[1]

The nominalist philosophers, who base our knowing, not on self-evident truths, but on an indubitable experience, and thus seek to provide knowledge with an absolute resting-place while still maintaining mistrust in regard to our understanding, can be grouped in two categories—that of the mystics and that of the empiricists. For the one category as for the other, it is not rational self-evidence but experience—whether it be mystic ecstasy or simple sensation—that is capable of establishing immediate contact between subject and object—to the point that in it subject and object become indistinguishable.

Ecstasy, which comes only occasionally, does not permit of the working out of a science, of a system of communicable truths: it can only ally itself with scepticism so far as concerns discursive knowledge. Empiricism, if it is to lead to knowing, must transfer the structures of rationalism to the plane of sensible experience.

It is not clear ideas that, combining to form self-evident truths, will constitute the ultimate basis of all knowing: it is sensations, immediate data of sensible intuition, that will furnish simple ideas and guarantee the existence of connections between those ideas. Sensations cannot deceive us: they do not differ from individual to individual, at least so long as we are concerned with normal human beings; and no previous education is necessary to ensure the conformity of sensations originating in the same object among observers placed in the same situation with regard to that object. The permanent features of human nature will explain the elaboration of ideas in their capacity as weakened impressions.

If we had to resort to the imagination and inventive genius of individuals in order to account for the formation of ideas, these would have only the status of hypotheses or extrapolations, which correct method would require us to submit to constant verifica-

[1] Cf. Chapter VI.

tion. Only the truths concerning particular existents would be assured and would furnish *the facts*, the unshakeable basis of all knowing. Any affirmation of a generality higher than that of the facts would constitute a mere opinion or theory, the soundness of which would have to be confirmed by the facts. These latter, on the other hand, would be beyond the reach of all criticism— atoms of knowledge just like the self-evident ideas, essentially invariable and independent of the individual and of his temperament, education and history.

From this viewpoint language would be an arbitrary human artefact, but almost without importance because purely conventional. The same experiences would be expressible in several languages, all quite interchangeable, for an agreement on conventions would facilitate the passage, by means of translation, from one to another. Basically nominalism, like realism, aims at the elimination of language as being a factor of distortion and misunderstanding. Both envisage knowledge as a direct contact between subject and object; from such knowledge would be excluded all subjective and disturbing elements; to it intuition, rational or sensible, would furnish its unshakeable foundation. On this view, error results from everything that is other than intuition, experience, the facts; but these, when clearly perceived, are indubitable. In order to avoid error, it is necessary to test the empirical content of every opinion, and that contains only so much of truth as experience permits us to check.

Realist rationalism and nominalist empiricism thus, despite their undeniable divergencies, especially regarding the status of language, appear as doctrines which, confronted with the same problem—that of the basis of knowledge—have recourse to analogous solutions. It is a question of furnishing a basis which shall be at once given and indubitable, a self-evident factor constituting in the mind of the subject an authentic manifestation of the object. The subject experiencing that self-evidence would, so to speak, be transparent. He will be 'open to being'. The illumination to which he subjects being must leave this latter 'in that which it is and such as it is'; [1] and this illumination will not subject it to the distorting influence of any particularity of the knowing subject. If the consciousness which feels the self-evidence were

[1] HEIDEGGER, *De l'essence de la vérité*, French translation by A. de Waelhens, Louvain, Nauwelaerts, 1949, pp. 84, 88.

merely a gap in being, a nullity, then the problem would be the more easily solved, for we should be certain that the idea coincides infallibly with the object of knowledge; in these conditions the traditional distinction between idealism and realism is no longer meaningful. And *de facto*—this has, perhaps, not been sufficiently stressed—once there is self-evidence, rational or sensible, with its double character of element of knowledge and authentic manifestation of the real, there is no ground for distinguishing the subject from the object; once there is self-evidence, they coincide. It would be useless to inquire, with reference to doctrines basing knowledge on self-evidence, whether they are idealist or realist, for, more often than not, the status of the self-evidence remains undecided. When, as with Spinoza, the self-evident idea does not coincide with its object but is in conformity with it, we end up with an ontological parallelism about which it would be equally useless to inquire whether it is realist or idealist.

In such doctrines opinion (which is not self-evident) is necessarily erroneous or at the least insufficiently elucidated. Either it will be linked with the evidence by a demonstration in due and proper form or it will be unable to claim the status of knowledge. For all uncertainty, all disagreement, are signs of error. We are entitled to form opinions only when we lack the impersonal evidence which would make it possible to reach a conclusion, when the circumstances force us to adopt a point of view, to take a decision which is indispensable for 'the actions of life'. Thus it is that opinions are habitually linked with practice, common sense and daily life, but have no place as of right in science, save perhaps on the footing of provisional hypotheses which must disappear as quickly as possible in order to give place to well-founded knowledge, like the scaffolding in front of buildings under construction: when the building is finished, not a trace is left.

Opinions fade before evidence, but they play an undeniable role and regain importance as soon as evidence cannot force itself on us. The mistrust of opinion in the grand philosophic tradition of the west goes hand in hand with confidence in the criterion of evidence and the importance of its field of application. What are the structures of the real and of knowledge which render self-evidence possible; how to conceive of man or of the human faculties illuminated by self-evidence; how the human language

expressing and communicating the self-evident is developed—
these are the grand problems of any absolutist metaphysic.

The rejection of absolutism is, above all, the rejection of the
criterion of self-evidence. But it is at the same time the rehabilita-
tion of opinion. If the absolute validity of the criterion of self-
evidence is not granted the difference between truth and opinion
is no longer one of kind but one of degree. All opinions become
more or less plausible, and the judgments that form the basis of
that plausibility are not themselves clear of all controversy. There
is no longer any knowledge that is objective or impersonal or,
what comes to the same thing, guaranteed by a divine mind.
Knowledge becomes a human phenomenon from which error,
vagueness and undue generalisation are never entirely absent.
Knowledge, always perfectible, is always imperfect. Truth is not
perfect coincidence with its object: unless it has no object—as in
the formalist conceptions of the deductive sciences—it is approximation and generalisation, and these alone make its communication possible. Knowledge finds itself placed in the cultural milieu,
in tradition and in discipline. The history of knowledge ceases to
be the history of the errors of the human mind and becomes that
of its progress. The past leaves its mark on the present, just as the
father lives on in the child: no more than in law is there in science
a break in continuity. Human knowledge never begins at zero
with a *tabula rasa*. The illusion of being the son of nobody, the
first thinker of a new dawn, the abolisher of the ancient idols and
the old tables of the law, is always accompanied by a supernatural
illumination. For if there is no inspiration by a divinity revealing
himself to the prophetic individual, what is it that enables the
innovator to break completely with the past, to hold himself out
as so far the superior of, and so much nearer the truth than, all his
predecessors? There can be no rationality without benefit of
continuity.

It is in the rules and criteria already worked out, in the methods
already tested—which can be bettered or replaced only for reasons
recognised as valid even by those who had hitherto accepted them
—it is in these that the innovator who improves and enriches
human knowledge, who widens and deepens the field of rational
knowledge, will find the arguments that will enable him to gain
acceptance for his point of view. There can be no human progress

without previous initiation. The child abandoned to himself, without parents and without masters, would grow into a rude, wild man, if ever indeed he attained the dignity of humanity at all.

In periods when the foundations of society seemed unshakable, when man on reaching maturity could believe that his reason had come to him fully armed at his birth, that it was a divine gift which education was hastening to obscure and tarnish—in such periods the individual, face to face with God and truth, was able, in the name of conscience and of science, to challenge all his past. But the imperatives of conscience and the affirmations of science, if they are not to be those of a madman or a visionary, ought to be capable of becoming the common property of all mankind. The individual's reason, in its theoretical and practical aspects, had authority to oppose the prejudices and errors of his place and time, when it had the guarantee of the divine reason which enlightened all reasonable men. But if such a guarantee comes to be wanting, is it not in his own past, in the traditions and disciplines into which he has been initiated, that the individual can find the guarantee of his own rationality?

The fundamental rule, which governs his theory as it does his practice, and respect for which manifests the rationality of his thought and his action, will be *the rule of justice*, which calls on him to treat alike beings and situations that appear to him to be essentially similar.[1] The various cultures and the various disciplines determine what this treatment is and work out the categories which, in such or such a field, give precise meaning to the vague notion of 'essentially similar'. What matters and what does not, the differences that are irrelevant and those that are decisive— none of this is settled haphazard or by some intuition, but is defined in conformity with the requirements and criteria in force in each technique and in each scientific discipline. The rule of justice furnishes the common, and purely formal, factor in rational activity. But the content to which the rule is applied, the manner of making specific what it leaves indeterminate—these are an affair of human opinions, opinions which bear the stamp of their holder's personality and, through it, of all his past, all his education and all the tradition which he continues and, in case of need, improves and renews.

[1] V. C. PERELMAN and L. OLBRECHTS-TYTECA, *Traité de l'argumentation*, Paris, Presses Universitaires de France, 1958, § 52, 'La règle de justice'.

Reason, the heritage and glory of every human being, is not that eternally invariable and fully developed faculty whose products are alleged to be self-evident and universally accepted. The rationality of our opinions cannot be guaranteed once and for all. It is in the ever-renewed effort to get them accepted by what in each field we regard as the universality of reasonable men that truths are worked out, made specific and refined—and these truths constitute no more than the surest and best tested of our opinions.

VIII

THE NEW RHETORIC[1]

1. CONCERN for a theory of argumentation can find justification in a tradition as old as that of Greek rhetoric and dialectic.[2] At the same time any theory of argumentation must break with the notion of reason and reasoning which comes from Descartes and has left its stamp upon western philosophy for three hundred years.

No one denies that the ability to deliberate and argue is a distinctive sign of rational being. And still for three centuries the logicians and theorists of knowledge have neglected any consideration of the means which bring a mind to accept an argument. This fact is due to the non-compelling character of arguments which give support to a thesis. Deliberation and argumentation are opposed by their very nature to necessity and evidence. We do not deliberate where the solution is necessary, we do not argue against evidence. The domain of argumentation is that of the likely, the plausible, the probable, to the extent that the latter escapes mathematical certitude. Now it was Descartes' idea, clearly expressed in the First Part of the *Discours de la méthode*, to hold 'almost as false whatever was only probable'. Making evidence the mark of reason, he wanted to consider as rational only the demonstrations which, setting out from clear and distinct ideas, extend the evidence of axioms to all theorems, by

[1] Written jointly with Mme. Olbrechts-Tyteca, it was published as the Introduction to *Traité de l'argumentation*, Paris, Presses Universitaires de France, 1958. It appeared in this translation by Francis Sullivan, in *Philosophy Today*, Vol. I, No 4, March 1957.

[2] Cf. C. PERELMAN, *Raison éternelle, raison historique*, 'L'homme et l'histoire,' *Actes du VIe Congrès des Sociétés de Philosophie de Langue française*, pp. 347-354. (Paris 1954).

means of apodictic proofs. Reasoning *more geometrico* was the model he proposed to philosophers, who wanted to construct a system of thought which could reach the dignity of a true science. A rational science cannot really be content with more or less likely opinions. It has to elaborate a system of necessary propositions which impose themselves on all reasonable beings, and about which agreement is inevitable. Disagreement, then, is a sign of error. 'Every time two men make a contrary judgment about the same matter,' says Descartes, 'it is certain that one of them is mistaken. What is more, neither of them possesses the truth, for if one of them had a clear and precise view of the truth, he would be able to expound it to his opponent in such a fashion that it would force the latter's conviction.' (*Regulae* II)

For the followers of the experimental and inductive sciences, what counts is not so much the necessity of propositions as their truth, *their conformity with facts*. The empiricist considers as evidence, 'not that which the mind does or must yield to, but that which it ought to yield to, namely that by yielding to which its belief is kept conformable to fact.' (J. S. Mill. *System of Logic*, p. 370). Although the evidence he acknowledges is not that of rational intuition but of sensible intuition and the method he approves is not that of the deductive sciences but of the experimental sciences, he is no less convinced that the only valid proofs are proofs admitted by the natural sciences.

Only that which conforms to scientific method is rational, in the broad sense of this word. And the works of logic which study the means of proof (works limited essentially to the study of deduction and usually completed by some indications about inductive reasoning, reduced moreover, not to constructing but to verifying hypotheses) rarely venture to examine the means of proof used in the human sciences. The logician, inspired by the Cartesian ideal, feels at home only in the study of the proofs that Aristotle qualified as analytic. No other means presents the same character of necessity. And this tendency is all the more strongly marked after a period in which, under the influence of the mathematical logicians, logic was reduced to formal logic, to a study of the means of proof used in the mathematical sciences. As a result, reasoning which is foreign to the purely formal domain escapes logic, and consequently escapes reason too. This reason, which Descartes hoped would let us solve, at least in principle, all the

problems which men face and for which the divine mind already
has the solution, has been more and more limited in its competence, so that whatever cannot be reduced to the formal presents insurmountable difficulties for it.

From this evolution of logic, and from the progress it has
unquestionably realised, must we draw the conclusion that reason
is quite incompetent in areas that escape mathematics? Must we
conclude that, when neither experience nor logical deduction can
furnish the solution of a problem, we can do nothing but abandon
ourselves to irrational forces, to our instincts, to suggestion or
violence?

In opposing will to understanding, insight to geometry, the
heart to reason, the art of persuading to that of convincing, Pascal
already was trying to side-step the shortcomings of the geometrical method that result from the fact that fallen man is no
longer solely a reasonable being. Similar purposes are behind
Kant's opposition between faith and science and Bergson's antithesis of intuition and reason. But whether there is question of
rationalist philosophers or of those called antirationalist, all of
them continue the Cartesian tradition by the limitation they put
on the idea of reason.

It seems to us, on the contrary, that this is an undue and quite
unjustified limitation of the domain where our faculty of reasoning
and proving comes into play. Indeed, Aristotle had already
analysed dialectic proofs alongside analytic proofs, those concerned with the likely alongside those which are necessary, those
employed in deliberation and argumentation alongside those used
in demonstration. The post-Cartesian notion of reason, however,
forces us to bring in irrational elements every time the object of
knowledge is not evident. Whether these elements are obstacles to
be overcome—such as imagination, passion or suggestion—or
suprarational sources of certitude—such as the heart, grace or
Bergsonian intuition—this view introduces a dichotomy, a distinction of the human faculties, that is wholly artificial and contrary to the real processes of our thinking.

It is the *notion of evidence* as characterising reason that must be
challenged if we want to make room for a theory of argumentation which admits the use of reason to direct our action and influence the action of others. Evidence is thought of as the force
before which every normal mind must yield and at the same time a

sign of the truth of whatever imposes itself because it is evident.[1] Evidence would bind the psychological to the logical, and allow passage from one of these levels to the other. Every proof would be a reduction to evidence, and what is evident would have no need of proof: this is the immediate application, by Pascal, of the Cartesian theory of evidence. (Pascal, 'Of the art of persuasion. Rules for demonstration.' *Oeuvres*, p. 380, Pléiade Edition.)

Leibniz already objected to such a limitation being imposed on logic. It was his wish that 'one might demonstrate or give the means of demonstrating all the axioms which are not primitive, without distinguishing the opinions men have of them, and without caring whether or not they give their assent thereto'.

Now the logical theory of demonstration developed along the lines traced by Leibniz, not those of Pascal, and did not admit that what was evident had no need of proof. In the same way, the theory of argumentation cannot be developed if every proof is conceived of as reduction to evidence. The object of this theory is the study of the discursive techniques that allow one to *bring about or increase the adherence of minds to the theses that one proposes for their assent*. It is characteristic of the mind's adherence that its intensity is variable. Nothing makes us limit our study to a particular degree of adherence that is characterised by evidence. Nothing permits us to think *a priori* that the degrees of adherence to a thesis are proportional to its probability, and to identify evidence and truth. It is good method not to confuse at the outset the aspects of reasoning relative to truth with those relative to adherence, but to study them separately. Preoccupation about their interference or their eventual correspondence might come afterwards. Only on this condition is it possible to develop a theory of argumentation that has a philosophical bearing.

2. In the last three centuries there have appeared works of ecclesiastics preoccupied with the problems raised by preaching. And the twentieth century can be called the century of publicity and propaganda, devoting many works to this matter.[2] Yet

---

[1] Cf. C. PERELMAN, 'De la preuve en philosophie' in *Rhétorique et philosophie*, pp. 123 ff. (Paris 1952).

[2] For a bibliography, cf. LASSWELL, CASEY and SMITH, *Propaganda and Promotional Activities* (Minneapolis 1935). Also *Propaganda, Communication and Public Opinion* by the same authors (Princeton 1946).

modern logicians and philosophers have remained totally disinterested in the subject. An authentic study of this matter would call for a return to the preoccupations of the Renaissance, and still further to those of the Greek and Latin writers who studied the art of persuading and convincing, the technique of deliberation and discussion. Such a study could rightly be called a *new rhetoric*.

Aristotle examines certain proofs in his *Topics* and shows how they are used in his *Rhetoric*. He calls them 'dialectic'—a terminology that might justify a rapprochement of the theory of argumentation with dialectics, which was conceived by Aristotle himself as the art of reasoning in which commonly accepted opinions (εὔλογος) are the point of departure. (*Topics*, Bk I, Chapter 1, 100a.) But a number of reasons make a rapprochement with rhetoric preferable.

In the first place, there is danger of confusion coming from a return to Aristotle. For even though the word 'dialectics' served for centuries to designate logic itself, since Hegel and under the influence of the doctrines he inspired, the term has acquired a meaning far removed from its primitive one and now generally accepted. The lot of the word rhetoric is quite different. It has so fallen out of philosophical use that it is not even mentioned in A. Lalande's vocabulary of philosophy.

But there is a much more important reason for our preference: it is the very spirit in which antiquity dealt with dialectics and rhetoric. Dialectic reasoning was considered as parallel to analytic reasoning, but it treats probable instead of necessary propositions. The very idea that dialectics is concerned with opinions—theses to which one adheres with a variable intensity— is not exploited at all. You might say that the status of opinion is impersonal, not relative to the minds adhering to them. By contrast, the idea of adherence and of minds to which a discourse is addressed is an essential ingredient of all the ancient theories of rhetoric. Connecting argumentation with rhetoric in this way underlines the fact that *it is in relation to an audience that all argumentation is developed*. In this framework the study of opinion in the *Topics* can be given its proper place. It goes without saying, of course, that a modern study of argumentation would go far beyond the limits of certain aspects of the ancients' rhetoric, while at the same time it would pass over certain aspects which held the attention of these masters of rhetoric.

The object of the ancients' rhetoric was above all the art of speaking persuasively in public. It concerned the use of spoken language, of discourse, before a crowd gathered in the market place, seeking its adherence to a thesis presented to it. Evidently then the goal of oratorical art, the adherence of minds, is the same as that of all argumentation. But there is no need to limit oneself to the spoken word or to limit one's audience to a crowd in the market place.

Rejecting the first of these limitations opens up a more philosophical horizon: the logician wants to understand the mechanism of thought, while a master of eloquence desires merely to form practitioners. We have only to cite Aristotle's *Rhetoric* to show that this way of looking at rhetoric has the support of some famous examples. What is more, the modern role of printing makes it important to lay special stress today on printed texts. On the other hand, the study of mnemonics and oratorical delivery can be passed over in the modern logician's approach to rhetoric. Such problems belong rather to schools of dramatic art. Any study of argumentation must be conceived in the broadest terms. It need not be a one dimensional thing, limited to discourse as we commonly think of it. Discussion between two individuals or even personal deliberation belongs to a general theory of argumentation. The scope of modern rhetoric will go far beyond that of classical rhetoric.

What must be retained from traditional rhetoric is the idea of *audience*, which immediately comes to mind when we think of discourse. Every discourse is directed to an audience; and too often we forget that the same is true of all writing. A discourse is conceived of in terms of an audience. But the material absence of readers can make a writer think he is all alone in the world, while as a matter of fact his text is always conditioned, consciously or unconsciously, by the persons whom he means to address.

Among the ancients, rhetoric was the study of a technique to be used on the common herd, impatient to get to conclusion quickly, to form an opinion, without taking the trouble of making a serious investigation beforehand. (Aristotle, *Rhetoric*, Bk I, Chapter 2, 1357a.) It is this aspect of rhetoric that explains why Plato in the *Georgias* (455, 457a, 463, 471) fought it so vigorously and contributed to its falling into disfavour in the opinion of philosophers. But here again, why not admit that argumentation can be addressed to any kind of audience, and not just to an illiterate mob? True, if an orator is going to fulfill his function he must adapt himself to his audience. Understandably, then, the discourse that is most effective with an incompetent audience is not necessarily the one that will beget conviction in a philosopher. When Plato in his *Phaedrus* (273e) dreams of a rhetoric worthy of a philosopher, what he recommends is a technique that could convince the gods themselves. When the audience changes, the argumentation changes too, and even though the goal at which it aims is always to act efficaciously on minds, in judging its value one cannot but take account of the quality of these minds it succeeds in convincing. For this reason particular emphasis should be given to the analysis of philosophical arguments, which are traditionally considered as the most 'rational'—since they are presumably addressed to readers over whom suggestion, pressure, or special interest hold the least sway. But the same techniques of argumentation are found on every level, whether it is discussion around the family table or debate in a very specialised circle. If the quality of the minds which adhere to certain arguments in highly speculative domains presents a guarantee of their value, the common structure they share with arguments used in daily discussion shows how and why those arguments are understood.

Argumentation itself is concerned only with *discursive means* for obtaining the adherence of minds, with the technique that uses language to persuade and convince. Such a limitation in no way implies that this is the most efficacious way of acting upon minds. Quite the contrary. The most solid beliefs are those which are not only admitted without proof but which are often not even made explicit. And when there is question of obtaining adherence, nothing is more certain than internal or external experience and calculations that agree with rules previously agreed upon. But recourse to argumentation cannot be avoided when these proofs are discussed by one of the parties, when there is disagreement about their meaning or interpretation, their value or their connection with controverted problems.

On the other hand, anything done to win adherence falls outside the field of argumentation to the extent that language is not used to support or interpret it. The man who preaches by his example without saying anything or the person who uses a caress or a slap can obtain considerable results. But such procedures are of interest to argumentation only when they are revealed by means of language, when there is recourse to promises or threats. There are cases when language is used, not as a means of communication, but for direct action, as a blessing or a curse. These instances pertain to rhetoric only when such action is integrated with argumentation.

One of the essential factors in propaganda is the conditioning of the audience by means of the numerous and varied techniques that make use of anything that can influence behaviour. This sort of conditioning has been developed especially in the twentieth century, but the usage was well known from antiquity. The Catholic Church has turned it to advantage with incomparable skill. These techniques exercise an undeniable effect in preparing an audience, in rendering it more accessible to the arguments that will be presented to it. But here again we have a viewpoint that escapes the field of argumentation, which restricts itself to conditioning done through discourse.

Finally, what Aristotle calls 'extra-technical proofs'—proofs which do not arise from oratorical technique—enter argumentation only when there is disagreement about the conclusions that one can draw from them. (*Rhetoric*, Bk I, Chapter 2, 1355b.) Incidentally, the ancients' term 'extra-technical proofs' is a happy reminder that our civilisation, characterised by its extreme ingenuity in techniques for acting upon things, has almost completely forgotten the theory of acting upon minds by means of discourse, which the Greeks considered, under the name of rhetoric, as the τέχνη par excellence.

3. Since the theory of argumentation is concerned with an efficacious action on minds by means of discourse, it might be considered a branch of psychology. If arguments are not compelling, if they do not necessarily convince but possess a certain force which can vary according to the audience, could one not judge them by the effect they produce? The study of argumentation would thus become one of the objects of experimental psychology: various arguments would be tested before various audiences sufficiently well known to draw from these experiments conclusions having a certain general validity. American

psychologists have not failed to develop such studies,[1] whose interest cannot be questioned.

But a philosophical approach is different. It seeks to characterise the various argumentative structures, the analysis of which must precede any experimental proof for testing their effectiveness. Moreover, we do not think that the laboratory method could determine the value of argumentation used in the human sciences, in law and in philosophy, for the very methodology of the psychologist already constitutes an object of controversy.

We likewise reject the approach adopted by philosophers who strive to limit reasoning power in social, political, and philosophical material by taking their inspiration from models furnished by the experimental or deductive sciences, which reject as valueless anything that does not conform to schemes previously imposed. Rather, we would seek inspiration from the logicians, imitating the methods which have been so successful for them for the past century.

Let us not forget that in the first half of the nineteenth century logic enjoyed no prestige, either in scientific circles or among the public at large. Whately could write, about 1828, that if rhetoric no longer enjoyed the esteem of the public, logic enjoyed its favours still less.[2]

Logic has sprung into life brilliantly during the last hundred years, when, instead of rehashing old formulas, it set out to analyse the means of proof really used by mathematicians. Modern formal logic was set up as the study of the means of demonstration used in the mathematical sciences. But as a result its domain is limited, for whatever is ignored by the mathematicians is foreign to formal logic. The logicians should complete their theory of demonstration by a theory of argumentation. They face the task of analysing the means of proof which the human sciences, law and philosophy make use of. They must analyse the argumentation presented by publicists in their journals, by politicians in their speeches, by lawyers in their briefs, by philosophers in their treatises.

[1] For example, H. L. HOLLINGWORTH, *The Psychology of the Audience.* (New York 1935).

[2] *Elements of Rhetoric, Preface.* (Oxford 1828).

IX

LOGIC, LANGUAGE AND COMMUNICATION[1]

THE object of logic is to study methods of proof. Formal logic sets out to study formal proof, proof, that is, whose validity is deemed to depend only on the *form* of the premisses and of the conclusion. We should from the outset remember that any logic assumes a conception of proof. This prior conception is a function of a theory determining the relations between that logic and our faculties of knowledge. The theory relating to formal proof should, in addition, state explicitly the contrast 'form-matter', set out its scope and fix its limits. It should in any case be noted that, for a formal system to be interpreted as logic and not as mere calculation, we must rule out *a priori* the possibility of drawing false conclusions from true premisses. This necessitates respect for the principles of identity and non-contradiction.

It is the idea of what ought to constitute strict formal proof that results in a system of formal logic being put forward as a formalised language. The desire to eliminate the ambiguities inevitable in the structure of a natural language, to adapt the elements of the system to the demands of infallible communication and of unambiguous application of the rules of formalised inference—this is sufficient explanation why today establishing a system of formal logic comes to the same thing as constructing an artificial language.

The purely formal part of such an artificial language—the part that can be described in advance of any interpretation of the

[1] Communication presented at the XIIth International Congress of Philosophy, at Venice, *Proceedings of the Congress*, vol. I, Sansoni Firenze, 1958.

language itself—is called the logistic system. Its establishment will conform to the following requirements:[1]

(1) enumeration of all the basic signs (linguistic atoms) that go to constitute the formulae of the language;

(2) indication of unambiguous rules of *formation* which, on the basis of the basic signs, make it possible to construct properly framed formulae, these being the only *expressions* considered as significant in the language;

(3) selection from among these expressions of those to be treated as *axioms*, that is as expressions whose validity is independent of any process of inference;

(4) determination of the *rules of inference* which make it possible to proceed from one or more expressions to an expression deduced immediately therefrom and to be inferred on the basis of those expressions, termed premisses. An inference will be regarded as *proved* and will constitute a theorem if it is the last of a finite series of expressions all of which are either axioms or expressions deduced immediately from those preceeding them, in conformity with the rules of inference.

In pursuance of these requirements, a change in the list of signs, in the rules of formation, in the axioms or in the rules of inference will give rise to a different artificial language. These strict requirements, with which no natural language complies, are inspired by the ideal of the formal logician, whose desire it is to be able to say, without possibility of dispute, whether any series of signs constitutes a significant (that is, properly framed) expression, and whether any series of expressions constitutes a proof. To this end it is essential that any hearer or reader should have available effective and incontrovertible means of checking the correctness of an expression and the regularity of the formal proof of a theorem, in such fashion that, if he grants all the elements of the system the proof is based on, it carries its own conviction.[2] Formal proof, in its full strictness, cannot rely on any interpretation of the logistic system. Only thus, and only in so far as it is independent of any appeal to intuition, can its purely formal character be recognised. The ideal of rigour has brought about a progressive reduction of logic to formal logic. The desire to create the conditions for unambiguous communication leads to

[1] Cf. A. CHURCH, *Introduction to Mathematical Logic*, Princeton University Press, 1956, Vol. I, pp. 48–56.
[2] A. CHURCH, *op cit.*, pp. 53–54.

the conception of a system of formalised logic as an artificial language. It would be useful to subject to discussion the philosophic presuppositions required to complement the working out of a formalised logic if logicians are to be assured that all ambiguity has been eliminated from the formal system itself, as well as from its possible interpretations. Such a discussion would also make it possible to determine precisely in what regard a formal system is inferior to human logic reasoning within the system's limits.

Let us establish to begin with that basic signs, even in an entirely formalised logistic system, can be identified neither with the sounds nor with the ink-marks indispensable for each act of communication, for in that case exhaustive determination of all the elements of the system would not be feasible. To get out of this first difficulty, logicians have put forward various solutions. Church flatly adopts a Platonist standpoint (which Russell,[1] incidentally, justifies at length), distinguishing the sign from the instances in which it appears, and eliminating *ex hypothesi* the difficulties that illegible marks, for example, might produce.[2] Tarski, following, I think, Lesniewski, understands by sign and by expression, not individual pieces of writing, but classes of pieces of writing of the same form.[3] He does not think it worth while to say when pieces of writing are or are not of the same form. Quine, because further removed from Platonism, is preoccupied with the problem and somewhat tempted to resolve the difficulties that arise by adopting the maxim of the *identity of indiscernibles*, relative in each case to the discourse that gives rise to it and to a degree dependent on the structure of that discourse.[4] In trying to avoid Platonism, he is obliged to ask himself questions neglected by other logicians, and can no longer rest content with working out a formal language without examining its philosophic presuppositions.

Be that as it may, the existence of an unambiguous logistic system assumes that no problem is raised by the identification of

[1] B. RUSSELL, *An Inquiry into Meaning and Truth*, London, 1948 (1st edition 1940), pp. 58–59.

[2] A. CHURCH, *op. cit.*, p. 51, distinguishes 'symbol' and 'symbol-occurrence'.

[3] See, for example, A. TARSKI, *The Semantic Conception of Truth*, in 'Philosophy and Phenomenological Research' (1944), Vol. IV, p. 370, n. 5.

[4] Cf. QUINE, 'From a logical Point of View', pp. 50–51, 71–72, etc.

the basic signs. On this point assurance is possible only by having recourse to evidence, applicable in this instance not to ideas, but to the signs and expressions of the formal system.[1] Yet is the criterion of evidence enough to account fully for the attitude of the mind in face of a formal system? It would, at a pinch, make it possible to satisfy the requirements imposed on a calculating machine, but such a machine is incapable of rectifying faults and errors in calculation, at any rate when these have not been foreseen by the man who built it. Whereas the human mind, when confronted with any sort of calculation governed by rules, is perfectly capable of doing so.

In order to grasp this, let us examine the following arithmetical examples:

$$(a)\ Z + 5 = 7$$
$$(b)\ 3 + = 9$$
$$(c)\ 3 + 8 = 11$$
$$(d)\ 5 + 3 = 7$$
$$(e)\ 1 + 1 = 2$$
$$2 + 1 = 3$$
$$2 + 1 = 3$$
$$4 + 1 = 5$$

In each case a child of ten who had learnt the elements of arithmetic would spontaneously correct the printing errors, sometimes even without having noticed them. In example (a) he would put '2' instead of 'Z'; in (b) he would put '6' after the plus sign; in example (c) he would take no notice of the abnormal space between the '+' and the '8'; in example (d) he would replace '7' by '8'; and he would see that in example (e) the repetition of the formula '2 + 1 = 3' is an error which must be corrected by writing '3 + 1 = 4'.

Take, on the other hand, the case of someone confronted with these examples and content with strictly following directions for calculation, analogous to those formulated for the construction of a logistic system. He would discard example (a) because it contains a sign foreign to calculation; examples (b) and (c) because inconsistent with the rules for forming correct expressions; example (d) because it is not a theorem; and the last line of example (e) because it makes use of the sign '4' which has not been defined in the system. A calculating machine, or someone model-

[1] Cf. Chapter VI.

ling his behaviour on that of a machine must, whenever the rules of the system are departed from, stop and wait to be rescued. Whereas a man who has grasped the system, and sees in the examples given a number of instances of the rules he has been taught, will be able, when necessary, to correct an error whether of printing or of calculation. For, while giving priority to the avowed intention of keeping to the rules of the system, he is in a position to put right the way that intention has been carried out, by distinguishing the spirit from the letter, reality from appearance. Instead of stalling, like a machine registering an error, the mind ranges the elements of the system into an order of importance and rectifies the error by substituting the *real* sign for the *apparent* one. It is incontestable that this mode of proceeding not only discloses a certain intelligence, but is also consistent with logic, conceived as fidelity to the rules. Note, moreover, that these corrections, because introduced within the framework of a formal system, will be made in a fashion no less assured than operations conforming to the rules of the system, notwithstanding that these latter would not permit of their being carried out. Formal systems build up the complex on the basis of their elements and proceed step by step. Furthermore, the logical mind is capable of modifying the elements themselves in order to bring them into conformity with the rules whose paramount importance it perceives. A theory of logic and a theory of knowledge will be incomplete and insufficient if they fail to take account of this superiority of the mind over a calculating machine, even by reference to a formal system.

But there is yet more. The logistic system we have put forward contains another defect, in that it makes no mention of the special role of the principle of non-contradiction. The mere fact of a theorem's being proved is, in effect, not enough to ensure its necessarily convincing the person who grants its presuppositions. For, if it were admitted that the system makes it possible to prove two contradictory theorems, confidence in each one of them would be shaken, and, as a logical reaction, confidence in the system itself would be challenged. Conviction does not solely, as the formalist assumes, follow a line from the axioms and rules of the system to theorems. The conviction that a proved theorem is not valid can convince us of the non-valid character of the system as a whole. The difficulty can be resolved only by accepting an order of importance between rules and, in any case, by subordinating the rules of a logistic system to the principle of noncontradiction. The contradictory system will have to be dropped, and replaced by another framed in such fashion as to avoid contradiction. The new system, albeit constructed by reference to this preoccupation, will be put forward by the theoretician limiting himself to the study of formal systems as being either as arbitrary as the one that preceded it (nominalist point of view) or else as being equally consistent with the eternal verities (realist point of view). In either case human and historic factors are entirely forgotten or regarded as negligible and as without influence on the problems of the logician.

The insufficiency of the strictly formalist attitude in logic will become clear as soon as the question of *interpreting* the logistic system arises. Now it must be emphasised that there can be neither language nor logic until the signs and the expressions have been interpreted and have had attributed to them a meaning thanks to which the axioms of the system become assertions.

If the principle of identity is to be applied in formal systems, every noun and every expression must have one single meaning which is fully defined and which varies neither in accordance with the context nor in pursuance of the usages of the formal language. To abandon this requirement of unambiguity would be to abandon the very reasons that justify the employment of logistic systems.

It is, therefore, necessary to furnish reasons exterior to any formal system, reasons that will render such a system an instrument of communication free of ambiguity.

There are those who find the guarantee they require in taking up a Platonist standpoint. Thus it is that for Frege—as also for Church who draws on him—the name of a thing has a meaning and a designation. Synonyms are nouns having a meaning which is the same, a meaning which, for Church, is a *concept*. Concepts, according to this view, are independent of any particular language: they have no linguistic status and the most that can be said of them is that they constitute the meaning of a noun in some conceivable language.[1] Frege gave the name of *ideas* to these objective entities, independent of all human thought.[2]

[1] Cf. A. CHURCH, *op. cit.*, pp. 4–7.
[2] Cf. G. FREGE, *Logische Untersuchungen*, Beiträge zur Philosophie des Deutschen Idealismus, 1918–1919, I, Der Gedanke, pp. 58–78, II, Die

Analogously, the realm of objective propositions turns up in the writings of logicians who had been thought to be positivists. Starting from sentences of a specified language S, Carnap introduces, by definition, propositions which these sentences designate and whose truth is deemed to be independent of any language.[1] Was Ducasse inspired by this definition when he identified a true proposition with a fact?[2] Russell, with greater prudence, defines the proposition as 'the class of all sentences having the same significance as a given sentence',[3] and endeavours to render the proposition independent of a specified language, conceiving it as a function of all the possible languages in which it could be expressed.

Why is it that all these logicians who identify logic with a formal language arrive at the conception of these extra-linguistic entities? It is because, thanks to those entities, logical relations become independent of any particular language, thus acquiring the desired objectivity and constituting structures such as any thought and any strict language have, on the contrary, a duty to reflect. The ontological status of these entities varies widely for those logicians who go to the trouble of making it explicit. Have we to do with an external world of Platonic ideas? Are all concepts and all possible propositions thought from all eternity by the divine intelligence? Is it a question of objective structure of the universe, pre-existent to the language that reflects it?[4] The Platonist logicians alone do not hesitate to shoulder their philosophic responsibilities. The rest back and fill.[5] They are unwilling to take on the ontological presuppositions of their own methodology.

To illustrate this point, let us take the notion of truth. The formalists have all adopted the semantic conception of truth

[1] R. CARNAP, *Introduction to Semantics*, Harvard University Press, 1942, p. 90.
[2] C. J. DUCASSE, *Propositions, Truth, and the Ultimate Criterion of Truth*, 'Philosophy and Phenomenological Research' (1944), Vol. IV, p. 320.
[3] B. RUSSELL, *op. cit.*, p. 166.
[4] Cf. L. WITTGENSTEIN, Tractatus Logico-Philosophicus, London, 1922.
[5] See in this connection QUINE, *op. cit.*, Chapter VI. Logic and the Reification of Universals, especially pp. 127–129.

Verneinung, pp. 143–157. See in this connection my article 'Metafizyka Fregego', Kwartalnik Filozoficzny, Cracow, 1937, pp. 119–142 (in Polish with French summary).

developed by Tarski.[1] This conception sets out to elaborate the Aristotelean idea of truth-correspondence ('To say that the thing that is is not, or that the thing that is not is, is false: whereas to say that the thing that is is, and that the thing that is not is not, is true'. *Metaphysics*, 1011b)—an idea adumbrated by Plato (Cratylus, 385b). This is expressly connected with saying, that is, with a language. According to Tarski this conception cannot even be strictly formulated except in languages whose structure has been precisely specified.[2] Yet we observe that some logicians who call themselves positivists or near-positivists, such as Carnap, Ducasse or Russell,[3] speak of truths independent of all language. How are we to explain this odd phenomenon?

The answer is that the idea of truth, when it is conceived as correspondence between what one says and what is, leads inevitably to a rationalist view of the world in which experience builds itself up—spontaneously, so to speak—into clear and distinct ideas. Whether a man is a Platonist, like Frege, or has empirical tendencies, like Russell, he will assume that intuitions, rational or sensible, furnish a knowledge which will spontaneously build itself up into statements (clear and distinct ideas, basic propositions) which are completely devoid of error.[4] The problem of the passage from truth to belief or from belief to truth is solved by its being immediately obvious. The language that the logician ought to preoccupy himself with is the one that serves his needs perfectly because it is sufficiently transparent not to hamper the establishment of unshakeable and perfectly communicable convictions. The problems arising from natural languages as vehicles of social communication are only of secondary interest in this context, since they do not prevent the working out of a logic conceived as formalised language without ambiguity.

But is it possible for this ideal of non-ambiguity, essential in formal logic, to be entirely satisfied within the limits of formal logic? To answer this question, let us take our stand on the most elementary part of modern logic, propositional calculus which contains propositional variables having classically two values,

---

[1] Cf. TARSKI, *op. cit.* and Der Wahrheitsbegriff in den formalisierten Sprachen, 'Studia Philosophica', I (1935), pp. 261–405.

[2] TARSKI, *op. cit.*, p. 347.

[3] B. RUSSELL, *Human Knowledge*, London, 1948, p. 129.

[4] Cf. B. RUSSELL, *Inquiry*, pp. 81, 137 *et seq.*

true and false. Frege is one of the rare logicians for whom true and false are thoroughly individualised objects, for which true or false propositions are the names.[1] According to him propositional variables can have only these two objects as values. But for the great majority of logicians, the values of propositional variables are held to be declarative sentences, true or false, which express assertions.[2] Now formal logic is incapable of saying when one finds oneself faced with an assertion. Propositional variables cease, for this reason, to be unambiguous notions, for how are we to affirm the unambiguity of a formal system whose variables can range over an imperfectly determined field of variation?

To illustrate the difficulty logicians are thus faced with, let us take the Fifth Commandment, 'Thou shalt not kill'. Is this a case of a declarative sentence? The form alone does not permit of an answer: it is in the light of the context that we recognise that we are dealing not with a future indicative but with an imperative. Let us try to cast this commandment into the form of a declarative sentence, true or false. Here are a few formulae that might, at first sight, comply with this condition: 'Yahwe has given instructions not to kill', 'Killing is a sin', 'It is immoral to kill', 'In killing, one breaks the Fifth Commandment'. Which of these four formulae constitute true or false sentences, possible values of the propositional variables? There is no way of answering without elaborating a theory of knowledge greatly exceeding the scope of formal logic.

We can understand why, in order to preserve the independence of formal logic, Quine would rather not speak at all of propositional variables. But in the event of their being granted, he prefers Frege's solution, treating it not as consistent with objective entities—the true and the false—but by application of his maxim of the identity of indiscernibles.[3] Within the frame of the propositional calculus, there is no need to distinguish between propositional concepts of the same truth-value.[4] But this solution is not good enough when we try to *apply* the propositional calculus. In effect, to determine the truth-value of a sentence, its meaning should not give rise to argument. But this simply cannot be

[1] Cf. G. FREGE, *Ueber Sinn und Bedeutung*, 'Zeitschrift für Phil. und phil. Kritik' (1892), Vol. 100, pp. 34–35.

[2] Cf. A. CHURCH, *op. cit.*, p. 23.

[3] Cf. QUINE, *op. cit.*, pp. 108–113.   [4] *Ibid.*, p. 71.

guaranteed if that meaning is set out in a natural language. When Yahwe orders men not to kill, what meaning must be given to that order? Its interpretation is not automatic because the same book of Deuteronomy orders the putting to death of those who transgress certain commandments of Yahwe and gives directions for ritual sacrifices. It must be, then, that putting to death and sacrificing are activities different from that of killing, assuming that Yahwe's intentions are not contradictory. To render a system coherent, it is often necessary to interpret its terms, without strictly observing the rule of the non-ambiguity of expressions of the same form. The several meanings of one and the same expression will be distinguished: corresponding to the maxim of formal logic concerning the identity of indiscernibles is that of the differentiation of formally similar expressions when treating them as identical leads to incoherence. In that case we are, of course, quitting the realm of formal logic, but can it be said that the activity of one who interprets a system is foreign to logic? When it is a case of proving that a law has not been violated, the execution of the proof will very often depend on determining the precise meaning of the law. Juridical logic, which studies reasonings that are conclusive in law, ranges outside formal problems when its object is to study the validity of an interpretation of the law. In such cases it does not, as might be thought, reduce itself to a kind of applied formal logic, for in law recourse is often had to methods of proof that are not *demonstrative*, but *argumentative*. It is often forgotten nowadays that argumentation is equally inspired by logic: and Aristotle, the father of formal logic, made a study, alongside *analytic* proofs, of the proofs which he termed *dialectic*, and which he examines in the Topics, the Rhetoric and the Refutations.

The considerations here summarily submitted for discussion induce us to believe that the problems of logic, language and communication cannot be treated from a viewpoint limited to the lessons—valuable indeed, but only partial—that can be drawn from the exclusive study of formal logic. Reasoning and proof do not consist solely in calculating, and logic cannot rest content with the study of formal proof, which itself assumes its true significance only in the more general context of a theory of argumentation.

An attempt to construct an ontology and a theory of knowledge having regard only to the requirements of formal logic results in a form of realism or in a form of nominalism, both of which are foreign to the way in which in fact our language develops and the problems of social communication present themselves. The logic that provides the norms of our intellectual attempts at proof constitutes neither a divine language nor an arbitrary one. It has, like all the other human disciplines, been introduced into the general process of knowledge, integrated with our philosophic and scientific traditions, and evolved by reference to the problems presented to it. Formal logic may have developed and progressed in virtue of the meticulous analysis of the methods of proof employed in mathematics: yet mathematics do not constitute the only discipline in which the question of establishing proof arises. There is legitimate scope for undertaking in the non-formal disciplines the same work of analysis that has made possible the extraordinary progress of formal logic since the middle of the last century. It is permissible to hope that this effort, by widening the viewpoint of the logician, will enable him the better to understand the techniques of proof employed in the natural and social sciences, in law and in philosophy.[1]

[1] Cf. C. PERELMAN and L. OLBRECHTS-TYTECA, *Traité de l'Argumentation*, Paris, Presses Universitaires de France, 1958.

X

THE SOCIAL CONTEXTS OF ARGUMENTATION[1]

ANY sociology of knowledge, inasmuch as its object is to study the conditioning of knowledge by elements of social reality, is led, by reason of the very nature of things, to distinguish, among kinds of knowledge, some which escape this conditioning or feel its effects in a reduced degree. In contrasting the natural and the human sciences, or quantitative with qualitative knowledge, we construct a classification of kinds of knowledge based essentially on the idea we form of their greater or smaller independence by reference to the social conditions in which they have developed.

I would like to suggest another way of proceeding, which seems to me both more satisfying from the theoretical point of view and more fertile in its sociological applications. It consists in taking as starting-point a technical distinction between *demonstration* and *argumentation* and in deriving consequences of a sociological order from the very conditions in which all argumentation, or any particular argumentation subjected to examination, is put forward.

Modern logic, especially formal logic, is devoted to the study of demonstration, which, basing itself on true premises—or premises assumed to be true—must eventuate as of necessity in conclusions that are either true or calculably probable. Demonstrative proof, consisting as it does solely in this transition from premises to conclusion, seems to evade social conditioning.

Contrariwise, argumentation, the theoretical study of which has been dropped by logicians for more than three hundred years,

[1] From *Cahiers Internationaux de Sociologie*, Nouvelle Serie, No. XXVI, 1959.

offers a vast field of investigation to the sociologist of knowledge. The theory of argumentation studies *the discursive techniques which make it possible to evoke or further people's assent to the theses presented for their acceptance.*[1] The result—an essential fact for the sociologist —is that the development of all argumentation is a function of the audience to which it is addressed and to which the speaker is obliged to adapt himself. By speaker I mean the person putting forward the argumentation, whether orally or in writing. By audience I mean all those whom the argumentation is aimed at, whether hearers or readers.

The diversity of audiences is extreme. They can vary quantitatively from the speaker himself (who in interior deliberation divides himself into two) by way of the single auditor of dialogue and all particular audiences, right up to the totality of beings capable of reason—that universal audience which is then not a concrete social reality but a construction of the speaker based on elements in his experience. They can vary in countless other ways —according to age, sex, temperament, competence and every sort of social or political criterion. They can vary, above all, in accordance with the functions they exercise, and more particularly according as the role of the auditors is to reach a conclusion of whatever kind, or simply to form an opinion or acquire a disposition towards some action as yet contingent and undetermined.

Every argumentation in fact aims at a change in the mind of the auditors, whether it be to modify the theses themselves to which the auditors adhere or simply the intensity of that adherence as measured by the eventual consequences it tends to produce in action. The outlook of argumentation, unlike that of demonstration, does not make it possible entirely to separate thought from action,[2] and it is easy to understand that argumentation should sometimes be favoured, sometimes banned and often regulated by those who hold power or authority in society.

Every society possesses institutions and provides for ceremonies promoting common social feeling—the cult of the heroes

---

[1] Cf. C. PERELMAN and L. OLBRECHTS-TYTECA, *Traité de l'Argumentation,* Paris, Presses Universitaires de France, 1958, p. 5.

[2] Cf. C. PERELMAN, *Les Rapports Théoriques de la Pensée et de l'Action,* in *Entretiens Philosophiques de Varsovie,* International Institute of Philosophy, Warsaw, Ossolineum, 1958, pp. 23–28.

and sages who constitute the acknowledged models, or the transmission of approved values by means of the education of children and adults.

In certain societies the practice of argumentation is in various sectors the monopoly of persons or bodies especially authorised for that purpose. Sometimes it is subject to prior authorisation or censorship. Almost always there are fields in which argumentation is in danger of being illegal, of violating some legislation protecting public or private interests. In order to speak it is necessary in a great many cases to have some qualification, to be a member or representative of some group. Sometimes argumentation is under restrictions as to its duration, its subject or the time at which it may be presented. In this matter there are customs and regulations, and the codes of civil and criminal procedure can profitably be examined from this point of view.

The effective exercise of argumentation assumes a means of communication, a common language, without which there can be no contact of minds. This language is the product of a social tradition which will have different rhythms in the case of a natural language and in that of a technical language common to the members of a discipline or profession, different in the case of a people's language and in that of a language kept as the private preserve of the initiate.

Given a language understood by his audience, the speaker can develop his argumentation only by linking it to theses granted by his auditors, failing which he is likely to be guilty of begging the question. It follows that all argumentation depends for its premises—as indeed for its entire development—on that which is accepted, that which is acknowledged as true, as normal and probable, as valid. Thereby it anchors itself in the social, the characterisation of which will depend on the nature of the audience. The theses granted will sometimes be those of common sense, as that is conceived by the audience, sometimes those of a particular discipline, scientific, juridical, philosophical or theological. It is an indispensable condition for the efficacy of argumentation that the theses that must serve as its basis should be known and understood.

The epistemological status of these theses may vary. Sometimes affirmations developed within a scientific discipline will be involved, sometimes dogmas, sometimes common-sense beliefs, sometimes approved rules or precepts of conduct, sometimes quite simply propositions that have been granted at an earlier stage in the discussion by those taking part in it. All these theses, whatever their status, have this much in common that one cannot, without risk of appearing ridiculous, set them aside unless reasons are furnished to justify such behaviour. Laughter is the sanction against unjustified departure from the norm in argumentation, and on account of this reaction the normal becomes socially normative. It follows that in argumentation, contrary to what happens in de-monstration, we do not justify anything whatever, for producing arguments in support of a thesis amounts to an implicit admission that it is not above discussion. It would be most instructive to follow, through the history of a society or of a particular disci-pline, the evolution of what, in that society or discipline, is con-sidered to be a matter of course, to be normal and reasonable; and to bring out the origins of and reasons for this evolution. The historicity of reason is always closely connected with its becoming part of a tradition, in which innovation must always produce its letters of credence. That is why so often the best justification of a course of conduct—the one that dispenses with the need for any other reason—consists in showing that that course is in con-formity with the recognised order, that it can avail itself of un-questioned precedents. Precedent plays a quite primary role in argumentation, the rationality of which is linked with the ob-servance of the *rule of justice*, which demands equal treatment for similar situations.[1] Now, the application of the rule of justice assumes the existence of precedents to teach us how situations similar to the one confronting us now have been dealt with in the past. These precedents, just like the models by which a society is inspired, make part of its cultural tradition, which can be recon-structed on the basis of the argumentations in which they have been employed.

When we invoke a precedent we are assimilating the new case to an old one, we are stressing the similarities and ignoring the differences. If the assimilation is not accepted at once, an argu-mentation may be admitted to be indispensable. Now, in order to determine which arguments are relevant in the particular case, to determine when an argument is to be regarded as strong or weak,

[1] Cf. C. PERELMAN and L. OLBRECHTS-TYTECA, *Traité de l'Argumentation*, § 52: 'La règle de justice'.

the rule of justice comes in afresh. It is because of its introduction that the value of arguments—and these, unlike demonstrative proofs, are never conclusive—is itself a function of the ways in which they have previously been employed, of the admissibility and effectiveness which were allowed to them in similar contexts of the past. The rule of justice thus appears as the constituent principle of historic reason,[1] whereas the principles of identity and non-contradiction, by virtue of their more formal character, furnish the key-pieces of an invariable and eternal reason.

I would like to conclude this brief communication with a few reflections coming more directly within the context of this discussion inasmuch as they leave the plane of the social conditions of argumentation for that of our way of looking at it. What I have in mind is the variations undergone by the theory of argumentation, by rhetoric and topics, in the course of the history of western thought, and the hypotheses tending to explain these variations as a function of social conditioning.

As we know, apart from an odd eighteenth-century work or so devoted to juridical topics, the theory of argumentation was almost entirely neglected by post-Cartesian logic and philosophy. The problems dealt with by this theory were studied in Graeco-Roman antiquity, in the Middle Ages, and above all during the Renaissance, by authors concerning themselves with rhetoric and the Topics, examining the proofs characterised by Aristotle as dialectical in contrast to the analytic proofs of formal logic which aim not at argumentation but at demonstration.

The evolution of rhetoric and of the theory of argumentation follows the fate of the epistemological status of *opinion* as opposed to *truth*. According as it is claimed that all truth presents itself as the most defensible opinion or that opinion is nothing but mock truth, the position allotted to rhetoric and argumentation will be more or less important. The controversies which opposed the sophists to the Eleatics, the Pythagoreans and the followers of Plato, provide us with the earliest writings on this subject. The question is whether truth is the outcome of dialogue, discussion and the confrontation of opinions, or whether there exist direct

[1] Cf. C. PERELMAN and L. OBRECHTS-TYTECA, *De la Temporalité comme Caractère de l' Argumentation*, in *Il Tempo, Archivio di Filosofia*, Padova, Cedam, 1958, p. 125.

and immediate means of attaining truth, the employment of which would be preliminary to any rhetoric, this latter being transformed from a technique of discussion and discovery into a technique of presentation and persuasion concerned far more with the form than with the basic ground of discourse. Whereas Aristotle and his successors, as also the philosophers of the Middle and New Academies, adopted a position more favourable to rhetoric, the Stoics, soon to be followed by the Neo-Platonists and the Christian thinkers, saw in rhetoric no more than a process of exposition. More and more, discourse, instead of convincing, was required primarily to please, and rhetoric ceased to be a philosophical technique and became a literary method, a role it was to play throughout the Middle Ages. The centuries of the Renaissance saw the highest flight of rhetoric, which had become the centre of humanist thought. For the most varied thinkers, it was at that epoch the humane technique *par excellence*, the technique uniting thought and action. But the resort to self-evidence characteristic of the sixteenth and seventeenth centuries—first to religious evidence as felt by the conscience of the good Christian, then to the rational evidence of Cartesianism and finally to the sense-evidence of empiricism—removed all philosophical importance from rhetoric as a technique of argumentation. Rhetoric became the study of stylistic methods and such it was to remain until the Romantic movement which subordinated the techniques themselves to the poet's inspiration. Positivism, as it developed during the second half of the nineteenth century, marked the lowest point of rhetoric, which was removed from the syllabus of the French state schools in 1885. In compensation, under the influence of pragmatism and in consequence of the increasing part played by the philosophy of language in contemporary thought, studies in rhetoric—as a technique at once of argumentation, persuasion and presentation—have multiplied, more particularly during the last twenty years.

Is there a correlation between this development and the accompanying social and historical conditions? Hypotheses have been propounded on this question by several authors concerned with different epochs. The dawn of a régime of liberty and democracy, it is suggested, promotes the rise of rhetoric and its philosophical importance, whereas the setting-up of an authoritarian state entails its decline. It is from this point of view that we now judge the controversy between the sophists and Plato;[1] that Gwynn[2] explains the decline of rhetoric following the establishment of the Roman empire; that the role of mediaeval rhetoric[3] is presented; and that the rise and decline of Renaissance rhetoric[4] are explained. Is it not in the same way that the contemporary renewal of the theory of argumentation should be explained?

I hope that these few hints will serve as a starting point for deeper studies by sociologists and historians interested in the problems of the sociology of knowledge.

[1] E. Dupréel, *Les Sophistes*, Editions du Griffon, Neuchâtel, 1948, p. 28.

[2] Aubrey Gwynn, *Roman Education from Cicero to Quintilian*, Oxford, Clarendon Press, 1926.

[3] R. McKeon, Rhetoric in the Middle Ages, *Speculum, A Journal of Mediaeval Studies*, Vol. XVII, January 1942, pp. 1–32.

[4] E. Garin, *L'Umanesimo Italiano*, Filosofia e vita civile nel rinascimento, Bari, Laterza, 1952, particularly pp. 103 *et seq.*

XI

THE DIALECTICAL METHOD
AND THE PART PLAYED
BY THE INTERLOCUTOR
IN DIALOGUE[1]

IN his *Gorgias*, Plato mentions the reason for which he considers dialogue to be best suited for the presentation of philosophical theses.[2] The long and continuous discourse conforming to the precepts of rhetoric aims essentially at convincing its listeners through a multiplicity of procedures of the widest possible variety, each supporting the others and impressing through their effect as a whole, rather than through the soundness of any one of the arguments put forward in particular. This is not the case with dialogue conceived in accordance with the method of Platonic dialectic. The reasoning here advances step by step; each step has to be tested and must be confirmed by the approval of the interlocutor. One does not proceed from one thesis to the next, before having obtained the consent of the listener, guaranteeing the truth of each link in the argumentation. Such, at least, is Plato's ambition, as displayed in the introduction to the discussion between Socrates and Callicles:

'. . . if you agree with me in an argument about any point, that point will have been sufficiently tested by us, and will not require

---

[1] Communication presented during the Athens Meeting (April 1955) of the International Institute of Philosophy, devoted to 'Dialogue and Dialectics'. It appeared in this translation in the *Proceedings of the Thirtieth Indian Philosophical Congress*, Nagpur, 1955.

[2] PLATO—*Gorgias*, 471 d.

to be submitted to any further test. For you could not have agreed with me, either from lack of knowledge or from superfluity of modesty, nor yet from a desire to deceive me, for you are my friend as you tell me yourself. And therefore when you and I are agreed the result will be the attainment of perfect truth.'[1]
Pareto, whose interpretation of Plato is unsympathetic, makes fun of this way of arguing:

'The good Plato,' writes Pareto, 'has a simple, easy and effective way of obtaining universal consent or, if you prefer it, the consent of the wise. He has it granted to him in his dialogues by an interlocutor whom he makes say anything he himself desires. Thus, this consent is in reality nobody else's but Plato's and it is accepted without difficulty by those whose imagination he flatters.'[2]

Is this interlocutor then nothing but a mere puppet whose strings are pulled by the author in whatever way seems to him the most appropriate? In that case, what would be the value of the dialectical method, not only for the readers but for Plato himself as well? Goblot provides an answer to this question that makes it possible for him to specify the scope of this method:

'Dialectic proceeds by way of questions and answers so that one never passes from one assertion to the next without first having gained the approval of the interlocutor. The dialectical art consists in never failing to secure this approval. This method of dialogue is essentially oral and requires the participation of at least two persons. Why does Plato think nevertheless that it could be applied to a written work, where the same person, the author, presents the questions as well as the answers? Does his own approval entitle him to proceed any further? Plato takes it for granted that no interlocutor could answer differently from the one whom he lets speak. That is the art of dialectic in a nutshell.'[3]

Should Goblot's interpretation prove correct, and were the development of the dialogue influenced in no way by the personality

[1] PLATO—*Gorgias*, 487—trans. by B. JOWETT, Oxford University Press, 3rd ed., 1931.
[2] Cf., PARETO—*The Mind and Society*, Ed. by ARTHUR LIVINGSTON, Trans. by ANDREW BONGIORNO and ARTHUR LIVINGSTON, 4 vols. New York, Harcourt, Brace 1935, § 612.
[3] GOBLOT—*La logique des jugements de valeur*, Paris, Colin, 1927, pp. 16–17.

of the one who is giving the answers—the latter representing nothing else but the reaction of a normal mind confronted with self-evident truth—the dialogue form is nothing but a snare, exposing us, as is shown by Pareto's argument, to the danger of being misled, since it is possible to ascribe to the interlocutor a part which he does not play. In this perspective, Plato's dialectic constitutes an outline of a deductive system in which the theses would follow from each other, thanks to an inner mechanism which, in its modern form, might lead to construction of dialectical machines on the pattern of computing machines. The dialectical *method*, correlative, in our mind, with thinking in dialogue form, would metamorphose into a monolithic dialectical *system* in which, the consequences would follow automatically from the initial premises, leaving no room not only for the personality of the respondent but even for the personality of the dialectician himself. Dialectic and analytical logic would coincide. The dialectical procedure would become as compelling as formal demonstration. In order to achieve this, it would have to enjoy the same univocity of the terms to which it is applied, and the same indisputable character of its operative rules. Turning into logic, dialectic becomes a system of necessary sequences, but this is achieved at the cost of abandoning any conformity to an actual dialogue, whose development is conditioned by the personality of the interlocutors as well as by their intentions.

For Aristotle, it is analytical reasoning that possesses those qualities of univocity and of necessity that today we consider as belonging to formal demonstrations. When an agreement exists with respect to the theses from which the dialogue departs and upon the rules of inference, the teacher will have every reason to use the schemes of analytical reasoning in stating the system and presenting its consequences. The pupil plays but a passive part; he has only to follow and understand each step of the discourse. According to Aristotle, it is in the absence of agreement on the elements of such a deductive system—agreement resulting from a convention, intuition or any form of self-evidence—that recourse to dialectical proofs may become inevitable.

These latter alone make reasoning about the primary principles of each science possible:

'For it is impossible to discuss them at all from the principles

THE DIALECTICAL METHOD AND THE PART PLAYED BY

proper to the particular science in hand, seeing that the principles are the *prius* of everything else: it is through the opinions generally held on the particular points that these have to be discussed, and this task belongs properly, or most appropriately, to dialectic: for dialectic is a process of criticism wherein lies the path to the principles of all inquiries.'[1]

The deductive method may be the best when setting forth the results of a science whose outlines are already settled, but in order to discover, as well as to test, the outlines of a developing science, the method of dialectical proofs should be used. Since it is a question of considering various possible formulations of principles and of weighing carefully their advantages and inconveniences, this investigation must perforce adopt the form of a dialogue containing questions and replies, objections and rejoinders, whether this be undertaken by several persons or be confined within the limits of a private deliberation. The dialectic method, inasmuch as it is heuristic and critical, thus stands quite naturally connected with thought in the form of a dialogue.

The confrontation of opposing theses in a dialogue may be carried out in several manners, differing essentially according to the intentions of the participants.

When the interlocutors are moved by the sole desire to win the argument, to perplex the adversary, and to make their own point of view prevail, we are confronted with the kind of dialogue farthest removed from philosophical preoccupations. This has received the name of *eristic* dialogue. The sole purpose of the eristic dispute is to get the better of the adversary, which implies complete indifference to the truth. Thus, in his *Euthydemus*, which is the very archetype of eristic dialogue, Plato makes Socrates describe such a scene:

'Whichever he answers, said Dionysodorus (the eldest of the sophists), leaning forward as to catch my ear, his face beaming with laughter, I prophesy that he will be refuted, Socrates.'[2]

In a *critical* dialogue the thesis is put to test by the effort to prove its incompatibility with other theses granted by the person who is putting it forward. It is inner coherency which provides

[1] ARISTOTLE—*Topics*, 101a–101b, trans. Ross, Oxford University Press, 1937.
[2] PLATO—*Euthydemus*, 275a, transl. B. JOWETT.

the criterion for critical investigation; this does not necessarily presuppose the existence of several interlocutors, for any one may examine for himself the theses to which he is inclined to adhere by confronting them with the rest of his beliefs in order to see whether they are incompatible or not.

Dialogue ceases to be critical and becomes *dialectical*, acquiring thus a constructive philosophical interest, from the moment when, over and above the inner coherency of what they have to say, the interlocutors endeavour to agree on what they consider to be true or, at least, on the opinions they acknowledge as the most secure.[1] The search for truth, as it is seen by Plato, becomes with Aristotle an argument setting out from propositions that are not necessarily admitted, though in general they are, and whose conclusions are not merely no longer obvious but those ones most consistent with prevalent opinion.

Notice that the Aristotelian distinction between eristic, critical and dialectical argumentation, dealt with in the passage cited above constitutes but an ideal formulation of aims inextricably interwoven, with varying intensity, in actual debates, where the interlocutors endeavour, to be sure, to make their thesis prevail but, as often as not, also believe that thesis to be free from contradiction and the one most consistent with truth. A minute study of interlocutors' attitudes and intentions would alone enable us in particular cases to sort out the different varieties of motivation involved; and even this could be done only with a likelihood which seldom approaches certainty. The distinction nevertheless draws our attention to three kinds of criteria which could be valuable in appraising debates and the value of conclusions deriving from them.

It would seem at first sight that critical dialogue could be judged by purely formal criteria; this would certainly be the case if its aim were to establish a formal contradiction between the theses granted by one of the interlocutors: it would suffice to be able to specify such of these theses as contained operational rules, and to endeavour by means of a calculus, to establish the contradiction. But things are far from being so simple. For critical discourse aims less at establishing formal contradictions than at indicating the existence of incompatibilities which occur only in respect to

---

[1] ARISTOTLE—*De Sophisticis Elenchis*, 165b, 1–5.

certain situations. Thus the rule prescribing obedience to one's parents becomes incompatible with the rule forbidding one to kill only if one of the parents orders his child to commit murder. Hence, in order to establish incompatibility it is not sufficient to possess knowledge of the rules admitted and of the sense attributed to them by the interlocutor. One must know the situations which he is inclined to take into account.

Were there any need for a clear sign enabling one to contrast the criterion of eristic dialogue with that of the other kinds, it would be found in the existence of a judge or arbiter charged with giving the casting vote between the antagonists, rather than in the intentions and procedures of the adversaries themselves.[1] Because the purpose of the debate is to convince not the adversary but the judge; because the adversary does not need to be won over in order to be beaten; for this very reason the eristic dispute is of no great interest to the philosopher. The judge's decision may well depend on certain conventionally accepted criteria whose social import may be indeniable. That is not how philosophical opinions are formed.

Philosophic dialogue is, *par excellence*, dialectical; indeed it determines the very characteristics of a dialectical method. Agreement between the interlocutors may serve as a point of departure for argument, not because there might be any question of the concurrence of two divergent opinions but simply because this agreement would be the expression of a generalised adherence to the opinions under discussion. The agreement between the interlocutors rests upon what in their milieu is considered as well-grounded, and as requiring to be accepted until there is proof to the contrary. The point of departure for a dialectical argumentation does not consist in necessary propositions, valid everywhere and for all time, but in propositions effectively admitted in a given milieu; in a different setting, in a different historical and social context, these propositions may no longer meet with general approval. The dialogue might have come to an end as soon as these basic propositions were established, provided formal reasoning had enabled us to infer all the consequences that are of importance. However, these basic propositions will serve, most of the time, not as axioms of a deductive system but as arguments

---

[1] For the purposes of his study, Aristotle identifies eristical and sophistical argumentation, but we cannot admit this simplification.

supporting other theses that one endeavours to put forward. Neither their value as arguments, nor their use as examples or as elements of analogy, gives rise to a compelling conclusion, since the explicit adherence of the interlocutors is indispensable at every step, in order to allow the reasoning to proceed. New theses, connected with the preceeding ones, will follow, blending themselves into the totality of generally accepted opinions—such, at least, is the ambition of the authors of philosophical dialogues.

The peculiarity of the dialectical method, as it appears in dialogue, consists in the fact that the theses tested and the conclusions adopted are neither obvious nor fanciful, but represent opinions considered, in a given milieu, as the soundest. It is precisely this aspect of dialectical argumentation which enables one to regard the interlocutors in this kind of dialogue as not merely expounding their own point of view, but as expressing the 'reasonable' opinion of their society.

Controversy concerning these opinions bring about an extension or modification of the field of the reasonable. What is reasonable, in fact, is not limited to what is expressed by means of carefully worked out deductive systems; it extends to every thesis a thinker claims to display for the community of man, starting from those generally accepted in the surroundings he knows and in which he was brought up. In this case, there is no criterion for judging this form of dialogue and the conclusions which follow from it, save the philosophical vision of the interlocutors. In dialectical argumentation, it is conceptions considered as generally accepted that are confronted and contrasted with each other. Because of that, the dialectical method is the method *par excellence* of any philosophy which realises the social, imperfect and incomplete aspect of philosophical knowledge, instead of relying upon intuitions and self-evident truths considered as irrefragable.[1]

---

[1] Cf., De la preuve en philosophie, in C. PERELMAN and L. OLBRECHTS-TYTECA, *Rhetorique et Philosophie*, Paris, Presses Universitaires de France, 1952.

XII

ACT AND PERSON
IN ARGUMENT[1]

IN order to specify the import of the following observations, it will be well to indicate briefly the framework in which they are located. Man living in society has discussions with his fellows and tries to bring them to share some of his views and to perform certain actions. Relatively rarely does he have recourse solely to coercion in order to do this. In general, he seeks to persuade or to convince; and to this end he reasons, in the broadest sense of the term, and presents proofs. In those cases in which the means of proof consist in rigorous demonstration, they are studied by a well-defined science: logic. But to the extent that it has developed into a purely formal science which determines the conditions of correct deduction, it appears that a great many of the proofs utilised in law, ethics, philosophy, political debate, and daily life cannot be considered relevant to logic in the strict sense.

All these arguments evidently might be relegated to the sphere of mental suggestion and denied any kind of rationality. This has been, more or less explicitly and to a greater or less extent, the viewpoint of a great many logicians and philosophers. But the consequences of this point of view can be quite serious, for it tends to put all kinds of informal procedures of argument on the same footing, whether those of the confidence man or the philosopher; and, on the other hand, this point of view places the system of logic, as well as of science, beyond all the rest of mental life and almost without contact with it. It seems to us, on the contrary,

[1] Written in collaboration with Mme. OLBRECHTS-TYTECA. Appeared in this translation in *Ethics*, Vol. LXI, No. 4, 1951.

that it is worth while to study more closely those argumentative procedures which are of such social and philosophic importance. We have given the name 'rhetoric' to the discipline which we thus propose to revive, in recognition of the fact that, at least in Greek antiquity and particularly for Aristotle, the object of rhetoric was precisely the study of these techniques of nondemonstrative argument, its end being to support judgments and thereby win or reinforce the assent of other minds.[1]

It soon appeared to us that all argument presupposes that those to whom it is addressed agree on a certain number of data. This agreement may serve as a point of departure for further agreements, but it may also be questioned, in which case the discussion turns on the justification of this agreement, on the basis of other elements presumed to be accepted.

This viewpoint involves another: we will constantly need a notion correlative to agreement, that of the audience. For what is accepted by certain persons is not necessarily accepted by others; and so the audience may extend from the individual himself—in the case of deliberation with one's self, which in several respects can be considered as a special case of discussion with others—through the whole series of particular audiences to the universal audience. Of course, the universal audience never actually exists; it is an ideal audience, a mental construction of him who refers to it. We could easily show that this so-called 'universal audience' varies with the epoch and with the person: each creates its own idea of the universal audience. This fact explains the interest of the sociology of knowledge.[2]

Any audience accepts a certain number of data which it will call 'facts', 'truths', 'presumptions', or 'values'. A fact is important in argument because it is considered as forming the object of universal agreement: it *must* be accepted by everyone. If someone says, 'I opened this book', we would doubtless see in this the statement of a fact. But at any time this status may be taken away from it by objections such as 'No, the book was opened by someone else', 'The book opened itself', or even 'There is no book there at all, but only loose pages', etc. What is understood by

[1] Cf. C. PERELMAN and L. OLBRECHTS-TYTECA, 'Logique et rhétorique', *Revue philosophique*, Nos. 1–3 (Paris, 1950).
[2] Cf. C. PERELMAN, 'Sociologie de la connaissance et philosophie de la connaissance', *Revue internationale de philosophie*, No. 13 (Brussels, 1950).

'fact' thus furnishes us the first example of an agreement always subject to revision. It likewise shows us that as long as this agreement is not questioned, it does not occur to anyone to demand a justification of it; as long as the agreement lasts, the fact can serve as a point of departure for further argument, such as 'I opened the book; therefore I intend to read it'. It can be seen at once how this conception of fact differs from that of the scientist or philosopher who would seek to extricate the facts which underly a theory and the immediate premises, logically or genetically prior, which serve as foundation for his conceptual system. It is true that rhetoric, as a discipline, likewise presupposes the existence of facts appropriate to it. These are audiences, arguments and adherences. The conception of these may, moreover, always be modified. That on which we ask agreement is that there exists argument which, starting from certain given opinions, seeks to win new opinions or to reinforce other opinions already obtained.

All audiences accept values as well, whether abstract values, such as justice, or concrete values, such as one's country. These values are generally accepted only by a particular audience. Some of them are considered universal values, but it could doubtless be shown that they are so regarded only on condition that their content is not specified. Besides, it is not so much the values to which they adhere as the manner in which they arrange the values in a hierarchy, which makes it possible to describe a particular audience. Indeed, audiences accept not only facts and values but also hierarchies, constructs of reality, and connections between facts and values—in short, a totality of common beliefs, which we shall call 'places', in recognition of the ancient usage of the term 'commonplaces'. These make it possible to argue with more or less effectiveness. An argument always introduces elements of this sort. For example, to support the fact, challenged by an interlocutor, that I opened this book, others might suggest presumptions (e.g., that an open book has been opened by someone) or values (e.g., truth, to which it is claimed I pay respect and conform my conduct). In the end, the matter might be resolved by admitting that it is indeed a fact; but it is so regarded only on condition that it is again separated from the arguments by which the agreement was obtained.

We have said that among the elements of agreement are found certain structures of reality which are considered as accepted. We may divide them into two broad categories: connections of succession, such as the relation of cause to effect, and connections of co-existence, such as the structural properties of a single body. Philosophical argument may seek to reduce some of these connections to others, which are considered more fundamental. But, from our viewpoint, any effort at systematisation being at least premature, it is proper to recognise the broad types of connection which are explicitly used in discussion and are implicit at other times.

One of the connections of coexistence which may be considered as very generally accepted by all sorts of audiences and which seems to us to have a great importance is that of the relation of the person to the act which is attributed to him, a relation which is the prototype of a large number of connections of coexistence.

The makeup of the human person and its separation from his acts is tied to a distinction between what is considered important, natural and characteristic of the being under discussion and what is regarded as a transitory and external manifestation thereof. The makeup of the person always gives us a rule, in virtue of which the essence may be distinguished from its manifestations.

Since this connection between the person and his acts does not constitute a necessary link or possess the same sort of stability as the relation between an object and its qualities, a simple repetition of an act may involve either a reconstruction of the person or a reinforced adherence to the previous makeup. The precariousness of the relation determines a constant interaction between the act and the person.

Of course, the conception of what constitutes the person may vary considerably according to the epoch and according to the metaphysics to which one connects the construction. It is very likely that the argument of primitive peoples made use of a much broader conception of the person than ours has become. They doubtless would include therein all the incidentals, such as the shadow, the totem, and detached fragments of the body. Whereas we must make use of special connections in order to join these elements to the person, primitive man would have to use disassociation in order to isolate the personality in the limited sense from this more extended personality.

The person, as we will consider it, will be that which occurs in different epochs and according to different authors, so that we will not have to ask ourselves, in this more general investigation, how the person is defined or what are the elements which, for practical purposes, enter into its makeup or which, according to the psychologists, should theoretically enter into it.

It may be useful to show by an example that phenomena of this sort may or may not be regarded as a part of the person rather than merely as a purely external manifestation, i.e., an act. A woman's beauty can be considered as a quality constitutive of the person rather than as a transitory and contingent manifestation of it. In this regard it should be noticed that the fact that such a phenomenon is attached to the makeup of the person rather than treated as an accidental manifestation, i.e., as an act, may be considered one way of placing this phenomenon in a hierarchy in relation to others. As a general rule, the more important traits are integrated into the makeup of the person. That is to say, the manner of formation of the person may be the object of the uncertain and limited agreement of a given group, although this will always be susceptible of revision.

We must emphasise a primary characteristic of the person, namely, that the person introduces an element of stability. An argument concerning the person takes advantage of this stability, since we presume it in interpreting the act as dependent upon the person, or we deplore the fact that this stability has not been respected, when someone is reproached for inconstancy or an unjustified change. A large number of arguments attempt to prove that the person has not changed, that the change is merely apparent, or that it is the circumstances which have changed, etc.[1]

But the stability of the person is never completely assured, though certain linguistic techniques help to emphasise the impression of stability. The use of proper names allows the continuity of the person to be presumed; other ways of speaking manifest a permanent trait of the person. Thus the insertion of a typical category ('your stingy father'), the use of an epithet ('Charlemagne of the flowery beard') or the hypostasis ('his generosity has contributed . . .')—each of these reinforces the impression of the stability of the whole person by emphasising a

[1] Cf. the study by N. LEITES, 'The Third International on Its Changes of Policy', in the collective work edited by H. LASSWELL, *Language of Politics: Studies in Quantitative Semantics* (New York: George N. Stewart, 1949).

characteristic of the person which is regarded as permanent. In this regard we may note the role in argument of what are called 'figures of speech'—a role which confers on them an important place in all rhetoric aimed at achieving the adherence of minds.

The person, considered as the support underlying a series of qualities, as the author of series of acts and judgments, and as the object of a series of evaluations, is thus this enduring being around which clusters a complete series of phenomena to which it gives coherence and significance. But, on the other hand, this person is himself known in virtue of his actions and his manifestations, for there is a deep community between the idea which we have of the person and our knowledge of the totality of his acts. Indeed, we are faced with a constant inter-relationship between the act and the person.

Both moral life and legal life need these two notions, both as they are joined together and in their relative independence. Ethics and law judge the act and the agent at the same time; and neither would be satisfied to consider one of these elements alone. By the very fact that it is the individual, and not his act, which we judge, it is granted that he is linked to the acts which he committed. But, on the other hand, if we are interested in the person, it is on account of acts which can be characterised independently of him. If the notions of responsibility, merit and guilt emphasise the person, those of norm and rule are primarily preoccupied with the act. But this separation of the act and the person is never more than partial and unstable. The merit of a person may be seen independently of his acts, but this would be possible only in a metaphysics in which the reference to acts is given by the context. On the other hand, if the rules prescribe or forbid certain acts, their moral or legal import consists in the fact that they are addressed to persons. The terms of the relation of act and person are sufficiently independent to permit each of them to be used in isolation at certain times, but they are sufficiently connected that their joint interaction characterises entire areas of social life.

The distinction between the act and the person and the interaction of these two notions are not utilised by moralists alone. They permit the introduction into all thought of distinctions which are important for argument and play an outstanding role, even if they are not explicitly invoked, as will be shown by the two examples which follow.

173

The first of these examples is furnished for us by a little dialogue imagined by Stevenson:[1]

A (*speaking to C, a child*): 'To neglect your piano practice is naughty.'

B (*in C's hearing*): 'No, no, C is very good about practising.' (*Out of C's hearing*): 'It's hopeless to drive him, you know: but if you praise him, he will do a great deal.' [And Stevenson adds] Here B is not opposed to the general direction of A's influence on C, but wishes to change the manner in which it is exerted.

A judges the act of C and decides that C does not conform to the rule, since he neglects his piano. B forms a judgment on the person and says that he works well, hoping to see him conform to the flattering picture which is presented to him. Both seek the same result, and at first glance they seem opposed only because the first blames that which the second praises. But let us note that the two arguments are not the counterparts of each other. Actually, the blame puts the emphasis on the violated norm, and the person is involved only because of this violation; in the second case the accent is put on the person in the attempt to encourage him in spite of his action.

The second example is furnished us by a text of Chevalier de Méré,[2] in which he distinguishes two modes of expression: 'Among all the servants, those who served him well were rewarded' and 'Among these numerous gentlemen, those who were judged worthy were pleased by his recognition.' Méré here opposes a delicate mode of expression to another which expresses the same fact. According to the second formula, the person seems to be rewarded, not his act. A merit is recognised, not a service— which seems more honourable, at least in Méré's surroundings. Moreover, the persons are placed in the esteemed class of gentlemen; and, finally, a reward is alluded to only in an indirect manner, by the appreciation of those who benefit from it. In the same way it is implied that they have the added merit of being able to appreciate the recognition of their master, i.e., a reciprocal recognition

---

[1] C. L. STEVENSON, *Ethics and Language* (New Haven: Yale University Press, 1945), p. 128.

[2] CHEVALIER DE MÉRE, *Œuvres complètes* (Paris: Collection des Universités de France, 1930), Vol. III, 134.

is indicated. In general, to proceed in this way ends in an evaluation of the person; the acts fall into the background.

After these general considerations, we will examine successively the influence of acts on the conception of the person and that of the person on his acts.

The reaction of the act on the agent is of such a nature as to modify constantly our conception of the person, whether it is a question of new acts which are attributed to him or of former actions which are referred to. Both play an analogous role in argument, although greater weight is given to the more recent acts. Except in limited cases, of which we will speak, the makeup of the person is never completed, not even by his death. However, certain makeups necessary for consistency are much more constant than others. This is the case particularly with historical personages. It is this which was well recognised by Mr. Aron, when he wrote: 'Another, when he is present, reminds us constantly of his capacity to change; when he is absent, he is the prisoner of the image of him which we have formed. And if we distinguish what our friends are from what they do, this distinction fades away to the extent that they sink into the past.'[1] In place of speaking of a distinction which fades away, we would rather say that the reaction of the acts on the person no longer has occasion to manifest itself. Nevertheless, this constancy is only relative: not only might new documents give rise to a revision, but, completely apart from any new fact, the evolution of the personality of the historian or a change of public opinion might modify the conception of a personage, owing to the inclusion in his makeup of acts considered unimportant until that time or by the minimisation of acts formerly judged significant.

This conception, which stresses the uncertainty of the makeup of the person, is sharply opposed to a 'thinglike' conception thereof, whereby each act is considered merely as a sign which reveals an unchangeable personality, which exists prior to its manifestation. Thus it happens that the person is separated from his acts, as the fire is distinguished from the smoke; but the systematic utilisation of such a conception would appear rather strange to us. Witness this passage from Isocrates, which speaks of men as

[1] G. ARON, *Introduction à la philosophie de l'histoire* (Paris: Gallimard, 1948), p. 80.

things: 'If some sign distinguished vicious men, it would indeed be best to punish them before they had done any harm to their fellow citizens. But since people cannot recognise them before they have harmed someone, it is at least proper for everyone to hate them and regard them as an enemy when they are discovered.'[1] In this way the punishment would not be proportionate to the seriousness of the offence but to the wickedness which the offence reveals. But it often happens that an act obliges us to reconstruct our conception of the person and to place a person in a category different from that to which he had been believed to belong. This revision, with the transfer of value which accompanies it, is often expressed by the assertion of a qualification applying to the person.

Everyone knows the famous passage by Pascal: 'There are only three sorts of persons: some who have found God and serve him; others who search for him, but have not found him; and still others who neither search for him, nor have found him. The first are reasonable and happy; the last are mad and unhappy; those in between are unhappy but reasonable.'[2] The act serves to characterise the person, to make him a reasonable being or a madman; we should notice, however, that this characterisation of the person must serve to disqualify certain behaviour. It is the act which determines our conception of the agent, but the interrelation is such that, to that extent, we end up with an evaluation of the act.

The value which we attribute to an act leads us to attribute a certain value to the person, but this is not merely a higher or lower evaluation. In the case in which an act determines a transfer of value, this is correlative with a revision of our conception of the person, to whom we explicitly or implicitly attribute certain tendencies, aptitudes, instincts, or sentiments.

In the relation of act to person, we understand by 'act' anything which may be considered as an emanation of the person; in addition to actions, these might be judgments, modes of expression, emotional reactions, or involuntary mannerisms. In this way, in placing value on a judgment, an evaluation is thereby accorded to its author. The manner in which he judges permits the judge to be judged, and, in the absence of accepted criteria applying to the object, it is extremely difficult to prevent the interaction of the act

[1] ISOCRATES, *Against Lochites*, sec. 14.
[2] PASCAL, *Œuvres*, ed. La Pléiade, *Pensées*, 364 (ed. Brunschvicg, 257).

and the person in this area. The judgment which is applied to both is, at the same time, quite often dependent upon the idea which has been formed of the subject discussed. To call a man 'frivolous' because he has treated frivolously things which are considered important constitutes a well-founded judgment only in the eyes of those who agree on the importance of what has been neglected; thanks to this mechanism, an ambiguity is introduced into the debate, whereby certain cases are prejudiced by judging the persons.

Very rarely is the effect of the act on the person limited simply to a higher or lower evaluation of the person. More often the person serves as what might be called a steppingstone, permitting the passage from known to unknown act, from the knowledge of past acts to the anticipation of future ones. Often the argument concerns acts of the same nature, as in Calvin: 'Is it plausible that we would plot to overthrow kingdoms—we, from whom a seditious word was never heard and whose life was known to be simple and peaceful, when we lived under you, Sire?'[1] Often acts of the past must render likely acts which are a little different. In his speech against Callimachus, Isocrates argues that one who had borne false witness would not hesitate to produce false witnesses in his own favour.[2] However different they may be, one always tries to make known acts and presumed acts fall into the same category.

One may base an argument on habitual acts which are sufficiently numerous to characterise a way of being; but it is also possible to use a unique act or a single judgment, the importance of which is underlined. The uniqueness of the act is no obstacle to proceeding in this way, unless use is made of techniques, of which we will speak later, which seek to separate the act sharply from the person. It is by making use of a single act that the establishment of heresy on a lone issue makes the entire doctrine of a condemned theologian suspected. Likewise, Simone Weil argues from the fact that we find a defence of slavery in the writings of Aristotle, to the condemnation not only of all Aristotelianism but also of the Thomistic movement which is inspired by it.[3]

Past acts and effects produced by them may acquire a certain

[1] JOHN CALVIN, *Institution de la religion Chrétienne* (Geneva, 1888), p. 14.
[2] ISOCRATES, *Against Callimachus*, sec. 57.
[3] S. WEIL, *L'Enracinement* (Paris: Gallimard, 1949), p. 260.

firmness and form a sort of asset which their author would not wish to lose. Enjoyment of a good reputation must be taken into consideration, and Isocrates does not hesitate to invoke it in the defence of his client: '[I] would be the most unhappy of men if, having paid out a good bit of money to the state, I were said to covet that of others or to take no account of your opinion—when people see that I have been much less concerned not merely with my fortune, but even with my life, than with the good reputation which you give me.'[1] Past care for the reputation becomes a guaranty that nothing would be done that would bring about its loss. Previous actions and the reputation which results from them become a sort of capital which is incorporated in the person. It becomes a sort of acquired asset which one may invoke in his own defence. We should notice in this respect that, although the rhetorical argument may never be conclusive, the very fact that people affirm that it must not be overlooked and must be attended to is itself the sign of its rationality and its value for a universal audience.[2]

In the preceding pages, although we have discussed the effect of the act on the agent, we have been induced to allude also to the effect of the agent on the act. But the idea which we form of the agent is itself founded on previous acts and it often happens that the idea we form of the person is the point of departure for the argument, serving to anticipate certain unknown actions, to interpret them in a certain way, or to transfer to them the judgment applied to the person.

An example is furnished us by a joke attributed to the Belgian statesman, P. H. Spaak. After a press conference, a reporter pressed him: 'Is it really true, what you have just told us?' and Spaak retorted, 'With a good head like mine, could I tell you something which wasn't true?' We should mention in this regard that there is a humour in argumentation which results from the application of argumentative schemas beyond their conditions of normal application. The study of this sort of joke, which need not be confused with general use of humour in persuasion, should show us certain schemas of argument. It doubtless permits us, as

[1] ISOCRATES, *ibid.*, sec. 63.
[2] Cf. C. PERELMAN, 'La Quête du rationnel', in *Études de philosophie des sciences en hommage à F. Gonseth*, p. 141.

well, to specify their conditions of application. Mr. Spaak's joke caricatures the passage from the person to the act as it is currently practised.

In reasoning concerning a person, as concerning things, we constantly infer his future behaviour from what is known of him and his past and move to unknown cases from those which are known. But it is more interesting to declare that the behaviour of persons may be predicted not merely on the basis of our past experience but on the basis of the idea of a moral impossibility, furnished by a system of beliefs, which is completely parallel to the physical impossibility furnished by a scientific system. It is thus that Pascal tells us, concerning miracles, 'There is a great deal of difference between not being for Christ and saying so, and not being for Christ, though pretending to be. The first may do miracles, the second not, for the first are clearly seen to be against the truth; but not so the others, and thus miracles are more clear'[1] and 'him who is a covert enemy, God would not permit to do miracles adversely.'[2] Diabolical miracles are possible, because they fool nobody; but it is not possible, conversely, that God should permit hidden enemies of Christ to fool the faithful with miracles.

The interpretation of acts in terms of the image we form of the person constitutes a more specific aspect of argument in this area. The context which the person supplies and which permits better comprehension of his acts most often appears in terms of the notion of 'intention'.

When we pass from the knowledge of a person's previous acts to considerations concerning future ones, the role of the person stands out, but it constitutes merely a sort of privileged link in the totality of facts which are invoked, whereas the notion of intention puts the emphasis much more on the permanent character of the person. The intention is, indeed, intimately tied to the agent, being the emanation of his personality or the result of his will— that is, of that which characterises him most fully. Since the intention of others is never known directly, we simply presume it through what is known of this person and his permanent characteristics. Generally the intention is presumed in virtue of repeated and consistent acts, but there are cases in which merely the idea

[1] *Pensées*, 751 (ed. Brunschvicg, 836).
[2] *Ibid.*, 753 (ed. Brunschvicg, 843).

which we form of the agent permits his intentions to be determined. The same act, performed by someone else, would be considered as different and esteemed otherwise, because it would be believed to have been done with a different intention. So recourse to intentions constitutes the heart of the argument and subordinates the act to the agent, whose intention permits the understanding and evaluation of the act. It is thus that Calvin, recalling that the afflictions of Job could be attributed simultaneously to three authors—God, Satan and men—finds that God has acted properly, whereas Satan and the men were to be condemned because their intentions were different.[1] But the idea we have of the intentions depends entirely on what we know about the agents.

All moral argument based on intention constitutes a morality of the agent, in opposition to a morality of the act, which is much more formalistic. The above example shows clearly the mechanism of these arguments because it brings in agents, as well, characterised as God and Satan, but there is no moral controversy which does not make use of such a mechanism. The intention of the agent and the motives which determined his action are often considered as the reality, which is hidden behind purely external manifestations. It is assumed that knowledge of them must be sought through appearances, for they alone have importance in the final analysis.

Here is another little dialogue by Stevenson, the effect of which, according to the author, is to disqualify the interlocutor and to remove all value from his advice:[2]

A: You ought to vote for him, by all means.
B: Your motives for urging me are clear. You think that he will give you the city contracts.

It is not without interest to oppose to this dialogue by Stevenson, and the conclusion which he draws from it, a passage by Pareto:

A certain proposition A can not be good unless it is formed by an honest man; I show that he who made this proposition is not honest, or that he was paid for doing it; thus I have shown that the proposition A is harmful to the country. This is absurd; and

[1] CALVIN, op. cit., Book I, chapter xviii, par. 1.
[2] STEVENSON, op. cit., p. 128.

anyone who uses this reasoning has departed completely from the domain of reasonableness.[1]

To hold that the dishonesty of the author or the fact that he had a peculiar interest constitutes an argument invalidating his proposition or to reject this argument completely as irrelevant are two extreme positions which are equally over-simplified. In the first case, account is taken only of the person and the intentions attributed to him, to the neglect of the examination of the proposition advanced; in the second, only the proposition is looked at, apart from what is known concerning its author. Actually, in daily practice, we take account of both these factors, for what we know concerning the author permits us to understand the proposition better and to estimate its proper value. This shows that in this area practice is a great deal more varied than the analysis of theoretical thinkers, and the effect of the agent on the act is of an infinitely variable intensity. It is only at the extremes that it may be accorded an exclusive influence or entirely eliminated. We will see that one of these extremes is located in the region of theology and the other in that of science, inasmuch as science is considered as a system in itself.

We may cite on this subject a very interesting study by Mr. Asch,[2] who criticises the procedures generally used in social psychology to determine the influence of prestige. These consist in asking subjects to what extent they agree with a judgment. Ultimately, the same judgment is presented to the same subject, but with a modification of the subject's knowledge of the author of the judgment. Mr. Asch shows quite well that the results attained do not at all demonstrate, as is generally supposed, that evaluations are modified exclusively in relation to the prestige accorded to the author. Indeed, the judgment estimated is not at all an invariable element which is evaluated by taking account of the prestige of the different authors to whom it is attributed. The judgment is not the same because, when it is attributed to one author rather than to another, it changes its significance; there is no simple change of value but a new interpretation, for the judgment is put in the new context of our knowledge of the person

---

[1] PARETO, *The Mind and Society*, ed. A. LIVINGSTON (London, Cape, 1935), Vol. II, para. 1756.

[2] ASCH, 'The Doctrine of Suggestion, Prestige, and Imitation in Social Psychology', *Psychological Review*, IV (1948), 250–76.

who is supposed to have enunciated it. There are, then, judgments, as there are acts, which we interpret by what we know concerning their author. The influence attributed in recent years to prestige and its power of suggestion is manifest less irrationally and simply than is generally supposed.

It is this interpretation of acts as dependent on what is known concerning their author which makes us understand the mechanism of prestige, and the transfer of value which it effects from the person having prestige to the most diverse of his acts. 'What genius does not vindicate the works of his youth!' Malraux exclaimed.[1] And, indeed, anyone who considers the early works of a great artist cannot help seeing in them the foreshadowing of his future greatness. Thus recognition of outstanding value in a person even validates acts which precede the time when it becomes indisputably manifest. The author of works of genius created at different times *is* a genius; and this characterisation attaches the acts to a stable quality of the person which shines as well into the years previous to the period of production of masterpieces as into the years which follow. It is not sufficient to say that the past guarantees the future—for the future may very well validate the past—but the stable makeup of the person does permit us to prejudge his acts and particularly his judgments. 'There are persons,' says Méré, 'who recognise true merit and to please them is a good indication; but there are many more who do not have good judgment, and satisfying them should not cause too much rejoicing.'[2]

We thus see how prestige may serve to validate acts, to give rise to inclinations to imitation, and to work out the idea of a model from which conduct may be copied. The use of this argumentative mechanism in knowledge has given rise to both the use and the abuse of arguments from authority.

When Cicero asked us to scorn works of art and wrote: 'In your opinion what would be said by L. Mummius, who had such complete scorn of Corinth, if he saw one of these dandies lovingly fondling some chamber-pot made of Corinthian bronze?'[3] this argument has no interest unless L. Mummius has some prestige. In addition, we should notice that this scorn for Corinth, which can serve as a model, is at the same time an element of this prestige,

---

[1] MALRAUX, *Saturne: Essai sur Goya*, la Galerie de la Pléiade (Paris: Gallimard, 1950), p. 18.

[2] MÉRÉ, *op. cit.*, I, 77.   [3] CICERO *De paradoxe* 2.

for very often the authority to whom we refer is at the same time being justified. If there is no prestige, argument from the model becomes worthless. In the *Rhetorica ad Herennium* we find a humorous example which requires us to distinguish between an argumentative scheme and the conditions of its application. This work tries to give an example of an argument which is feeble because it argues from what is done to what ought to be done. It concerns a passage from the *Trinummus* by Plautus: 'It is very disagreeable to rebuke a friend for a fault, but it is often useful and profitable: for today I shall rebuke my friend for what he has done.'[1] The argument has scarcely any value because it is stated by a comic character, the old Megaronides. But this is not always the case. To be convinced of this, it is sufficient to remember the confessors of the faith.

Argument based on the idea that a model must be followed is stronger to the extent that the authority is not contested. When it is a question of divine authority, this authority even makes it possible to determine standards of goodness and of truth.

Very often the authority is based on competence as the only reason for the argumentative value of certain expressions. When the teacher says to his pupil, 'I don't understand what you are saying', this usually means, 'You have expressed yourself badly' or 'Your ideas are not very clear on this point'. Again, incompetence may be made use of as a criterion for the disqualification of everyone who is considered less competent than those who disclaim their own competence. This is the import of the argument used by Chevreul, president of the Parisian Academy of Sciences, when the attempt was made to disqualify the testimony of handwriting experts from the discussion of the authenticity of the manuscript presented by Michel Chasles.[2] This form of argument can have an outstanding philosophic importance, since it may destroy the competence not only of an individual or a group, with respect to a certain matter, but of humanity as a whole. When one denounces in himself the deficiences of reason, this may be done in order to affirm the deficiencies of human reason in general. He does not present himself as an exception: quite the contrary, he creates the

---

[1] *Rhetorica ad Herennium* ii, 23, 35; cf. PLAUTUS *Trinummus*, Act I, scene 1, vs. 5.

[2] VAYSON DE PRADENNE, *Les Fraudes en archéologie préhistorique* (Paris: Nourry, 1932), pp. 397–398.

impression that others are in the same situation as he. In the extreme case, if all men are in the same situation, the problem is deemed insoluble.

Schopenhauer shows quite well the abuse of this argument which might occur, using the artifice of feigning incompetence in a ticklish situation.[1] Here we pass from rhetorical arguments to eristic and even sophistical argument. But it is because rhetorical argument has some value that it may be utilised in bad faith, just as counterfeiting would be inconceivable unless there were authentic bills having some value. And if sophistical argument differs from honest argument by the bad faith which is employed in it, in order to establish this bad faith in another we make use of the ensemble of rhetorical methods of argument which permit us to conclude from the acts to the intention. Sophistical argument thus provides double confirmation of the value and importance of rhetoric, for its value is confirmed both by those who imitate it in bad faith and by those who make use of it to discredit the pretences of an adversary.

In analysing successively the effect of the act on the agent and that of the agent on the act, we have been led to emphasise first one and then the other. But this is merely the artifice of analysis. The interaction is constant and is quite often explicitly seen.

We may gain the benevolence of the judges, we read in the *Rhetorica ad Herennium*, 'by praising the courage, wisdom, kindness, and brilliance of their judgments, and by consideration of the esteem which they will merit, and the expectations which they must fulfil.'[2] Thus we pass from the consideration of past judgments to an evaluation of the jury and from the good jury to the anticipated favourable verdict, which will itself elevate the prestige of the judges. Successive evocation of the act and the person, then of the person and the act, does not leave the mind at the point at which it started. The cumulative effect of these interrelationships is clear, as long as no use is made of a separating technique. We shall call this the 'snowball' interaction. This may take place even in the case of a single act, since a work which does honour to its author will be itself all the more prized as the author is highly

---

[1] SCHOPENHAUER, 'Eristische Dialektik', Kunstgriff 31 (*Sämtliche Werke* [Munich, Piper ed.], VI, 423).

[2] *Rhetorica ad Herennium* i, 5, 8.

esteemed. But the snowball interaction is better revealed when there is a difference either in the time or in the nature of the acts to be performed. Its effect is then to allow the person or the agent to be a basis for expectations quite superior to those which his previous acts would have justified, had this interaction not taken place. We find an example of this in the reasoning which Whately cites, whereby, on the basis of the marks of divine benevolence in this world, we conclude concerning the splendour of the afterlife by way of the intermediate conclusion that God is benevolent.[1] No less than the intervention of a person is required to permit the passage from an observable realm to one entirely different, from the real world to the world of the future life. But there is more: the benefits which we expect in the afterlife infinitely surpass those we enjoy here below, which serve as the beginning point for a snowball argument.

Of course, the snowball interrelation implies that the act and the person mutually affect each other in the same direction. However, the interaction may operate in opposed directions. It is generally in such cases that use is made of certain techniques which prevent the interplay. It is these which we are going to analyse in the remainder of our study.

The techniques which break or curb the interaction of the act and the person must be utilised when there is an incompatibility between the act and what is known concerning the person, that is to say, when the act requires a profound modification of our conception of the person which we refuse to make or when the person should confer on the act a value incompatible with the consequences which it involves, that is to say, with other connections which also influence its value.

The most effective technique for preventing the reaction of the act on the agent is to consider the latter as completely good or evil, that is, as a god or a demon. The most effective technique for preventing the reaction of the agent on the act is to consider the latter as a truth or the expression of a fact on which there is complete agreement, at least in the present circumstances. We will begin by examining these two techniques, which we will call 'separation' techniques.

The introduction into our thought of a perfect and divine being

[1] RICHARD WHATELY, *Elements of Rhetoric* (Oxford, 1828), p. 62.

gives the possibility of completely detaching the person from the act. Nevertheless, the notion of God is not always used in this manner, far from it. We are familiar with a series of arguments in which God is presented as operating in order to acquire prestige and is deemed to have done certain things to show his power, or as a sign of his power, which, being manifest in a natural order, permits belief in his actions in another order.[1]

Leibniz likewise refuses to neglect the works and consider only the creator. 'And so', he writes, 'I am very far from the sentiment of those who maintain that there are no rules of goodness and perfection in the nature of things, or in the ideas which God has of them, and that the works of God are good merely for the *formal reason* that God has made them. . . . *The creator is discovered by consideration of creation.*'[2] Leibniz thus wishes to apply the same reasoning to God as to man. In the double transition from the person to the act and from the act to the person, the first transition is prior, since God is involved. But Leibniz does not wish to leave it at this; he wishes as well to understand why the world is good and to pass from the creation to the creator. But let us not forget that it is in virtue of the highly privileged first movement that he knows that the present world is the best of all possible worlds. However, if he makes use of the value of the creation to glorify the creator, he also knows how, in some cases, to prevent the action of the act on the agent, by making use of divine perfection. This he explains to us in the *Essay on Theodicy*, by imagining a man of extraordinary reputation in the following situation. He writes:

'A man might give such great and strong proof of his virtue and holiness that all of the most apparent reasons which could be held against him to charge him with a proposed crime, for example, larceny, or an assassination, would have to be rejected as the calumnies of false witnesses, an extraordinary accident which occasionally lays suspicion on the most innocent. Thus in a case in which all others would be in danger of condemnation, or questioning . . . this man would be unanimously acquitted by his judges.'[3]

---

[1] PASCAL, *Pensées*, 560 (ed. Brunschvicg, 643).

[2] LEIBNIZ, *Discours de métaphysique* (Paris: Vrin, 1929), pp. 26–27.

[3] LEIBNIZ, *Essais de théodicée*, in Works, ed. Gerhardt (Leipzig, 1932), VI, 70–74.

In this case, Leibniz continues, there would be no new law but the application of a 'good logic of probability', since 'this person has such admirable qualities, that in virtue of a good logic of probability we must have more faith in his words than in that of numerous others'. Leibniz has used a human example as a basis for this justification, which he considers as rational, of a technique consisting in refusing all unfavourable effects of the act on the agent; but by that very fact, when the same technique is applied to God, it operates perfectly: 'I have already remarked that anything which might be opposed to the goodness and justice of God, is merely an appearance, which would be damaging to a man, but which becomes as nothing when applied to God and when weighed with the demonstrations which assure us of the infinite perfection of his attributes.'

We just as often encounter the independence of the person in relation to the act when it is a matter of negative values. Bossuet makes use of it in this curious passage:

'We Christians must recognise that neither the sciences, nor a great mind, nor the other gifts of nature are very considerable advantages, since God permits them to be completely possessed by devils, his chief enemies, and thereby renders them not merely unfortunate, but even worthy of infinite scorn; that in spite of all these outstanding qualities, and miserable and impotent as we are, we are enviable to them, because our great God chooses to regard us with pity.' [1]

It is qualities which are involved here, but the mechanism is the same as with acts. These qualities cannot modify the idea which we hold of the demon, but rather they are tainted thereby—they are devaluated and do not constitute 'very considerable advantages'. The act or the quality is interpreted or minimised so that it cannot affect the agent, and it is completely subordinated to the nature attributed to the latter.

From the moment an act expresses a fact, the value which is attributed to it is completely independent of that of the person, so that we find ourselves in a situation the opposite of that in which the person is shielded from his acts. 'A factual error subjects a wise man to ridicule', La Bruyère tells us. But this is evidently on

[1] Bossuet, 'Sermon sur les démons', in *Sermons* (Paris: Garnier), II, 11.

condition that the fact is incontestable. No man has enough
prestige to make us believe that $2 + 2 = 5$ or accept any testimony which seems to us contrary to experience. It is a matter of
weighing the evidential value of the experience.

In this regard, Locke reminds us that
'to a man whose experience has been always quite contrary, and
has never heard of anything like it, the most untainted credit of a
witness will scarce be able to find belief: as it happened to a Dutch
ambassador, who entertaining the king of Siam with the pe-
culiarites of Holland . . . amongst other things told him 'that the
water in his country would sometimes in cold weather be so hard
that men walked upon it, and that it would bear an elephant if it
were there.' To which the king replied 'hitherto I have believed
the strange things you have told me, because I look upon you as a
sober, fair man: but now I am sure you lie!'[1]

In this account, experience and the generalisations which seem
to be authorised by it are considered as a fact which surpasses any
influence of the person. His act, since it is deemed incompatible
with convictions drawn from experience, is treated as a falsehood,
which is, in turn, considered a fact. The person can do nothing
about it. And, conversely, the act is not without effect on the
person, since the validity of all his previous assertions is damaged.

Anything which is considered as a fact is independent of the
action of the person; this is why the status of the fact is shaken by
using one means or another to attach its assertion to the character
of the witness. Everyone knows the famous tale of the magician
who was trusted by the king and had him put on clothes which, he
said, were seen only by men above reproach. The king and his
courtiers saw nothing but did not dare to say so until one day
when a child, in his innocence, cried, 'Why is the king naked?'
The spell was broken. The magician had enough prestige to make
perception serve as a criterion of everyone's morality until the indisputable innocence of a child destroyed this favourable prejudice. From the moment the perception was no longer tied to a
judgment of value, everyone gave it its usual importance.

When does a judgment express a fact? As long, we have seen,
as it is believed to be valid for a universal audience and (to avoid

[1] LOCKE, *An Essay concerning Human Understanding* (London: Routledge,
1894), Book IV, chap. xv, par. 5.

all discussion in this regard) has been included in a special discipline whose foundations are presumed to be accepted and whose
criteria have been made the object of an explicit or implicit convention.

There is a number of scientific or practical techniques which
attempt to obtain objectivity by separating the act from the agent
either to describe it or to judge it. Behaviourism is one example;
another is supplied by all competitions in which the contestants
are judged on measurable performances or in which the work is
judged without the name of its author being made known. In law
a great many arrangements seek to characterise acts independently
of the person committing them and even without concern for his
intentions. In ethics such recourse to the fact without consideration of the intention is much less frequent. Still it is apparent that
an ethics such as the Japanese, which is much more formalistic
than Western ethics, may be considered as a morality of the act.
Ruth Benedict cites a long list of Japanese school directors who
committed suicide because the flames of a conflagration, with
which they had nothing to do, threatened the portrait of the
emperor which ornaments each educational institution.[1]

Detachment of the act and refusal to introduce into its evaluation any consideration concerning the person seem much more
rationalistic than does the inverse technique. We have seen that
Pareto ridicules the introduction of considerations concerning the
author into estimation of the foundation of a proposition. In this
he merely follows Bentham's view. We may note in this regard a
remark by Whately, of which we cannot help admiring the insight
on this point. 'If the measure is a good one', says Bentham, 'will it
become bad because it is supported by a bad man?' And Whately
replies, 'It is only in matters of strict science, and that too, in
arguing to scientific man, that the characters of the advisers (as
well as all other probable arguments) should be wholly put out of
the question.'[2] Nevertheless, whatever the value of Whately's
considerations, it cannot be denied that preoccupation with
objectivity leads to the detachment of the act from the person
because it is more difficult to obtain agreement concerning persons than concerning acts, or at least this seems to be the situation
in virtue of the notion of a 'fact'. Someone is usually called 'fair'

[1] R. BENEDICT, *The Chrysanthemum and the Sword* (Boston, 1946), p. 151.
[2] WHATELY, *op. cit.*, pp. 162–64.

because he judges the act without taking account of the person. It is true that this procedure often possesses indisputable advantages, the principal one being the facilitation of the agreement on criteria. But it must never be forgotten that it is no more than a procedure and may have serious disadvantages. The best proof of this is the recent attempts to individualise punishment.

The cases in which the interaction of the act and the person is entirely broken in one sense or another are relatively rare in social life, for they are merely limiting cases. Most techniques which are used for this are not separation techniques but curbing techniques, which have the effect of restraining this interaction without completely annulling it.

One of these techniques is prejudice or, perhaps better, bias. An act committed by someone does not react on the conception which we have of this person, in so far as favourable or unfavourable prejudice permits maintenance of an adequation between the act and the person. The act is interpreted and judged in such a way that it need not modify our idea of the person, which, as we have already seen, supplies the context whereby the act is better understood whenever the act is not perfectly univocal. But if prejudice does permit the removal of a threatening inconsistency, it cannot be used when the inconsistency is too obvious.

The effect of bias or prejudice is quite often a blindness towards the value of an act and the transfer to it of other values stemming from the person. Avoidance of prejudice is thus a healthy separation between act and person. But if we put ourselves in the point of view of the normal interrelation of act and person, which seems to us primordial, prejudice appears as a curbing technique, a technique which is opposed to the continual renewal of the image of the person and contributes primarily to the stability of the person.

When we look at the role of bias and prestige, we see that it is prestige which may be considered as the force which assures the action of the agent on the act. It has an active and positive role and occurs at an earlier stage than that at which bias enters. Bias itself corrects an inconsistency between the act and the person and occurs when the latter must be shielded against the act. But though prestige may prepare for bias, they are not always linked, for bias may be based on other kinds of previous arguments.

In order to avoid giving the impression that we judge certain acts as a function of the person or that we suffer from prejudice, certain precautions must often be taken. One of them is to preface an unfavourable estimation of an act with certain eulogies of the person, and conversely. These eulogies are sometimes directed towards other acts, but with the intention of praising the person and making clear our own impartiality.

If the technique of prejudice is insufficiently established and the act stands out in spite of everything, it is possible to make a separation between distinct realms of activity in such a way that an act done in one of them will be considered irrelevant to the idea we form of the person, whose image is determined by the action of another realm. In different societies and different environments, these realms would not be determined in the same way. For example, to be hard-working or faithful in marriage may in certain cases be determinant for the image we form of the person, while in others they would be relegated to the reserve realm of acts of scant importance. The extent of these inactive realms is the object of an agreement, generally tacit, which comes under the same heading as the values and connections admitted by the group and even contributes to its characterisation. It need hardly be said that the reserve realm of acts which are considered irrelevant may vary according to the person. Such acts as would be considered unimportant when attributed to a ruler would be essential to the idea we form of a person of lesser rank, and vice versa. It is the same with respect to the acts of a certain period of life—childhood, for example.

But we need not believe that the separation between the act and the person cannot be extended to the most important acts. Quite the contrary; in reality, the most important acts are also those which are watched, precisely because we know that they reflect on the image which we form of the person. But if we think that an act has been set up to create a certain impression, its indicative value is greatly reduced. This was emphasised by Schopenhauer, for whom the person colours and impregnates the least of his acts.[1] Indeed, it is in the little things which are least regarded that men indicate their true nature best.

In other cases, from the multiplicity of acts we retain only a single aspect, which alone is judged important. Sometimes we

---

[1] SCHOPENHAUER, 'Zur Ethik', in *Parerga und Para ipomena* (*Sämtliche Werke*, ed. Brockhaus [Leipzig, 1939], VI, 245).

split the person into fragments having no mutual interrelation or frustrate the influence of the act on the person by crystallising the latter at a particular stage of his existence. Jouhandeau traces the portrait of the woman who reduces her ego to what it once was and refuses to integrate her present actions into it, saying to her customers, 'I am in the past; it is only my mummy that mends your shoes, Monsieur.'[1] This technique is used much more often than would seem. Each time we make a rigid exception of past action, we crystallise the individual in some way. Thus shielded, he is endowed with some value but has lost his spontaneity.

Paulhan notices quite correctly the disagreeable impression we feel when we hear friends speaking of us.[2] According to him, this disagreeable impression is tied to the illusion of forecasts from the past. But it is not necessarily this which causes the impression, being rather the fact that our acts and our person are linked by others in a mechanical and unchangeable fashion, as if our person had been arrested at a certain stage of its development. It is disagreeable to hear someone say of us, 'He will certainly act nobly and sacrifice himself', because this act is presented simply as the consequence of the past and does not have the power to react on our future personality and re-create it for ourselves or others.

Along with these techniques of more general importance, whose richness we are very far from having exhausted, there are techniques of less importance, which merely seek to remove an incompatibility between the act and the person in a given circumstance.

One of them is recourse to the notion of an exception. The meritorious or blameworthy act which seems incompatible with what we otherwise know of the person is considered as exceptional, to prevent the further transfer of its value to the person. Still it is often necessary to explain how this exceptional behaviour could occur. If a friend wrongs us, we explain this behaviour by ignorance or awkwardness, in order to avoid seeing in it causes which would shatter our friendly relations. It is on a conception of the same sort that we base the respectful recourse 'from the pope poorly informed to the pope well informed'. We thereby understand that the judgment which is opposed is not attributed to an

[1] JOUHANDEAU, *Un Monde* (Paris: Gallimard, 1950), p. 34.
[2] J. PAULHAN, *Entretien sur des faits divers* (Paris: Gallimard, 1945), p. 67.

imperfect faculty of judging but to badly informed counsellors. It is thus possible to disapprove of the judgment, without modifying one's estimation of the person.

An extreme procedure consists in supposing that the act only apparently belongs to the person and that it was suggested or dictated by someone else or, still better, that someone else speaks through his voice. The person is reduced to the role of a witness. Bossuet asks, 'May corrupt preachers bear the message of eternal life?' And he replies, carrying on Augustine's analogy to the vineyard and the bush, 'The bush bears a fruit which does not belong to it, and is nonetheless the fruit of the vineyard for being supported by the bush', and 'Do not scorn the grapes on the pretext that it is found among the thorns: do not reject this doctrine because it is surrounded by evil: it still comes from God.'[1]

Sometimes separation established between the person and his acts is an attempt not to protect the person but to see that the acts are given their proper value and are not lowered by the envy or ill repute with respect to their author. Chevalier de Méré tells us that 'Caesar attributed his most admirable deeds to the favour of the Gods. However, Cato accuses him of believing in neither Gods nor Goddesses; Caesar merely understood the sentiments of the people'.[2] Demosthenes does not hesitate to use the same technique: 'Well, If I showed greater foresight than others in all circumstances, I do not mean to attribute it in any way to a special wisdom or some faculty on which I pride myself. No, these insights I owe to two causes which I shall explain: first, Athenians, to good luck . . . and second, to the fact that my judgments and my predictions are not paid for.'[3] In this example the tie is only partially broken. Demosthenes attributes his good advice to luck but also to his own honesty. Indeed, the first reason might turn against him: if luck rules, why should it continue to favour him in the future? Now what is important, namely, confidence in his present forecast, he attributes equally to the honesty which his adversaries lack.

Recourse to luck or the goddess of fortune is a profession of modesty which, though it need not be taken too seriously, does permit the reduction of the effect of the act on the person. We may

[1] BOSSUET, 'Sermon des pécheurs', op. cit., II, 489.
[2] MÉRÉ, op. cit., II, 109.
[3] DEMOSTHENES, On the Peace, secs. 11–12.

treat in the same manner other procedures, such as recounting a story as if it came from a third person or such as making judgments preceded by 'they say that . . .' in place of 'I suppose that . . .'—in brief, all those cases in which we attempt, as far as possible, to separate the act from the person in order to reduce the role of the latter to that of a witness or a mouthpiece.

It is in the realm of judicial debate that all these techniques are really applied to a happy hunting ground. It is there that we find all the procedures tying act and person or permitting the union of the two to be broken. The only conclusion which may be drawn from this is that the connection between act and person is merely a presumption and must never be considered a necessary tie. Among the techniques examined in the *Rhetorica ad Herennium*, the one known under the name of 'deprecation' is very interesting from our point of view. 'The accused admits the crime and its premeditation, but none the less implores mercy.' And the author adds: 'This could scarcely be done before a tribunal, unless we plead for a man who has been recommended by fine acts which are many and well-known.'[1] At the extreme case, it is demanded that account be taken only of former acts which are put in opposition to the recent acts of the person. The argument at the same time implies the unity of the act and the person—without which previous acts would have no significance to the trial—and attempts to destroy this unity with respect to present actions. So conceived, this deprecation presumes that laudable acts express the true personality better than those which are harmful. It thus employs a double convention—that which ties the act to the person and that which permits them to be separated under certain circumstances. The duality of this convention alone permits this form of argument. The question is to note whether the destruction of the tie of act and person seems sufficiently justified under the given circumstances; but it must be emphasised that this destruction is invoked only in cases of difficulty.

The connection between act and person seems to us the prototype of a series of ties which give rise to the same interactions and lend themselves to the same arguments: the connection between individual and group, the connection between an event and the

[1] *Rhetorica ad Herennium* i, 14, 27.

epoch in which it occurs, and many other connections of co-existence of which the most general is that of act and essence. We have been able only to outline our observations concerning the relations between the act and the person. The study of other connections, the aspects in which they resemble the first, and those in which they are different, would carry us beyond the limits of this article. We will be satisfied if the preceding pages strengthen our readers in the idea that rhetoric, conceived as the study of methods of argument, may clarify the most diverse areas of human thought, from literature to epistemology and metaphysics, by way of law, morals, and religion.

XIII

PRAGMATIC ARGUMENTS[1]

SOMETIMES we draw conclusions about a thing's existence or its value by considering what are thought to be its consequences. I shall say that an argument is pragmatic when it consists in estimating an action, or any event, or a rule, or whatever it may be, in terms of its favourable or unfavourable consequences; what happens in such cases is that all or part of the value of the consequences is transferred to whatever is regarded as causing or preventing them.

Here are two characteristic examples of the employment of this argument. The first comes from Hume's *Enquiry Concerning the Principles of Morals*:

Can anything stronger be said in praise of a profession, such as merchandise or manufacture, than to observe the advantages which it procures to society; and is not a monk and inquisitor enraged when we treat his order as useless or pernicious to mankind?[2]

The second is taken from Locke. He uses it to attack the doctrine of divine right and the spiritual authority of princes:

No peace and security, not so much as common friendship, can ever be established or preserved amongst men so long as this opinion prevails, that dominion is founded in grace and that religion is to be propagated by force of arms.[3]

---

[1] The second of two Special University Lectures delivered at University College in the University of London, March 1957. The lecture was translated from the French by Professor A. J. AYER and published in *Philosophy*, Vol. XXXIV, No. 128, January 1959.

[2] Section II, part 2.

[3] LOCKE, *The second Treatise of civil government* and *A letter concerning toleration*, Oxford, Blackwell, 1948, p. 135.

Arguments of this type play such an essential part in our thinking, that some have wished to reduce all forms of rational argument to them. Thus Bentham says:

What is it to offer a *good reason* with respect to a law? It is to allege the good or evil which the law tends to produce. . . . What is it to offer a *false reason*? It is the alleging for or against a law something else than its good or evil effects.[1]

This attempt to reduce all good reasoning, in the field of practical affairs, or even in that of the theory of knowledge, to the use of pragmatic arguments is characteristic both of utilitarianism and of pragmatism. So, the development of every philosophical system depends upon the use of special forms of argument. Other types of argument which in the normal way might interfere with this schema are eliminated, at least in the constructive part of the system; and it is this that gives philosophical thought its air of being demonstrative. Conversely, the opponents of the system in question will have recourse, in their criticism, to different forms of argument. In what follows we shall see how the choice of this or that type of argument bears upon philosophical controversy.

The transfer of the value of the consequences to their antecedents, which is the work of the pragmatic argument, usually comes about of its own accord. The argument does not, in fact, require any justification in order to be accepted by common sense. On the contrary, it is the failure to take it into account that is regarded as paradoxical and in need of explanation. Thus when Pascal found that the straightforward use of the pragmatic argument did not seem to make the passion for the chase intelligible, he hit upon another use of the same argument as a basis for his theory of distraction:

Those [he wrote] who think it very irrational for people to spend a whole day running after a hare which they would not have wanted to buy, display their ignorance of human nature. The hare in itself would not protect us from the spectacle of human misery and death, but the chase by distracting us does so protect us.[2]

[1] BENTHAM, *The Theory of Legislation*, ed. C. K. OGDEN, London, Kegan Paul (1931), pp. 66–67.
[2] PASCAL, *Pensées*, 205 (139 éd. Brunschvicg), in *Oeuvres*, éd. de la Pléiade, Paris, 1941.

The emotive transference which is carried out by the pragmatic argument looms so large that very often one believes that one is valuing something for its own sake, when in fact one is interested only in its consequences. This is especially to be noticed in the case where disagreement as to the advisability of some course of action is wholly due to the fact that each one of the disputants has taken only a part of the consequences into account.[1]

These consequences may be present or future, established or hypothetical; in some cases they will influence our actions, in others only our judgments.

The pragmatic argument may be based on a generally recognised causal relation, which may or may not be verifiable; or it may be based on a relation which is known only to a single person, who is prepared to give a justification of its working. This is how Odier in a work entitled *L'angoisse et la pensée magique* summarises the way in which superstitious people reason:

If we are thirteen at table, if I light three cigarettes with the same match—what happens? I am uneasy and am no longer good for anything. On the other hand if I insist on our being only twelve, or refuse to light the third cigarette, then I feel reassured and all my faculties are restored to me. Therefore it is legitimate and rational for me to behave in this way. My position is logical and I am self-consistent.[2]

We see from this that the superstitious person rationalises his behaviour by invoking arguments which should appear reasonable to his interlocutor; the desire to avoid being physically enfeebled does in fact supply a sufficient reason, when combined with the pragmatic argument, for behaviour which at first sight seems irrational. Since it is generally admitted that it is better, other things being equal, to avoid being in a state of anxiety and uneasiness, the discussion will in these circumstances be confined to the genuineness of the causal connection which the superstitious person claims to exist. But how is one to use the pragmatic argument when there is no agreement about the value of the consequences?

When the value of the consequences on which the pragmatic

---

[1] Cf. The remarks of D. VAN DANZIG in *Democracy in a World of Tensions*, ed. by R. McKEON, University of Chicago Press, 1951, pp. 54-5.

[2] C. ODIER, *L'angoisse et la pensée magique*, Neuchâtel 1948, p. 122.

argument is based is itself a matter of dispute, one has to have recourse to other argumentative techniques. Thus J. S. Mill, confronted with the difficulty that not everybody appreciates the
same types of pleasure, resolves it by ordering pleasures into a
qualitative hierarchy, which is based on a hierarchy of the
characters and abilities of those who enjoy them. The argument
which he uses for this purpose postulates a double hierarchy:[1]
from a hierarchy of persons an inference is drawn to a hierarchy of
their acts.[2] And in order to justify the hierarchy of persons, in its
turn, in a way that would not seem irrational in his own eyes, he
takes it as a proof of one man's superiority to another that his
knowledge is more extensive: that it incorporates all that the
other knows:

It is better to be a human being dissatisfied than a pig satisfied;
better to be Socrates dissatisfied than a fool satisfied. And if the
fool, or the pig are of a different opinion, it is because they only
know their own side of the question. The other party to the comparison knows both sides.[3]

The superiority which is attributed to the better informed man
is based on the commonplace that the whole is worth more than
one of its parts. It is to be remarked, however, that in applying it
here Mill assumes that his wise man has lived the life of a pig or a
fool and has tasted their pleasures.

If Mill's argumentation, whatever interest it may have in itself,
is at variance with classical utilitarianism, it is because it brings in
different methods of reasoning from the pragmatic argument and
so breaks Bentham's methodological rule, to which we referred
earlier on.

The pragmatic argument is not limited to the transference of a
given value from an effect to another event which is taken to be its
cause. It also allows one to pass from one domain of reality to
another, from the evaluation of an action to the evaluation of the
agent, from the fruit to the tree, from the utility of a certain course
of conduct to the utility of the rule that governs it. It allows one
further, and this is where it achieves its greatest philosophical

---

[1] C. PERELMAN and L. OLBRECHTS-TYTECA, *Traité de l'Argumentation*, Paris,
Presses Univ. de France (1958) § 76.

[2] J. S. MILL, *Utilitarianism*, ed. by J. PLAMENATZ, Oxford, Blackwell, 1949,
pp. 169–71.

[3] J. S. MILL, *op. cit.*

interest, to discover in the consequence of a thesis the proof of its truth. We know that pragmatists like William James and Dewey developed an 'instrumental view of truth' which James sums up as follows:

The true is the name of whatever proves itself to be good in the way of belief, and good, too, for definite assignable reasons.[1]

But it is interesting to remark that thinkers who are acknowledged to have an absolute view of truth, have not been ashamed to use the pragmatic argument as a means of getting their thesis accepted. When it comes to the point of laying down the orthodox doctrine concerning the relationship of free will and Grace, Calvin does not hesitate to write:

But in order that the truth of this question be more easily displayed to us, we must begin by setting an end to which all our discussion should be addressed. Well, the way by which we shall guard ourselves against error is to consider the dangers which exist on either side.[2]

Leibniz too brings out the pragmatic argument in support of his thesis that the soul is naturally immortal:

For [he writes] it is infinitely more to the advantage of religion and morals, especially in these times when many people have little respect for revelation by itself or for miracles, to show that the soul is immortal by nature and that it would be miraculous if it were not, than to maintain that our souls are naturally designed to perish, and that it is thanks to a miraculous grace, founded only on God's promise, that they do not.[3]

It is in the same spirit that success is put forward as a criterion of validity. There are a number of philosophies and religions in which achievement, happiness, salvation, are made to provide the ultimate justification for their systems and their dogmas, the sign of a correspondence with reality, of an agreement with the world order. The pragmatic argument is made use of in the most various traditions. The happiness of the sage, whether he be epicurean or stoic, guarantees the value of his doctrine; it is not only in ordeals

---

[1] W. JAMES, 'What Pragmatism Means', in *Essays in Pragmatism*, Hafner Publishing Company, New York, 1948, p. 155.

[2] CALVIN, *Institution de la religion chrétienne*, Genève, 1888, Bk. II, ch. II, § 1.

[3] LEIBNIZ, Works, ed. GERHARDT, V vol. Nouveaux essais sur l'entendement, p. 60.

and tournaments that the winning side is held to be in the right. And it is well known that Hegelian realism sanctifies success by assigning to history the part of a supreme judge. The fact that something exists, that it has been able to come to birth and to develop itself, that it has proved itself in the past, and hence promises to do so in the future, gives it a warrant of objectivity and rationality. Even existentialist philosophers, who claim to be anti-rationalist, nevertherless insist on seeing in the failure of an existence a clear sign of its inauthenticity. Gabriel Marcel in his plays goes out of his way to stress this idea.[1]

According to the pragmatic argument, the consequences govern one's opinion of that which determines them. When these consequences are divergent, we are presented with arguments which are favourable to both parties to the dispute. Aristotle tells us that the whole of Callipus's technique consisted in the appeal to such divergent consequences. He gives the following example:

Education exposes people to envy, which is a bad thing, and makes them learned, which is good.[2]

To escape this balancing of arguments on one side and another, Bentham puts forward the utilitarian calculus. All that is needed is to make a quantitative determination of the importance of every consequence, and to apply the rules of arithmetic. But this is not so easy, since one would have, in each case, to know the *totality* of the consequences to which the calculus is to be applied and to determine the *importance* of each of them; and sometimes one would have to pick out the *causes* to which they were to be attributed. To apply his calculus, Bentham was obliged as a matter of principle to rule out all other considerations than the pragmatic argument.[3]

By examining these presuppositions of 'the logic of utility', we shall be enabled not only to form an estimate of utilitarianism, but also, I hope, to throw some light upon the relations of a philosophical system with the use of certain types of argument.

It would never be possible to bring together the totality of the consequences, on which the application of the pragmatic argument depends, if every such consequence had in its turn to be evaluated in terms of its own consequences, for the series of these

---

[1] Cf. G. MARCEL, *Un homme de Dieu.*
[2] ARISTOTLE, *Rhetoric*, II, 1399a.
[3] Cf. BENTHAM, *Oeuvres*, Brussels 1829, t. I, p. 10.

consequences would be infinite. There are two ways by which one might try to escape from this impasse: one might admit the existence of ultimate elements, the values of which could be determined directly; they would serve as the last court of appeal for every pragmatic argument: or one might, more modestly, be satisfied with a *de facto* agreement on the value of the totality of the final consequences.

According to the first solution, one would have to trace the series of consequences to the ultimate elements, pleasures and pains, for example, which would supply a measure for the value of everything that caused them, they themselves being directly evaluated; since their value would be self-evident these elements would not give rise to dispute or argument. The second solution would not depend on metaphysics, for it would require us only to reach an agreement about the value of the consequences, without any *a priori* specification of their nature. It is true this agreement would record only a contingent matter of fact, and one that was precarious in that it could be put in question, if the occasion arose. But at least it would not raise any insuperable difficulties of principle.

In applying the principle of utility, it is assumed that the value of each of the consequences is invariable and the same for everybody; an even bigger assumption, which is required for the numerical calculus to come into play, is that these consequences can be represented by magnitudes which are not only comparable but even quantifiable by means of established techniques. The fulfilment of these conditions gives rise to innumerable difficulties. Even Bentham, who believed in the possibility of a utilitarian calculus, because he denied the existence of irreducible qualitative differences among pleasures and pains, found himself obliged to acknowledge that they were divisible into different species and that their value depended upon their intensity, their duration, their certainty, their propinquity, their fecundity and their extent.[1] These various factors exert, as it were, an objective influence upon the appraisal of pleasures and pains. But Bentham admitted further that since people's sensibilities differ, the same stimuli do not produce the same effects on everyone. Under these conditions, how can it be assumed that a calculus of pleasures is feasible, particularly if one recognises, as John Stuart Mill does, that there

[1] BENTHAM, *Theory of Legislation*, ed. OGDEN, p. 31.

are qualitative differences among pleasures and pains which make them incommensurable? The result is that one must have recourse to a comparison of the consequences and be satisfied with estimates and judgments of value which depend on the character of the subject as well as on that of the object which he is evaluating. But in that case the use of the pragmatic argument presupposes the existence of an agreement about the value of the consequences. As it will only be a matter of a *de facto* agreement which, for want of objective criteria, one cannot transform into an agreement of principle, it is not essential either that the consequences should be uniform in nature.

To believe in the possibility of the utilitarian calculus, one has to assume that its elements constitute invariable magnitudes, irrespective of the part that they play in the situation as a whole. But does it make no difference whether the thing which we are appraising be common or rare, or even unique? One will judge the same effect differently if it is isolated from its context, if a symbolic value is attributed to it, if it is seen as a step in a particular direction. According to the way in which we interpret it, the significance that we attach to it, the same fact will be viewed in a favourable or unfavourable light.

When the inhabitants of Tarragona came to tell Augustus that a palm tree had grown on the altar which was consecrated to him, and represented this event as a miraculous portent, the emperor chilled their enthusiasm by remarking simply that shows how often you light a fire there'.[1] An alleged miracle loses its worth when one sees nothing more in it than the effect of neglect. In a similar way, the same act will be judged differently according to the intention that is attributed to its author.

The existence of all these different ways of interpreting the same facts may explain why the pragmatic argument does not always lead to the same conclusions, why it requires a preliminary agreement on the nature and value of the consequences, though it is to be remarked that such an agreement, within a given cultural milieu, is more common than one might think.

If, instead of starting with a fact and estimating its consequences, we proceed in the opposite direction and start with an

[1] QUINTILIAN, *Institutio oratoria*, Book VI, 3, 77.

effect or group of effects, whether favourable or unfavourable, in order to apply the pragmatic argument to their cause, to what cause are we to attribute them? The answer to this question is hardly ever obvious and it can give rise to interminable controversies. Indeed, if the pragmatic argument allows us to evaluate things in terms of their effects, how in the production of the consequences can one assess the share that belongs to a single cause?

The ideal case would be that in which one was able to show that one event was the necessary and sufficient condition of another. This is what is envisaged in the following piece of argument from a medieval author:

Do you mind having lost this or that? Then, don't go out of your way to lose it; for you are seeking a loss if you wish to acquire what cannot be kept.[1]

Normally a given event will be only a necessary condition or a partial cause. To enable ourselves to transfer to it the whole weight of the effects, we should have to diminish the importance and influence of the complementary causes by treating them as accidents, as mere conditions, as occasional causes.

Besides, in the process of transferring the value of an effect to its cause, up to what limit in the causal chain is one supposed to go? As Quintilian already remarked 'by going up in this way from cause to cause and by choosing them suitably, one can get anywhere one wants'.[2]

A man who is accused of having committed a crime may try to throw the responsibility on to his education, his parents, his social environment. The attempt to fix responsibility for civil wrongs involves one of the most complicated theories in law. To whom is a tort to be imputed, who is responsible for causing it? Nothing is less obvious.

The same difficulty arises in theology. Who is to be charged with what is evil and defective in the universe? Clearly God means everything to be ordered for the best, yet, although he is all powerful, we observe that the world is not free from imperfections. We are driven to the intellectual device of attributing to

[1] Guigues le Chartreux, *Meditaciones*, Patrologia latina, t. CLIII, col. 610B.

[2] Quintilian, *Institutio oratoria*, Book V, 10, 84.

God, the immaculate first cause, only what is good and perfect in the world and not what is evil and defective.[1]

To sum up, seeing that an effect most often results from a combination of causes, and seeing that each of these in itself a member of a causal chain, is it possible to provide unquestionable criteria which would indisputably pick out the cause to which the pragmatic argument is to be applied? I believe in the possibility of a limited agreement on this matter, but not in the existence of a metaphysical definition of the cause, which would be valid in all circumstances, so that there would never be any question about identifying the cause to which the value of the consequences was to be transferred.

Finally, objection may be taken to the exclusive use of the pragmatic argument for determining values. It is clear that this presupposes the reduction of every fact to the consequences which provide the means of judging it. If these consequences are of a determinate kind, it is they that will furnish the common denominator to which every value will be referred: it is in terms of them that it will be assessed. The objection raised by those who are opposed to making the pragmatic argument the sole arbiter of questions of value is that it does away with the specific features of the notions of duty, wrong-doing, or sin, and so reduces the sphere of the moral or religious life. The value of truth, of sincerity, is not to be measured only by their fortunate consequences, and success is not the only criterion in every field. Montaigne remarks in his Essays that:

It is a rightly received opinion that advice should not be judged by the event. The Carthaginians used to punish their captains for bad strategy, even when it was redeemed by success. And the Roman people often refused to award a triumph for great and fruitful victories, because the conduct of the fortunate commander did not match his achievement.[2]

The antithesis to utilitarianism is formalism. Here judgments of value are based not on consequences, as in the pragmatic argument, but on a different criterion, namely the conformity with

[1] E. GILSON, Le thomisme, Paris, Vrin 1945, p. 223.
[2] MONTAIGNE, Essais, Bibl. de la Pléiade, Paris 1946, Book III, Chapter VIII, pp. 904-5.

certain rules which have to be observed whatever the consequence may be.

It is in this spirit that Simone Weil complains that so many arguments in favour of Christianity take the form of 'advertisements for Pink pills—before and after. They consist in saying "See what poor creatures human beings were before Christ".'[1]

In fact the result of appraising a thing only on the basis of its consequences is to reduce it to the level of a means which, whatever its efficacity, no longer has the prestige of that which is valued for itself. There is a world of difference between things that are valued only as a means and things that possess intrinsic value. Consider Goblot's analysis of love:

We are already in love when we imagine the loved one to be a source of inexhaustible happiness, the range of which is not determined or known. In this case the loved one is still a means, a unique and irreplaceable means to innumerable, undetermined ends. The state of true love is loving one friend for himself, as the miser loves his gold, when, the end no longer being considered, the means itself has become the end and the value of the loved one is no longer relative but absolute.[2]

The contrary procedure of transforming ends into means carries with it a tendency to devalue and depreciate them. If we make morality depend entirely upon consequences, we are regarding it simply as a technique, however important; we are taking a pharisaical view of morality.

It is this charge of pharisaism that is brought by Scheler in his 'Formalism in Ethics' against all those who confound good and evil in themselves with socially accepted morality, the workings of which he allows to have been perfectly well analysed by the utilitarians.

In Scheler's view 'the forms of behaviour which illustrate these axio-logical qualities (good and evil) receive praise or blame on the social level *only to the extent* that they *happen also* to be beneficial or harmful to the interests of the society. In other words, it is the utility or disutility of different forms of behaviour that qualify them for social praise or blame. These criteria can be applied to moral values, but they are *in no sense the conditions of the existence* of

[1] S. WEIL, *L'enracinement*, Paris, Gallimard, 1949, p. 213.
[2] E. GOBLOT, *La logique des jugements de valeur*, Paris 1927, pp. 55-6.

values, nor are they the element which would determine their
unity as being "moral" or "immoral" '.[1]

The pragmatic argument, according to Scheler, is limited by its
very nature to the assessment of what is socially useful or harmful;
it is far from yielding us an appreciation of true morality. This
objection, and others of the same kind, will always be raised when
there is a difference of level between the phenomena in question
and the consequences by which they are supposed to be assessed:
it will be said that such a method of assessment is a profanation of
higher values.

Our brief examination of the uses of the pragmatic argument
and of the criticism which it arouses has shown us that the
methodological limitation of techniques of reasoning to this single
type of argument cannot be defended unless we are able, when we
apply it, to cut short any tendency to discussion by an appeal to
intuition or self-evidence. The existence of a *de facto* agreement on
all disputable points may make it possible to restrict all our
reasoning on matters of value to a single technique, that is to the
application of the pragmatic argument: but a philosophical position, which would turn this *de facto* agreement into an agreement
of principle, needs to be guaranteed by self-evident intuitions. In
default of this guarantee or in the event of disagreement, other
techniques of argument will be brought in to allow us to settle the
questions at issue. And, as in all argument, the solutions adopted
will not be irresistible in themselves; their adoption is a matter of
one's being ready to answer for them when one has, in all honesty
and sincerity, weighed the pros and cons.

[1] SCHELER, *Der Formalismus in der Ethik*, p. 180.

INDEX

act, 56, 59; and essence, 195; and person, 171–195. *See also* agent, argument, fact, just, person

action: results of, 8; and thought, 108, 124, 155. *See also* practice, works

agent: and act, 173; judgment on, 174–175; in pragmatic argument, 199. *See also* act, intention, moral, person

agreement, 53, 99, 190, 207; and audience, 169; about consequences, 198–203; revision of, 170, 172; universal, 169

Anselm, St., 74

arbitrary, -iness: of decisions, 91; of definitions, 2–4; in justice, 14, 45–50, 56–57, 59, 70; of language, 122, 123, 153; of opinions, 115; of values, 57. *See also* decision, reasonable, reasons

argument(s), 170; from act to act, 177–178; from act to person, 175–178; from authority, 182–183; from double hierarchy, 199; from incompetence, 183–184; force of, 124, 157–158; from the model, 182–183; from person to act, 179–182, 194; pragmatic, 196–207; sophistical, 184. *See also* philosophy, rationality

argumentation: *versus* demonstration, 101, 102, 154; never conclusive, 134, 167; not constraining, 124; opposed to evidence, 134; practice of, 156. *See also* rationality

Aristotle, 12, 14, 61, 64, 70, 72, 102, 111, 136, 138, 139, 150, 152, 158, 159, 163–166, 169, 177, 201

Aron, G., 175

Asch, S. E., 181

assertions, 151; as a case of doing, 80

Aubry, Ch., 104, 106

audience, 101, 138–140, 155–157, 166, 169–170; universal, 87, 155, 169, 178, 188–189

Augustine, St., 74, 111, 128, 193

Augustus, 203

authority, 182–183

axioms, 89, 98, 99, 137, 166. *See also* self-evidence

Ayer, A. J., 111

Bachelard, G., 89, 117

Bachet, M., 75

Baruk, H., 75

basic minimum, 23

being, open to, 129

Benedict, R., 189

beneficence, 55, 58

Bentham, J., 69, 189, 197, 199, 201, 202

Bergson, H., 75, 136

bias, 190–191

Bossuet, B., 74, 187, 193

Brunschvicg, L., 89

Caesar, 193

Calippus, 201

Calvin, J., 177, 180, 200

Cardozo, B., 66

Carnap, R., 149, 150

Casey, R. D., 137

category, *see* essential

Cato, 193

cause, 171; in pragmatic argument, 196, 198, 199, 203–205

change, 10; justification of, 63, 85–86, 119–120; in language, 123; in methods, 131. *See also* inertia, *status quo*

charity, 8, 13, 23, 40–41, 54, 58, 60, 71, 73, 74

Chasles, M., 183

Chevreul, M., 183

Church, A., 144, 145, 148, 151

Cicero, 68, 182

classes, 23–24. *See also* essential, rank

code: Napoleon, 65, 90, 100, 105; Belgian civ. proc., 104; penal, 90, 100; Swiss civ., 100

commonplace, 170, 199

common sense, 93, 197

confused idea, 4; justice as a, 5–6, 11, 59, 61

connections: of coexistence, 171, 194–195; of succession, 171

consequences, 196–203, 205–206

contradiction, non, 147–148, 158

cuique suum, 9, 71, 77

decision, 88, 93; responsibility of, 92, 93; reasons for, 97, 123